THE
SCIENCE
BOOK

First published in 2015 by
Miles Kelly Publishing Ltd
Harding's Barn, Bardfield End Green,
Thaxted, Essex, CM6 3PX, UK

Copyright © Miles Kelly Publishing Ltd 2015

10 9 8 7 6 5 4 3 2 1

Publishing Director Belinda Gallagher
Creative Director Jo Cowan
Managing Editor Amanda Askew
Managing/Cover Designer Simon Lee

Senior Editor Rosie Neave
Assistant Editors Amy Johnson, Lauren White
Designers D&A Design, Rocket Design
Proofreaders Carly Blake, Fran Bromage,
Claire Philip
Image Manager Liberty Newton
Production Elizabeth Collins, Caroline Kelly
Reprographics Stephan Davis,
Jennifer Cozens, Thom Allaway

ISBN 978-1-78209-841-6

Printed in China

British Library Cataloging-in-Publication Data
A catalog record for this book is available
from the British Library

Made with paper from a sustainable forest

www.mileskelly.net
info@mileskelly.net

THE
SCIENCE
BOOK

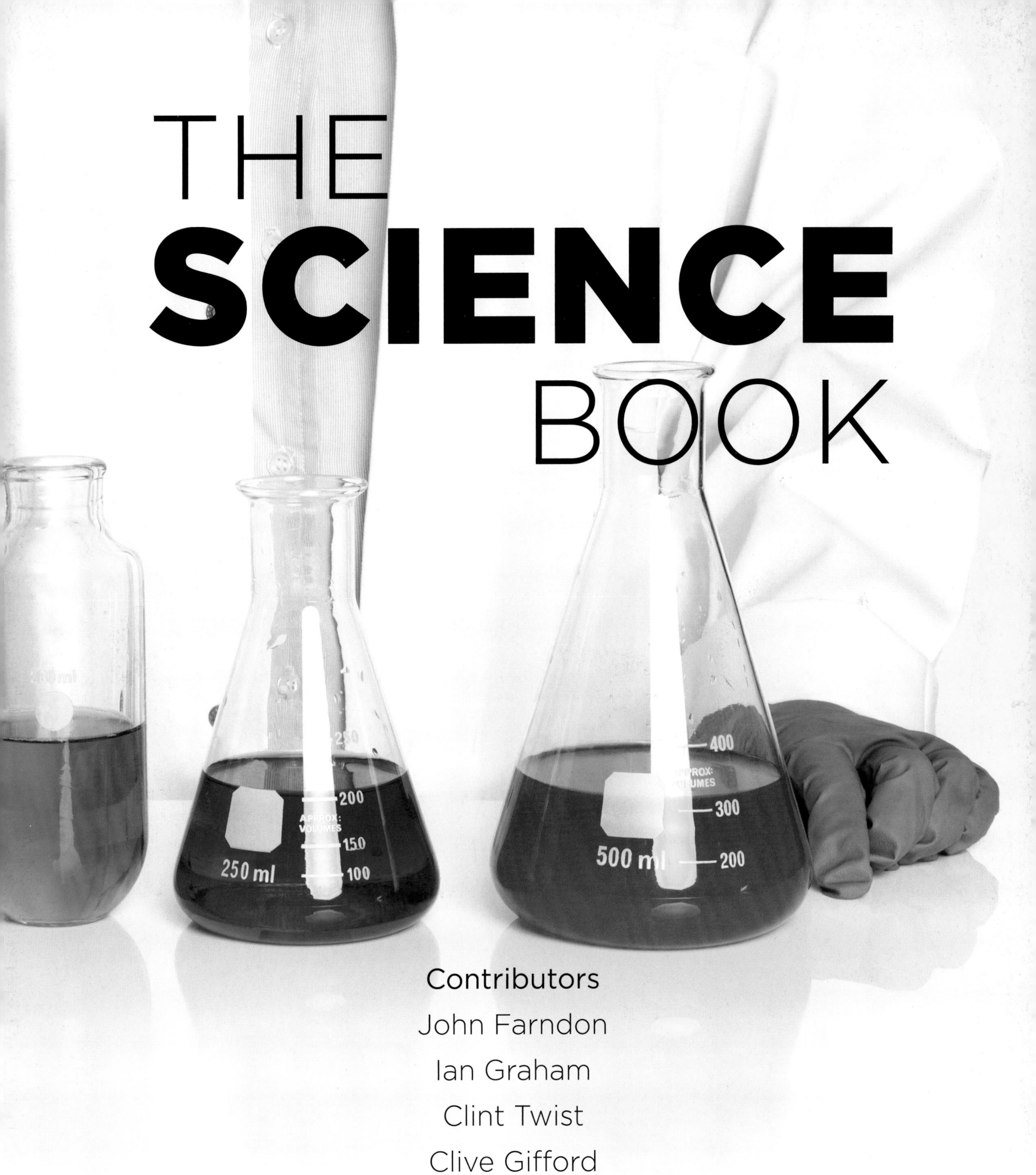

Contributors

John Farndon

Ian Graham

Clint Twist

Clive Gifford

Steve Parker

Miles
Kelly

Contents

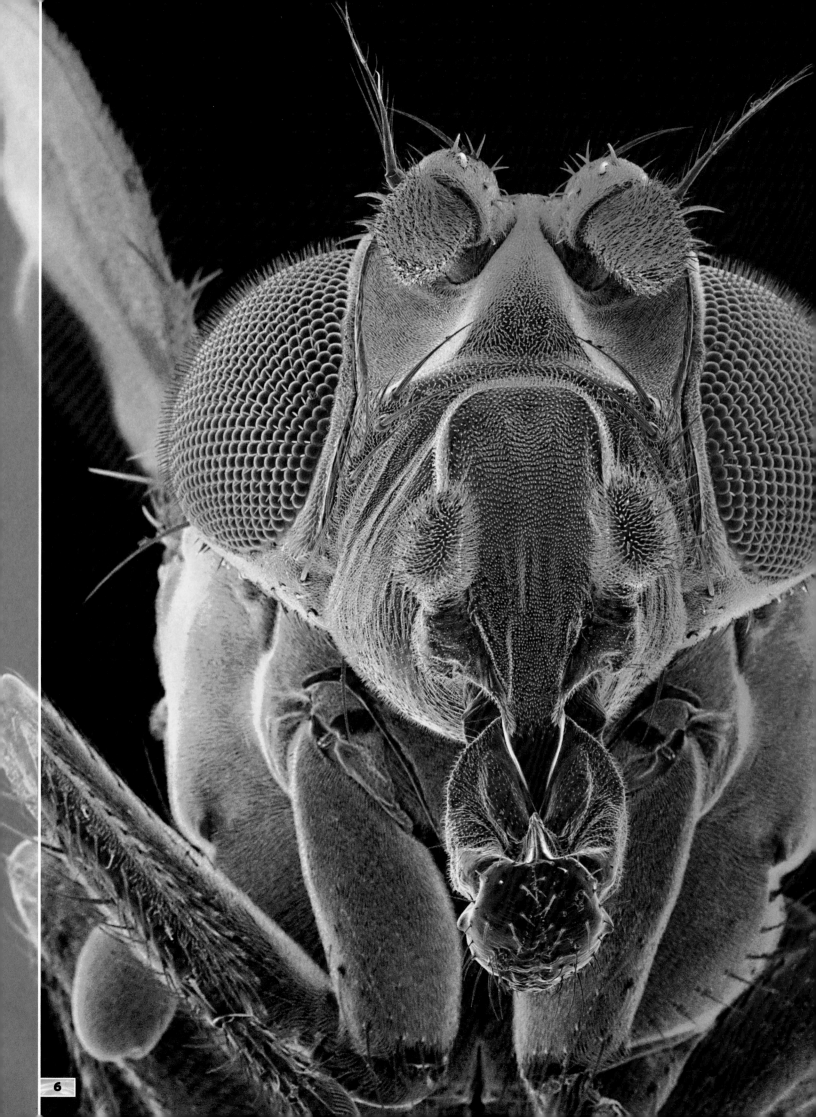

Incredible SCIENCE

Discover the breakthroughs that have shaped the world, and what science can reveal about our remarkable Universe.

◀ The power of a scanning electron microscope (SEM) homes in on the head of a tiny fruit fly, showing the 800 separate lenses that make up each of its two compound eyes.

Big BANGS

Explosions are the most powerful events in the Universe, capable of suddenly blasting apart anything from a rock to an entire giant star. They occur when heat, chemical, or nuclear reactions cause a dramatic and almost instantaneous expansion of gases. Some giant explosions, such as supernovae and volcanoes, occur naturally, but man-made explosions can also be very powerful.

Exploding star

The biggest explosion in the Universe is a supernova—the explosion that ends the life of a supergiant star. It may only be visible for a week, but can be seen far across the Universe, as bright as a galaxy of 100 billion stars.

▼ The Crab Nebula is the remnants of a supernova witnessed by Chinese astronomers in AD 1054.

Blow me down!

To demolish a building without damaging anything nearby, engineers have to make it implode (explode inward). To do this, they place explosive charges in carefully chosen weak points in the building, then set them off in a particular sequence.

▲ Experts need to place explosives very carefully to bring down an unwanted building, such as this 18-story apartment block in Shenyang, China.

Death trap

Land mines are bombs that can be buried just beneath the surface of the ground. Packed with a chemical called Trinitrotoluene (TNT), a land mine explodes by detonation—a powerful shock wave rushes through it, turning all the TNT almost instantly to gas. The gas expands violently, causing terrible damage. A detonator (a tiny explosive device inside the mine) triggers the explosion. Detonators are designed to be triggered when someone steps on the mine or drives a vehicle nearby.

EXPLOSIVE STRENGTH

The power of explosions is often measured in comparison to TNT by weight.

ITEM	POWER
1. Large hand grenade	3 oz (85 g) TNT
2. World War II bomb	6 lb (2.7 kg) TNT
3. "Bunker-buster" bomb	1 ton TNT
4. Hiroshima atom bomb	15 kilotons (15,000 tons) TNT
5. Hydrogen bomb	50 megatons (25 million tons) TNT
6. Mount Toba eruption	85 megatons TNT
7. Supernova	1,000 trillion trillion tons TNT

▶ An entire rock face in a quarry is blasted away by a line of simultaneous explosions.

Volcanic violence

The VEI (Volcanic Explosivity Index) rates the power of explosive volcanic eruptions on a scale from 0 to 8. The Mount St. Helens eruption of 1980 had a VEI of 5. When Mount Toba in Indonesia erupted around 75,000 years ago, it had a VEI of 8, so it was 10,000 times more powerful than Mount St. Helens and was one of the largest explosions on Earth, ever.

▼ Volcanic eruptions are the most powerful natural explosions on Earth.

Rock blast

To blast rock from the ground, quarries usually use dynamite. Invented by Swedish chemist Alfred Nobel (1833–1896), dynamite was the first High Explosive, and consists of sticks of sawdust soaked in nitroglycerin and wrapped in paper. Nitroglycerin contains so much oxygen that it detonates easily when heated. Typically, the heat source is a current of electricity running through a wire set into the dynamite.

Chemical Clash

When a candle burns, metal goes rusty, or a cake rises in the oven, a chemical reaction is taking place. When chemicals meet and react, they change each other to form new chemicals. But not all chemical encounters are quite so gentle.

CHEMICAL REACTIONS ARE CONSTANTLY TAKING PLACE WITHIN THE 100 TRILLION OR SO LIVING CELLS INSIDE YOUR BODY, SO THERE MAY BE MORE THAN 400 BILLION REACTIONS TAKING PLACE INSIDE YOU EVERY SECOND!

Exploding pop

Dropping Mentos mints into cola makes the drink suddenly fizz up in a fountain of froth. The Mentos react chemically with the cola, instantly creating bubbles of carbon dioxide gas, which turn the cola into a gushing foam. Other substances create bubbles in soft drinks, but the chemicals in Mentos make the reaction especially dramatic.

▲ Rusting corrodes tough steel into flaky, brown iron oxide as it reacts with oxygen in the air.

Acid danger

Strong acids are dangerous chemicals because they react so powerfully. Acids contain hydrogen, and when mixed with water the hydrogen atoms are turned loose as highly reactive "ions." Splashed on skin, acids can cause terrible burns by absorbing water in a reaction that creates a lot of heat. Strong acids can also dissolve metals.

▲ Mentos are covered in minute pits which act as nucleation sites—places that concentrate gas formation.

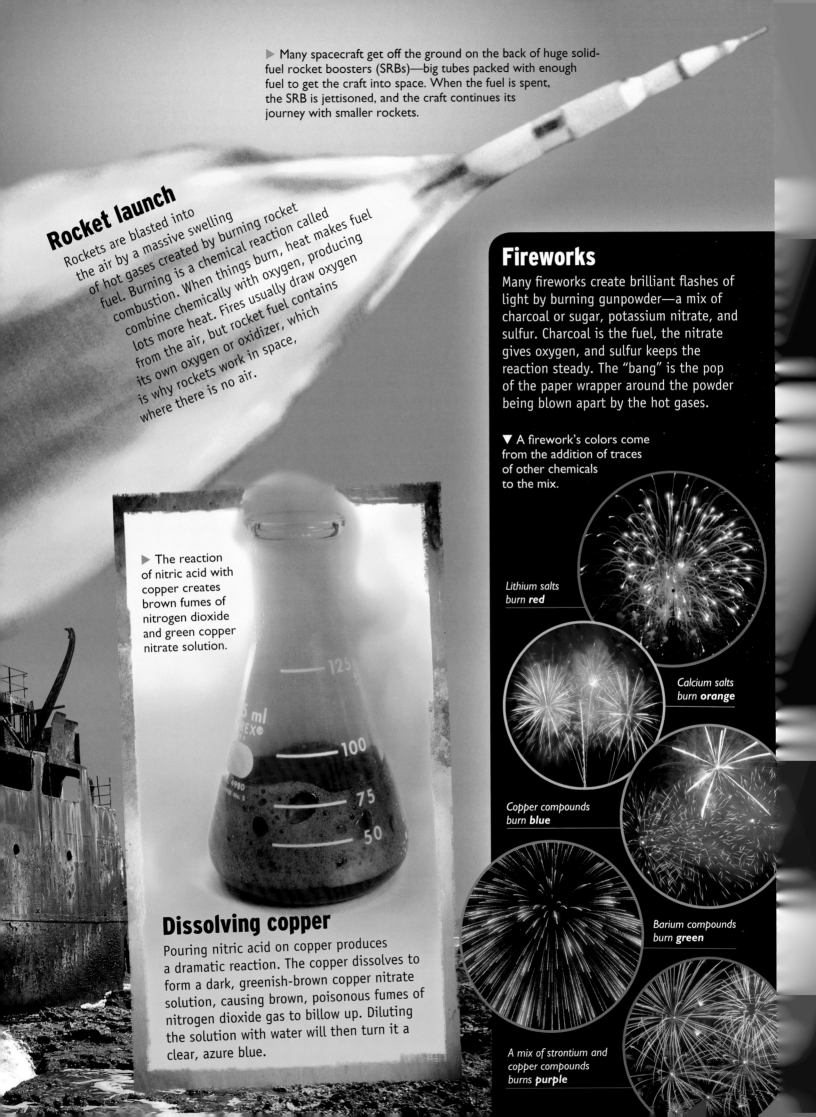

Many spacecraft get off the ground on the back of huge solid-fuel rocket boosters (SRBs)—big tubes packed with enough fuel to get the craft into space. When the fuel is spent, the SRB is jettisoned, and the craft continues its journey with smaller rockets.

Rocket launch

Rockets are blasted into the air by a massive swelling of hot gases created by burning rocket fuel. Burning is a chemical reaction called combustion. When things burn, heat makes fuel combine chemically with oxygen, producing lots more heat. Fires usually draw oxygen from the air, but rocket fuel contains its own oxygen or oxidizer, which is why rockets work in space, where there is no air.

The reaction of nitric acid with copper creates brown fumes of nitrogen dioxide and green copper nitrate solution.

Dissolving copper

Pouring nitric acid on copper produces a dramatic reaction. The copper dissolves to form a dark, greenish-brown copper nitrate solution, causing brown, poisonous fumes of nitrogen dioxide gas to billow up. Diluting the solution with water will then turn it a clear, azure blue.

Fireworks

Many fireworks create brilliant flashes of light by burning gunpowder—a mix of charcoal or sugar, potassium nitrate, and sulfur. Charcoal is the fuel, the nitrate gives oxygen, and sulfur keeps the reaction steady. The "bang" is the pop of the paper wrapper around the powder being blown apart by the hot gases.

▼ A firework's colors come from the addition of traces of other chemicals to the mix.

Lithium salts burn **red**

Calcium salts burn **orange**

Copper compounds burn **blue**

Barium compounds burn **green**

A mix of strontium and copper compounds burns **purple**

Wonder MATERIALS

Natural materials such as diamond and silk can be incredibly tough. But now scientists are creating a range of entirely man-made wonder materials. Some are incredibly light, others are incredibly strong, and some are both.

◀ The high-strength carbon fibers inside CRP help to absorb pressure. In a pole-vaulter's pole, CRP's combination of strength and flexibility gives a vaulter extra lift as it springs straight.

Carbon power

By embedding long fibers made of carbon in plastics, scientists make a material called carbon reinforced plastic (CRP). The plastic keeps it very light, but the fibers give it both strength and flexibility—perfect for the light, strong springiness needed for a pole-vaulter's pole. CRP is known as a "composite" because it combines plastic and carbon.

Jelly light

Aerogels are materials so light that they almost seem to float. Gels are jellylike materials that are mostly liquid. Aerogels are made by sucking liquid out of a gel and replacing it with gas. The gas filling not only makes aerogels amazingly light, but also very good barriers to heat.

CARBON FIBERS ARE FOUR TIMES STRONGER THAN STEEL WHEN PULLED, YET JUST ONE QUARTER OF THE WEIGHT.

▶ Aerogel stops the heat of the bunsen burner flame reaching the flower entirely.

▶ The LCROSS mission smashed a rocket with a wurtzite boron nitride nose into the Moon deliberately to throw up dust for scientists to analyze.

Tough titanium

Alloys are created by adding materials to a metal. Alloys of aluminum and magnesium are tough and light—which is why they are used to build aircraft. But the heat generated as high-speed jets tear through the air may be too much for aluminum alloys. So the fastest jets, such as the *F22 Raptor,* are made mostly from incredibly tough, superlight titanium alloys.

Super strong

Wurtzite boron nitride is the world's hardest material—harder even than diamond. It is used wherever materials need to be really, really tough and cost doesn't matter—from the heads of oil drills to the tips of "bunker-busting" bombs.

▲ With a superlight, superstrong titanium alloy fuselage (main body), the *F22 Raptor* can fly at speeds of up to 1,500 mph (2,400 km/h).

▶ The *Seabreacher* is a submersible made of Kevlar. It is so light and strong that it can burst out of the water like a dolphin.

The toughest threads

In 1961, DuPont chemist Stephanie Kwolek (b. 1923) discovered how to spin fibers from liquid chemicals such as oil. These "aramid" fibers are amazingly strong—threads of the aramid fiber Kevlar are five times stronger than steel. Kevlar has many applications, from helping to make puncture-resistant bicycle tires to strengthening cables used in suspension bridges.

▶ The fibers of Kevlar (a modified form of nylon) are incredibly tough for their weight, so they are used to make stabproof and bulletproof vests.

Deep

Freezing point, when water turns to ice, might seem pretty cold, but it can get much colder in locations such as Siberia and Antarctica. Elsewhere in the Solar System there are places that make Antarctica seem scorching. And in laboratories, scientists can create temperatures so cold that even atoms nearly freeze up.

1 Maximum chill

The coldest temperature possible is known as Absolute Zero. This is 0 Kelvin, or −459.67°F (−273.15°C). At this temperature atoms have no energy at all and do not even vibrate.

3 Supercold boomerang

Temperatures near Absolute Zero might only be achieved in a lab, but there is at least one place in the Universe that comes pretty close. In a cloud of gas known as the Boomerang nebula, the temperature is thought to be just 1K (−457.87°F, or −272.15°C).

−273.15°C   **−272.15°C**

−459.67°F   **−457.87°F**

MEASURING UP

Temperature is measured on three scales. In everyday life, people use degrees Fahrenheit (°F) or degrees Celsius (°C). You can convert from °F to °C using a simple formula: subtract 32, divide by 9, and multiply by 5. To convert from °C to °F, divide by 5, multiply by 9, and add 32. Scientists may prefer to use the Kelvin scale, which is identical to Celsius but starts at a different place. While 0°C is the freezing point of water, 0K (−459.67°F, or −273.15°C) is the lowest temperature possible and is called Absolute Zero.

2 Coldest ever

In 2003, scientists cooled sodium gas inside a magnetic container to the coldest temperature ever achieved on Earth. It was just half a nanokelvin— half a billionth of a degree—above Absolute Zero!

Chilled matter

Substances normally exist in one of three states—gas, liquid, or solid—depending on the temperature. But at 17 nanokelvins above Absolute Zero scientists can push gases into another state, known as a Bose-Einstein condensate (BEC). In a BEC, atoms have so little energy that if a beam of light is passed through them then it will come to a complete standstill.

▶ Ultracold rubidium atoms (top) briefly condense into a BEC (center) before evaporating again (bottom).

Inside this flask, helium gas has been cooled to the point where it turns liquid.

► Antarctica experiences the coldest natural temperatures on Earth.

Ice station
The coldest outside temperature ever recorded on Earth was −128.6°F (−89.2°C) at the Russian Vostok Station in Antarctica on July 21, 1983.

4 Helium liquefies
Helium remains a gas until incredibly low temperatures. It finally becomes a liquid at 4K (−452.2°F, or −269°C).

7 Brrrr!
On February 6, 1933, the temperature in one of the world's coldest towns, Oymyakon, in Siberia, plunged to a bitterly cold −90 °F (−67.7°C).

−269°C	−235°C	−89.2°C	−67.7°C	0°C
−452.2°F	−315°F	−128.6°F	−90°F	32°F

5 Icy moon
The coldest place in the Solar System is Neptune's moon, Triton. It is so far from the Sun that it receives none of its heat, and temperatures on its surface drop to −315°F (−235°C).

▼ Uniquely, water expands when it freezes, making it less dense, which is why icebergs float.

Neptune

Triton

8 Freeze!
Water normally freezes solid to become ice at 273.15K (32°F, or 0°C). The addition of salt or pressure keeps it liquid at slightly lower temperatures.

Super SCORCH

The more energy things have, the hotter they get. Our bodies get their warmth from the energy released by reacting chemicals. The Sun and stars get their immense heat from the energy released when atoms are forced together by the tremendous pressures in their cores.

Beneath the pale clouds, the surface of Venus is almost hot enough to melt tin.

3 On the boil

A liquid's boiling point is the hottest it can get without becoming a gas. The boiling point of water is normally 212°F (100°C). Beneath geysers, underground pressure allows water to be "superheated" to higher temperatures.

4 Trapped heat

Venus' thick atmosphere traps the Sun's heat, causing temperatures on the planet's surface to reach 896°F (480°C).

| 37°C | 41°C | 100°C | 480°C | 827°C |

| 98.6°F | 106°F | 212°F | 896°F | 1,521°F |

▲ This thermogram is created using infrared radiation. It indicates differences in temperature by color, from hot (white) to cool (blue).

2 Hot spots

In Dallol, Ethiopia, maximum daily temperatures averaged more than 106°F (41°C) for six years between 1960 and 1966!

5 Hot coals

The temperature of coal fires can vary, but coal can burn at up to 1,521°F (827°C).

1 Body heat

Your body temperature is normally around 98.6°F (37°C), except when you have a fever. Even then it only reaches 104°F (40°C)—much hotter would kill you.

These sulfurous volcanic pools lie in a region that experiences some of the hottest temperatures on Earth: Dallol, in Ethiopia.

6 Molten metal

The bonds between atoms in a metal are very strong, so most metals don't melt until they get very hot. Some steels melt at around 1,517°F (825°C), while tungsten doesn't melt until around 6,170°F (3,410°C).

8 Blue star

The hottest known star in the Universe is Eta Carinae. Its surface reaches more than 72,000°F (40,000°C), which is why it glows blue-hot.

10 Hottest ever

In February 2010, scientists working deep underground in New York, U.S., in the tunnels of the Brookhaven National Laboratory's RHIC (Relativistic Hadron Ion Collider) created the hottest temperatures since the beginning of the Universe. In the RHIC's tunnels, gold atoms smash into each other at almost the speed of light, briefly creating temperatures of 7 trillion°F (4 trillion°C).

▼ In 2005, astronomers realized that superhot Eta Carinae is not one star but two.

3,410°C   5,500°C   40,000°C

6,170°F   9,900°F   72,000°F

The Sun's atmosphere, or corona, reaches a blistering 1,800,000°F (1,000,000°C).

7 Sun burned

The temperature on the surface of the Sun is about 9,900°F (5,500°C). This extreme heat gives sunlight its yellow color—if the Sun were cooler, it would be more reddish. At the center of the Sun, temperatures reach more than 24 million°F (15 million°C)!

9 Big Bang heat

The hottest natural temperature was at the very start of the Universe, during the Big Bang, when temperatures briefly reached 3–5 trillion°F (2–3 trillion°C).

▶ Variations in microwave radiation in this computer map of the sky reveal the lingering glow of the Big Bang.

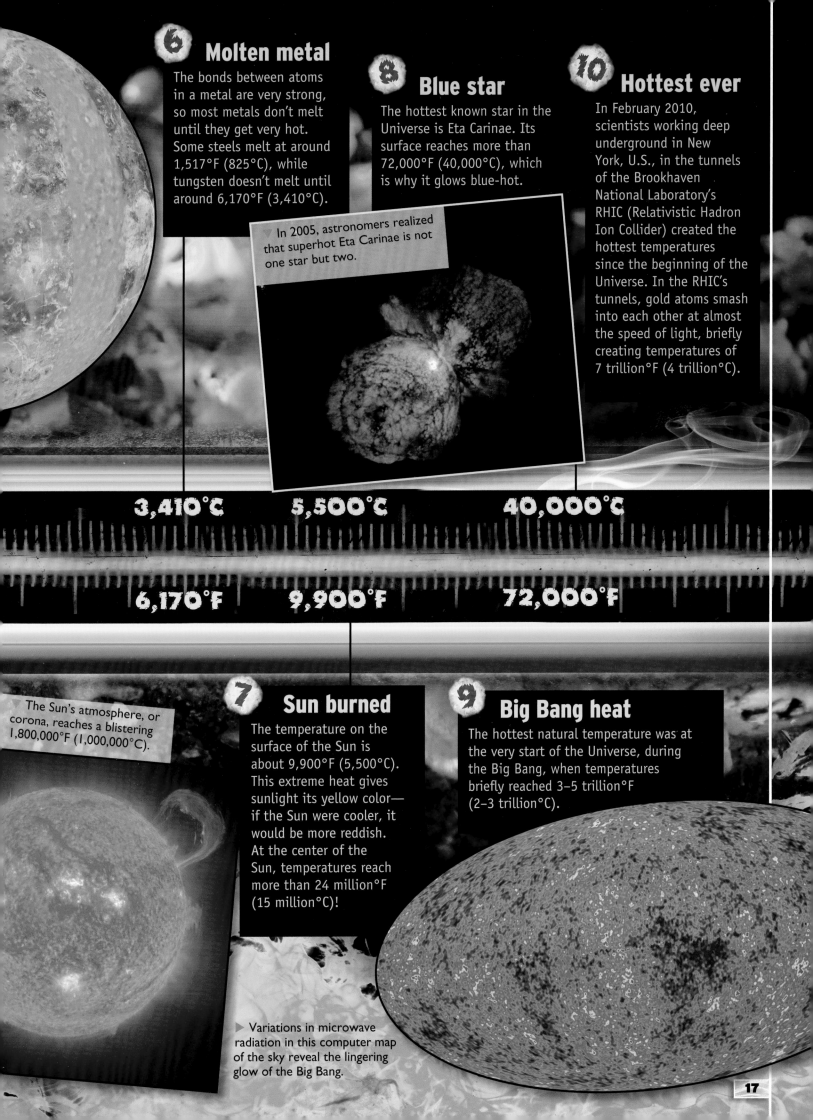

GIGANTIC Universe

To us tiny humans, Earth seems pretty big. A few centuries ago people thought it was the biggest thing in the Universe. But as telescopes reveal more, it's becoming clear that Earth is seriously small. Some things in space are so huge, they make our entire galaxy seem like a grain of sand on a beach.

Earth

Jupiter

1 Biggest planet

At 142,984 km across, Jupiter is the biggest planet in the Solar System. Its diameter is 11.2 times larger than Earth, and its volume is 1.43×10^{15} km³, so you could cram over 1,300 Earths inside Jupiter and still have room to spare!

Earth's diameter is 12,756.1 km. The volume of Earth is 1,083,210 million km³.

Earth

Jupiter

Sun

2 The Sun

The Sun dwarfs Jupiter. It is 1.4 million km across—109 times bigger than Earth. Its volume is $1,412 \times 10^{16}$ km³, which means you could get 1.3 million Earths inside the Sun.

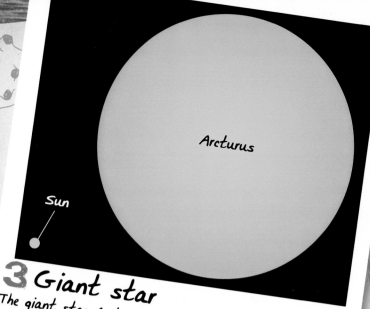
Sun

Arcturus

3 Giant star

The giant star Arcturus is 25 times the diameter of the Sun, and is the third brightest star in the night sky.

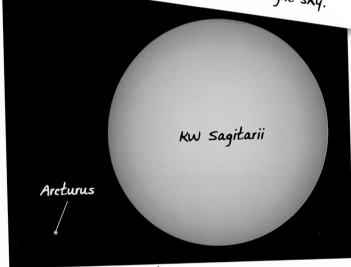
Arcturus

KW Sagitarii

4 Biggest star

The biggest star we know of is the hypergiant KW Sagitarii. At almost 2 billion km across it is 60 times bigger than Arcturus and more than 1,500 times bigger than the Sun!

LIGHT-YEARS

Dimensions in space are so vast that it's not practical to measure them in kilometers. Instead, astronomers measure things in light-years. Light always travels at the same speed—299,792 km/sec—so distances can be measured by the number of years it takes for light to cross them. A light-year is the distance light travels in a year, which is 9,460 billion km.

Milky way galaxy

If the Sun were the size of a grain of sand, the Milky Way would be the size of the Sun!

5 Our galaxy

Our Sun is just one of about 400 billion stars in the Milky Way galaxy. The Milky Way is 100,000 light-years across—a million trillion km.

6 Biggest galaxy

The IC 1101 galaxy is 5 million light-years across—50 times as big as the Milky Way.

7 Supercluster

The Milky Way is one of more than 2,000 galaxies in the cluster of galaxies known as the Virgo Cluster. But this cluster is tiny compared with superclusters such as the Perseus-Pisces supercluster, which is more than 300 million light-years across—3,000 times as wide as the Milky Way. If the Sun were the size of a grain of sand, this supercluster would be almost as big as the Solar System.

8 Sloan Great wall

The Universe is arranged like a gigantic spider's web. All the stars, galaxies, and clusters are concentrated in vast, thin walls. The biggest is the Sloan Great Wall, which is 1.37 billion light-years long—more than 12,000 times as wide as the Milky Way.

Mega IDEAS

As scientists explore the extremes of our world, they often need to use huge, complex pieces of equipment. Exploring the vastness of the Universe requires massive telescopes and research stations in space. Strangely, some of the biggest and most elaborate machines have been built to study things that are so tiny, they are invisible to the naked eye.

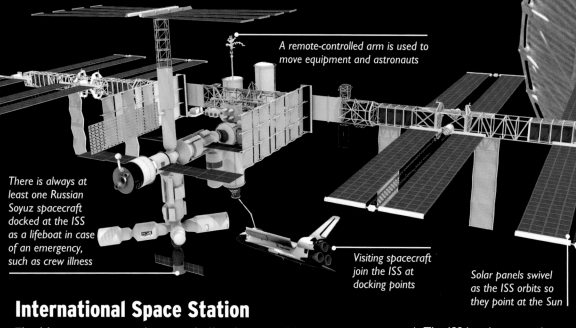

A remote-controlled arm is used to move equipment and astronauts

There is always at least one Russian Soyuz spacecraft docked at the ISS as a lifeboat in case of an emergency, such as crew illness

Visiting spacecraft join the ISS at docking points

Solar panels swivel as the ISS orbits so they point at the Sun

International Space Station

The biggest space station ever built, the ISS orbits between 173 mi (278 km) and 286 mi (460 km) above Earth. It is so big, it can be seen from the ground with the naked eye. Its parts were carried up bit by bit by dozens of space flights, then assembled in space by astronauts in more than 130 separate space walks.

▲ The ISS hurtles around Earth at an average speed of 17,239.2 mph (27,743.8 km/h), completing 15.7 orbits per day.

Human Genome Project

Every cell in your body carries instructions to keep you alive (and create your children), all contained on a tiny string of the chemical DNA. The instructions are in the form of thousands of chemical sequences called genes. The Human Genome Project was a huge international program to map the human genome (identify exactly where on human DNA every single gene occurs). The project began in 1990 and was completed in 2003.

▲ A computer image shows a tiny part of the map of DNA, with each bar showing one of the four chemical bases that make up the code.

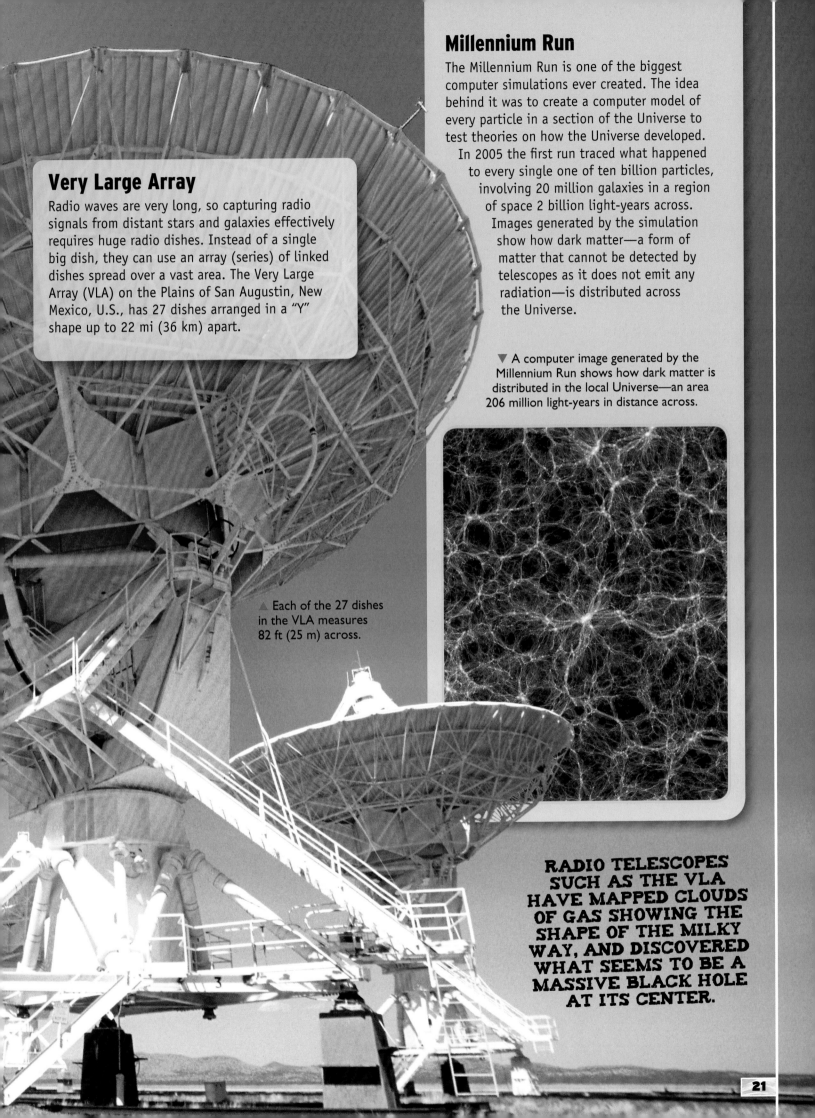

Very Large Array

Radio waves are very long, so capturing radio signals from distant stars and galaxies effectively requires huge radio dishes. Instead of a single big dish, they can use an array (series) of linked dishes spread over a vast area. The Very Large Array (VLA) on the Plains of San Augustin, New Mexico, U.S., has 27 dishes arranged in a "Y" shape up to 22 mi (36 km) apart.

▲ Each of the 27 dishes in the VLA measures 82 ft (25 m) across.

Millennium Run

The Millennium Run is one of the biggest computer simulations ever created. The idea behind it was to create a computer model of every particle in a section of the Universe to test theories on how the Universe developed. In 2005 the first run traced what happened to every single one of ten billion particles, involving 20 million galaxies in a region of space 2 billion light-years across. Images generated by the simulation show how dark matter—a form of matter that cannot be detected by telescopes as it does not emit any radiation—is distributed across the Universe.

▼ A computer image generated by the Millennium Run shows how dark matter is distributed in the local Universe—an area 206 million light-years in distance across.

RADIO TELESCOPES SUCH AS THE VLA HAVE MAPPED CLOUDS OF GAS SHOWING THE SHAPE OF THE MILKY WAY, AND DISCOVERED WHAT SEEMS TO BE A MASSIVE BLACK HOLE AT ITS CENTER.

Small WORLD

Looking at your skin through a magnifying glass reveals all kinds of details invisible to the unaided eye. However, scientists have now developed microscopes that allow us to see a world that is on a much smaller scale. Even a good magnifying glass only magnifies objects by a few times. The most powerful scanning tunneling microscopes (STMs) magnify things billions of times, and can reveal particles smaller than atoms.

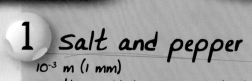

Pepper

Salt

1 Salt and pepper
10^{-3} m (1 mm)
To the unaided eye, pepper looks pretty much like salt, only dark brown. But a good light microscope shows just how different they are. Pepper is, of course, the seed of a plant. Salt is a mineral crystal.

2 Human hair
10^{-4} m (100 micron)
Your hair may feel pretty smooth and fine, but under a microscope you can see that each hair has a rough surface, and looks rather like a tiny tree trunk.

3 Red blood cells
10^{-5} m (10 microns)
The most powerful light microscopes can show the tiny red cells in blood, but to see their shapes clearly you need a scanning electron microscope (SEM). SEM pictures show that when red blood cells are healthy, they are a neat button shape.

4 Bacteria

10⁻⁶ m (1 micron)
You can just about see bacteria with light microscopes, but SEM pictures can show detailed close-ups.

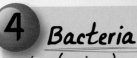

◄ Bacteria such as *Helicobacter pylori* live in many human stomachs, and can cause stomach upsets.

Coronaviruses cause anything from colds to gastric illnesses. They got their name because they look like crowns through an electron microscope.

5 Virus

10⁻⁷ m (100 nanometers)
Viruses are much tinier than bacteria and can only be seen with electron microscopes, such as the transmission electron microscope (TEM).

SCIENTISTS CAN MAKE ELECTRONIC DEVICES AS SMALL AS A SINGLE ATOM. VERY SOON, A POWERFUL COMPUTER NEED BE NO BIGGER THAN A GRAIN OF SAND.

6 Molecule

10⁻⁸ m (10 nanometers)
Atomic force microscopes (AFMs) and the most powerful TEMs can show actual strands of DNA.

◄ DNA can be seen clearly with a TEM, magnified almost half a million times.

7 Atom

10⁻⁹ m (1 nanometer)
To see an atom, you need a scanning tunneling microscope (STM).

MICROSCOPES

Light or optical microscopes use combinations of lenses to magnify things. They can magnify up to about 2,000 times. The smallest thing they can see is about 500 nanometers (500 billionths of a meter).

Electron microscopes can show things up to 20,000 times smaller. They don't use lenses at all—they fire electrons at their subjects and record the way the electrons bounce off. Instead of seeing an object directly, you look at a picture of it that builds up on a screen.

Scanning tunneling microscopes (STMs) and atomic force microscopes (AFMs) work by touch. AFMs run a sharp point that looks similar to an old-fashioned record needle over the subject. These microscopes can show atoms.

Microscopic Zoo

In recent years, scanning electron and tunneling microscopes have homed in on the world of insects and microbes to reveal them in amazing detail and clarity. Even the tiniest bugs appear as large and monstrous as creatures from another world. There are many, many more different species of these microscopic organisms than there are in all the rest of the living world put together.

◀▲ A tiny fruit fly seen through an SEM with a close-up of the "talons" on its leg (inset left).

Small fly

Magnified more than 800 times, this SEM image shows the two birdlike talons on the end of a fruit fly's leg. The hairlike stalks beneath the talons are covered with adhesive pads or "pulvilli." These allow the fruit fly to cling to vertical surfaces such as glass, which appear completely smooth to the naked eye. Scientists are hoping to develop artificial nanomaterials that adhere in a similar way.

Stomach bug

Transmission electron microscopes (TEMs) reveal the microscopic zoo living inside the human stomach. This is the bacteria *Helicobacter pylori* magnified 7,700 times. These bacteria get their name, "pylori," from the fact that they live in the pyloric (lower) part of many people's stomachs. Fortunately, they usually have no effect.

▲ *Helicobacter pylori* can move around by whipping its tail or "flagella."

Living jewels

Diatoms are algae that float in water and get their energy from the Sun, like plants do. They are so small, they can only be seen properly with an SEM. But SEMs reveal them to be astonishingly beautiful geometric "jewels." There are more than 100,000 different species.

▶ The spiny surfaces of these minute pollen grains help them stick to feathers and fur.

Plant packet

SEMs reveal the huge variety of different forms of pollen. Pollen is the dusty substance that flowers spread to help them reproduce. Each grain is a tough case holding male sex cells that must be delivered to the female ova or egg to create a seed for a new flower. Grains are so tough, they last tens of thousands of years, so archeologists can use SEM pictures of ancient pollen to identify plants that were growing long ago.

▶ A magnified head louse appears monstrous as it climbs along a human hair.

MICROSCOPIC NEMATODE WORMS MAKE UP 90 PERCENT OF ALL LIFE ON THE OCEAN FLOOR.

High life

In close-up, a head louse clinging to a human hair looks like a monster crawling along a tightrope. Head lice are tiny, wingless insects that live in the hair of living humans, lay their eggs on hair shafts, and feed entirely on human blood, sucked from the scalp.

▲ These fantastic, beadlike diatoms are only one hundredth of the width of a human hair.

▼ Protozoa such as this amoeba may be microscopic, but they are animals that can move around of their own accord.

The smallest animals

Protozoa are the smallest of all animals, made from just one cell. Most can only be seen under a microscope, yet they breathe, move, and reproduce like bigger animals. They live in water or damp places. Some protozoa can cause serious diseases. Others are helpful because they eat harmful bacteria and are food for fish and other animals.

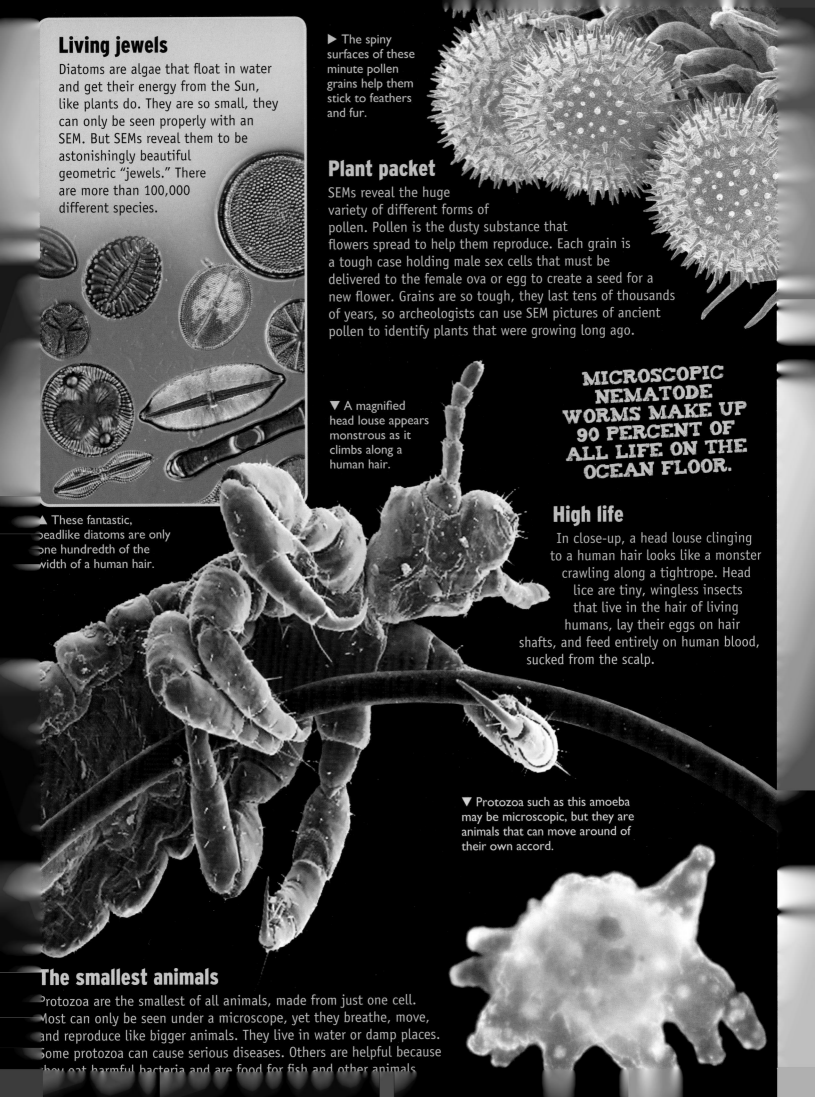

Light
FANTASTIC

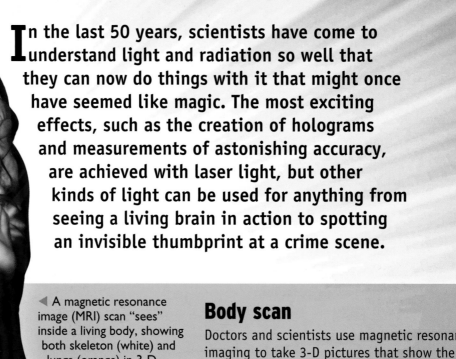

In the last 50 years, scientists have come to understand light and radiation so well that they can now do things with it that might once have seemed like magic. The most exciting effects, such as the creation of holograms and measurements of astonishing accuracy, are achieved with laser light, but other kinds of light can be used for anything from seeing a living brain in action to spotting an invisible thumbprint at a crime scene.

◀ A magnetic resonance image (MRI) scan "sees" inside a living body, showing both skeleton (white) and lungs (orange) in 3-D.

Body scan

Doctors and scientists use magnetic resonance imaging to take 3-D pictures that show the inside of the human body. It works by using powerful magnets to draw the nuclei (centers) of all the body's atoms into alignment. The magnet is then switched off. As the nuclei twist back to their normal position, they send out photons (particles of radiation). Detectors pick up the photons and a computer can then build up the 3-D image.

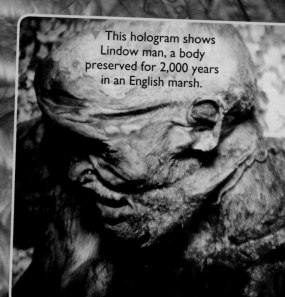

▼ This hologram shows Lindow man, a body preserved for 2,000 years in an English marsh.

Hologram magic

Holograms are 3-D images made by splitting a laser beam in two. One half, the reference beam, goes to the camera. The other bounces off the subject, breaking up the neat pattern of laser light waves. The camera records how this broken pattern interferes with (differs from) the reference beam, and this data can be used to project a 3-D image using lasers.

Nonmoving holograms have been around for half a century, but scientists are developing solid-looking moving holograms. In time, they may be able to create holograms that look like the real object.

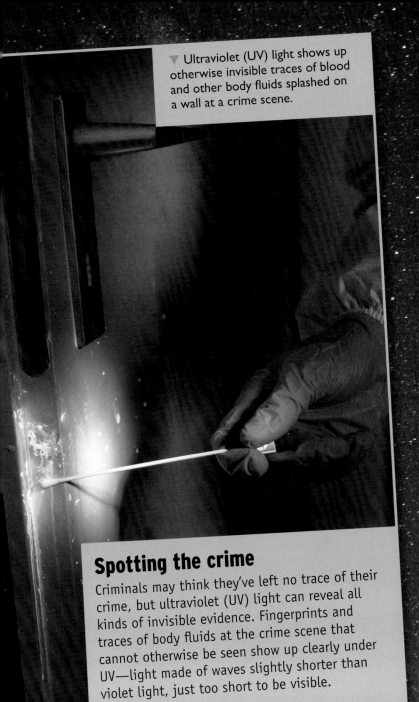

▼ Ultraviolet (UV) light shows up otherwise invisible traces of blood and other body fluids splashed on a wall at a crime scene.

LASER LIGHT

The first laser beams were created in 1960 by Theodor Maimann. Laser light is like no natural light in the Universe. All natural light is said to be "incoherent" because it is a chaotic mix of lots of photons (particles of light) of different wavelengths. In laser light, the photons are all identical and in sync. The result is an intense beam of light of just one color, which is much harder to scatter than ordinary light. In fact, laser light can be bounced off the Moon and back and still stay in a single, tight beam.

Spotting the crime

Criminals may think they've left no trace of their crime, but ultraviolet (UV) light can reveal all kinds of invisible evidence. Fingerprints and traces of body fluids at the crime scene that cannot otherwise be seen show up clearly under UV—light made of waves slightly shorter than violet light, just too short to be visible.

Making stars

Shifting dust in the air makes it hard to get a clear view of space beyond. That's why stars appear to twinkle. Astronomers use computers to adjust telescope images for the dust, using bright stars as a reference—a technique known as Adaptive Optics (AO). But there aren't always bright stars in the part of the sky astronomers need to study, so instead they create their own guide star using a laser. As the laser is shone up into the sky it creates a little "star" where it hits sodium gas and makes it glow.

◄ An observatory sends out a beam of laser light to create a sodium laser guide star in the sky for astronomers.

Laser precision

The precision of a laser beam means it can be used to take incredibly accurate measurements. For example, geologists can bounce lasers off satellites to measure the distance between continents an ocean apart to within a few millimeters. LiDAR (Light Detection and Rangefinding) is an amazing way of building up an instant 3-D map, in which a survey plane or satellite moves over a target and scans it with pulses of laser light. Detectors then pick up the reflections and use them to build up a 3-D image.

Extreme
Conditions

Some scientists learn about the world in laboratories, but others venture into the most extreme conditions to gather data and make observations. To find out more, some scientists will fly into the heart of a hurricane, endure months in the bitter chill of the Antarctic, walk into an active volcano, crawl into deep caves, dive to the depths of the ocean, climb towering rain forest trees, and much more. Where there is something to be learned, scientists will go.

Hot and hazardous

Volcanoes are incredibly dangerous up close. Although a protective suit provides a shield against the heat and fumes, it will not save a person in the event of an eruption. The two most famous volcanologists (volcano experts) of all time, Maurice and Katya Krafft, were killed, along with 41 journalists, when they were filming on Japan's Mount Unzen in 1991. Without warning, the volcano blasted out an avalanche of searingly hot gas and ashes that engulfed them in seconds.

Volcanologists test material from a live volcano.

DANGEROUS DINNERS

Cooking in chemist Helen Maynard-Casely's kitchen is a dangerous business. She uses ordinary ingredients such as cream, sugar, and bread, but she subjects them to extreme pressures and temperatures to see what happens to them. She might chill cream with liquid nitrogen at −274°F (−170°C), or squeeze burnt toast hard enough to turn the carbon it contains into diamonds. Her colleague, Colin Pulham, at the Edinburgh Centre for Science Under Extreme Conditions, in Scotland, makes diamonds by blasting carbon with dynamite!

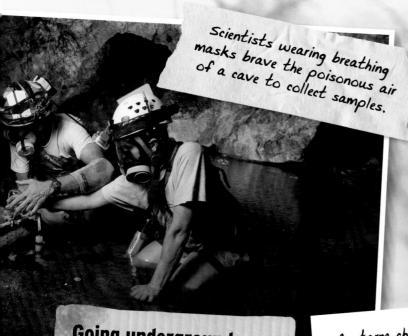

Storm chasers

Tornadoes are incredibly powerful storms. Their twisting funnels of winds can blast a building apart or whip a truck into the air. But they are localized and very brief, rarely lasting more than 15 minutes. Scientists such as Chuck Doswell and Dr. Josh Wurman have to chase the tornadoes they study at high speeds—and risk being caught in the storm themselves. The chase is so exciting that many people now pursue tornadoes just for the thrill, but authorities fear someone may soon be killed.

Going underground

Professor Hazel Barton is willing to go into Earth's depths to pursue her studies of bacteria that live in extreme conditions. Bacteria such as these can only be found in the most inaccessible caves. To study them, Professor Barton has to squeeze through narrow passages and swim through underwater lakes where visibility is practically zero and the air is often poisonous.

A storm chaser hurriedly sets down a weather probe in the path of an oncoming tornado.

The probe will measure conditions right in the heart of the tornado.

This tiny hammerhead shark being studied by a marine biologist is harmless, but it has much bigger, more ferocious relatives.

Ocean peril

Exploring the ocean can be difficult and even life threatening. In the surface waters, there is not only the danger of drowning, but also the threat of serious injury from potentially lethal creatures such as sharks, jellyfish, and stonefish. Deeper down, the water is bone-chillingly cold and pitch-dark—and the pressure is enough to crush a car.

Feel the FORCE

Force is what makes things happen. It can push things or pull them, speed them up or slow them down, draw them together or split them apart. Without forces, nothing would start or stop. Some forces—such as the force required to move your eye across this page—are tiny, while others are incredibly strong. Machines give us much more force than our bodies are capable of alone, but the most extreme forces are natural.

▼ The *Emma Maersk* dwarfs any passing craft, and is powered by an engine that weighs more than 2,500 tons.

Muscle cars

Power is a measure of not only force but also how fast it is delivered. A kilowatt (kW) of power is a force of one newton delivered at one meter every second. A small family car can get by with less than 50 kW of power, but to accelerate quickly, high-performance cars need a lot of force, very fast. That's why the *SSC Ultimate Aero TT*'s engine generates an incredible 960 kW of power.

Ship power

The more weight that must be moved, the more force you need, so the world's most powerful motors are on the world's heaviest ship—the *Emma Maersk*, which is driven through the ocean by the mighty Wärtsilä-Sulzer RTA96 diesel. It produces more than 83 megawatts (million watts) of power—as much as 10,000 high-performance cars!

MEASURING FORCE

One newton is the force that makes a mass of one kilogram accelerate at one meter per second every second. It's roughly equivalent to the force you'd use if you threw a big pebble into the sea.

45 N	The force required to push an adult over
670 N	The force of a karate chop breaking a plank
300–730 N	The gravitational force holding you on the planet
2,000 N	A good kick on a football
2,900 N	The force of a karate chop breaking a concrete slab
7,000 N	The force of an accelerating car
500,000 N	The force of a large locomotive
770,000 N	The thrust of a jumbo jet's engines
33,000,000 N	The thrust of the *Saturn V* rocket
200 million trillion N	The gravitational pull between the Moon and the Earth
350 billion trillion N	The gravitational pull between the Sun and the Earth

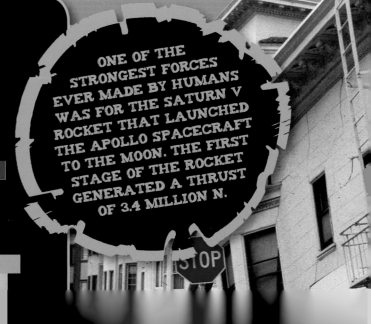

ONE OF THE STRONGEST FORCES EVER MADE BY HUMANS WAS FOR THE SATURN V ROCKET THAT LAUNCHED THE APOLLO SPACECRAFT TO THE MOON. THE FIRST STAGE OF THE ROCKET GENERATED A THRUST OF 3.4 MILLION N.

STOP

The *SSC Ultimate Aero TT* is the most powerful sports car ever, and can reach a speed of more than 270 mph (430 km/h).

Fundamental forces

There are many kinds of force. "Contact" forces directly push or pull, for example when someone hits a ball. Others act "at a distance," with no direct contact. All the fundamental forces of the Universe—gravity, electromagnetism, and the two nuclear forces that hold atoms together—act at a distance. Forces like this depend inversely on the distance between the affected objects—that is, they get weaker the further apart they are.

Star quake

There are forces in the Universe that make anything on Earth look minuscule. On December 27, 2004, a flash of energy burst from the star SGR 1806-20 in what is called a "star quake." This quake had a power of 10,000 trillion trillion trillion watts. If the star had been even 10 light-years away from Earth it would have shaken the Earth to bits. Luckily, it was much further away!

▲ The energy burst from the star SGR 1806-20 in 2004 was so huge, it was visible from Earth.

▼ Buildings were sent crashing down by the San Francisco quake of 1989.

MOUNTAIN SHAKING

Even the thrust of a rocket such as the mighty *Saturn V* is dwarfed by the natural forces involved in earthquakes. The faintest tremor has 60 million watts of power, while the most powerful earthquake ever, which hit Chile in 1960, generated 11 million billion watts. With this kind of force, earthquakes can lift up and knock down entire mountains.

STRANGE Brains

Most scientists are sensible, rational people, but sometimes they are working on ideas too complictated for most regular people to understand, so they can come across as being a bit peculiar. A few scientists become so obsessed with their research that their behavior seems truly eccentric (to put it mildly). Here are a few of the strangest scientists ever.

ELIXIR OF LIFE

The German alchemist, physician, and theologian Johann Konrad Dippel (1673–1734) was convinced he could find an elixir that would give people eternal life—and bring dead people back to life. He lived in Castle Frankenstein in Germany and tales of his experiments with corpses inspired Mary Shelley's famous story of Doctor Frankenstein and his monster. Dippel also invented Prussian Blue, the first of the chemical dyes that are used to give most clothes their colors today.

▲ Johann Dippel thought he could find a liquid that would bring the dead back to life.

He's electric

Serbian-born American Nikola Tesla (1856–1943) was the genius who gave us our modern electricity supply by pioneering the use of Alternating Current (AC) to send power over huge distances. However, some of Tesla's theories were slightly more eccentric. His idea of transmitting energy through the air without wires is now becoming a reality, but thankfully his plans for a giant death ray have not come to fruition.

▶ Nikola Tesla's many unusual ideas included using magnetic coils to turn Earth into a huge steerable spaceship.

I CAN FLY!

Some of the bravest—or craziest—scientists have been those who attempted to fly. There are many who tried strapping on wings to jump from high places and never lived to tell the tale. One of the most daring and successful was German flier Otto Lilienthal (1848–1896). Lilienthal made more than 2,000 pioneering hang glider flights in the 1890s. Sadly, a flight in 1896 proved fatal, but his experiments were crucial to the Wright brothers' famous first plane flight seven years later in 1903.

▶ Otto Lilienthal in 1893 on one of his glider flights in the hills near Berlin, Germany.

Kevin Warwick shows off the cyborg arm that responds to his thoughts.

The cyborg

Cyborgs are creatures of science fiction—they are half-human and half-robot. But British scientist Kevin Warwick (b. 1954) is turning himself into a cyborg for real. He isn't mad, though—he wants to experiment on himself to find ways of helping disabled people. He has implanted electronic devices into his arm that link his nervous system directly to a computer, so that he can operate the computer just by thinking.

ROCKET MAN

One of the pioneers of space technology, German-born American engineer Wernher von Braun (1912–1977) was obsessed with rockets from a very young age. Aged 12, von Braun packed his toy wagon with firecrackers and lit them, causing him to shoot across the street while his neighbors looked on in horror. The incident resulted in him being arrested by the police. However, von Braun was not so much mad as just dedicated to his science.

Wernher von Braun was responsible for the development of the V2 rocket in Germany, and went on to become a leading figure in the American space program after World War II.

BLACK Hole

Black holes are places where gravity is so strong that it sucks everything in, including light. They form when a star or part of a galaxy gets so dense that it collapses under its own gravity, shrinking to an infinitely small point called a singularity. Gravity around the singularity is so ferocious that it sucks in light, space, and even time.

WE CAN'T STUDY THE POINT AT WHICH LIGHT DISAPPEARS IN A BLACK HOLE IN SPACE, BUT SCIENTISTS AT THE UNIVERSITY OF ST. ANDREWS, SCOTLAND, CREATED A VIRTUAL BLACK HOLE IN THE LABORATORY USING PULSES OF LASER LIGHT.

Old supernova

Some black holes form when an old giant star collapses into a supernova. Astronomers can't actually see black holes, but sometimes they can detect their presence from their effect on other objects. Stars often form pairs, or binaries. If one star is a black hole, astronomers might be able to see the effect of its gravity on the visible companion star. They may also spot X-rays bursting from matter ripped off the companion star by the power of the black hole.

▶ An artist's impression of a black hole (right) ripping matter off its companion star (left) in a binary pair.

Supermassive

In the center of the Milky Way, in a region called Sagittarius A*, 20 million stars are packed into a space just 3 light-years across, and hurtling round at incredible speeds. Calculations show they must be in the grip of the gravity of an object two to three million times as heavy as the Sun yet only twice as big. It must be what astronomers call a "supermassive black hole." There is thought to be one at the heart of every spiral-shaped galaxy.

▲ Astronomers think the pink cloud near the galaxy NGC 4438 may be a bubble of gas belched out by a supermassive black hole at the galaxy's center. NGC 4438 is one of a pair of galaxies known as the Eyes Galaxies.

The powerful magnetic forces created by a black hole inside the galaxy Pictor A shoot out an X-ray jet thousands of light-years long.

Jet propulsion

Black holes don't just suck things in. As they mash up the matter they draw in, they can spew out giant jets of the remnants—electrons and other subatomic particles. The gigantic black hole at the heart of the M87 galaxy is shooting out an astonishingly brilliant beam of these remnants for thousands of light-years into the darkness, like some kind of galactic searchlight.

Tunnel through time

Some scientists think black holes may be linked to white holes. White holes, if they exist, would be the opposite of black holes—places where matter and radiation spew out into space like a fountain. A few scientists think that black holes and white holes could be linked by a tunnel through space and time called a wormhole. If there are such things as wormholes, it might be possible to slip through them to travel vast distances through space instantly, or even to travel through time to the future or the past.

INSIDE A BLACK HOLE

In every black hole there is a point of no return, called the event horizon. Beyond this point, time has no meaning and not even light can get out.

If you saw someone falling into a black hole, you would never see them reaching the event horizon. Instead, you would see them going slower and slower and getting redder and dimmer until they finally faded away altogether.

If you fell into a black hole, you would be stretched out like spaghetti because the pull of gravity on your feet would be so much stronger than on your head. Astronomers believe you'd become so "spaghettified" that you would eventually be ripped apart.

As you are being ripped apart, time would speed up dramatically—you'd see the future flashing by outside the black hole. But you couldn't get out, or get a message out, since even light cannot escape a black hole.

35

A MASSIVE Mystery

Deep beneath the countryside on the border of Switzerland and France is a circular tunnel more than 16 mi (27 km) long. Inside it is the world's largest machine—the Large Hadron Collider (LHC). It is basically a long, ring-shaped tube in which hadrons (subatomic particles) are accelerated round and round, reaching incredible speeds, and then smashing together. What scientists hope to see in the smashed bits may answer fundamental questions about the Universe, such as why things have mass, momentum, and inertia.

▼ The LHC has to run at incredibly low temperatures. This is the refrigeration or cryogenics unit.

▶ This computer simulation of the detector screen in the LHC shows what may happen if a Higgs boson (see far right) is found, sending out a spray of subatomic particles as it breaks up.

◀ The LHC uses powerful magnets to accelerate particles through a tube in opposite directions at high speeds and then smash them together head-on. Special sensors track the new particles created briefly as the smashed particles break up.

A crash test shows the effects of momentum dramatically—the car starts to crumple just before the test dummy is catapulted forward.

THE SEARCH FOR THE HIGGS BOSON

Forces such as electromagnetic radiation are transmitted by tiny "messenger" particles known as bosons. But scientists don't really know what mass is, or why things have inertia and momentum. It may all be down to a particle called the Higgs boson. This is how it might work:

Imagine a celebrity arriving at a party. As she swans in, fans (the Higgs bosons) crowd round her, giving her mass. The crowd makes it hard to get her moving, so she has inertia, but once they all start moving it's hard to stop them, so they give her momentum, too.

The mysterious Higgs boson is one of the things scientists are hoping to see among the smashed bits of particles in the LHC.

Momentum

Once an object is moving, it won't stop unless forced to because its mass propels it on. This is called momentum. It's what keeps the planets orbiting the Sun, and what carries a speeding roller coaster up the next incline. There's no more convincing demonstration of momentum in action than a crash test. When the test car slams into a wall, the momentum of the car and the dummy try to carry them on, which is why they smash into the wall with such force.

In order to throw the heavy shot, the shot-putter has to overcome all its inertia.

Inertia

It takes force to get something moving, because an object's mass keeps it rooted to the spot. This is called inertia. That's why a shot-putter has to be so strong to get the heavy shot moving.

Mass

Momentum and inertia both depend on mass—the amount of matter involved. The heavier something is (the more massive it is), the more momentum and inertia it has.

Energy UNLEASHED

The nucleus of most atoms is fairly stable—but not always. Sometimes nuclei can partly disintegrate (radioactivity) or split in two (nuclear fission). Under severe pressure, different nuclei may fuse together (nuclear fusion). When any of these things happen, it unleashes matter and energy, known as radiation. The Universe is filled with natural radiation, and it's the energy of nuclear fusion that makes stars shine. Humans have learned to harness this energy, both to generate power and to create nuclear bombs—the most devastatingly powerful weapons of all time.

Solar power

The Sun shines because it is so big that the pressure in its core is huge—enough to force the nuclei of hydrogen atoms to fuse to make helium. The energy released by each individual fusion may be tiny, but there are so many atoms involved that the heat generated is enormous. This nuclear fusion drives temperatures in the Sun's core to 27 million°F (15 million°C) and makes the surface glow white-hot.

RADIOACTIVITY

The nucleus of an atom is made of two kinds of particle—protons and neutrons—and there are three main kinds of radioactivity:

Alpha decay is when an alpha particle (two neutrons and two protons) breaks away from the nucleus.

Beta decay is when a neutron splits to form a proton, emitting a beta particle (an electron) and a particle called an antineutrino.

Gamma rays are not emitted from the nucleus, but are a kind of electromagnetic radiation emitted from electrons like light, but they are very energetic and dangerous.

NUCLEAR FISSION

Conventional fuel is too bulky for submarines to carry for long voyages underwater, so many big subs are now powered by nuclear reactors. The reactors generate heat from the fission (splitting) of uranium atoms, which are large and easily split. The heat creates steam to drive the submarine's turbines. Just a few small rods of uranium fuel power a sub for many long voyages.

◄ Nuclear power allows submarines to stay on patrol underwater for long periods.

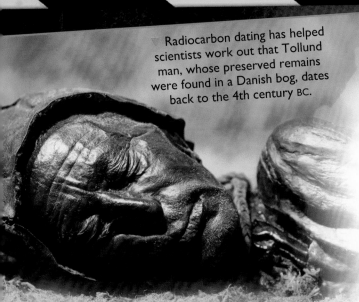

Radiocarbon dating has helped scientists work out that Tollund man, whose preserved remains were found in a Danish bog, dates back to the 4th century BC.

Carbon dating

Some variations of atoms, called isotopes, are more likely to disintegrate radioactively than others. The radioisotope carbon-14, for example, is present in all living things, but when they die, the isotopes begin to disintegrate. The rate of disintegration is so steady that by measuring the proportion of carbon-14 isotopes left in remains of once living things, scientists can tell exactly how long they have been dead. This process is called radiocarbon dating and it is one of the most valuable archeological techniques.

Radiation danger

Exposure to radiation can be very dangerous. Gamma radiation is the most dangerous because the particles are small enough to penetrate the skin. The larger particles of alpha and beta radiation are less immediately dangerous, but if you eat any food containing them, they can also cause illnesses from nausea to cancer, and may even result in death.

▶ Thermonuclear bombs use a small fission bomb to set off a massive hydrogen fusion bomb. It starts with a gigantic fireball, such as this one in a test in the Pacific in 1958.

H-bomb

The nuclear bomb that destroyed Hiroshima in Japan in 1945 depended on the fission of big atoms such as uranium and plutonium. But even more terrible bombs were created by the fusion of tiny hydrogen atoms. The hydrogen was encased in a small bomb that was exploded first to create the pressure to fuse the hydrogen atoms. These hydrogen or H-bombs are now known as thermonuclear weapons.

◀ The accident at the Chernobyl Nuclear Plant, Ukraine, in 1986 was one of the worst ever, releasing radiation that was carried by wind far across Europe. The red color in this satellite image of the area around the nuclear plant indicates radioactivity.

Birth of the
UNIVERSE

10^{27} °C		10^{12} °C
10^{-32} sec		3 min

0 seconds
First the Universe was a tiny hot ball that grew as big as a football, then cooled to (just) 10 billion billion billion°C.

10^{-43} seconds
In the "Planck" era, the four basic forces (gravity, electromagnetism, and the two nuclear forces) were joined as a single force.

10^{-12} seconds
The Universe became a sea of particles such as quarks and gluons, which began to gain mass.

10^{-32} seconds
The forces split into four and space swelled quadrillions of times in less than a fraction of a second, from something smaller than an atom to bigger than a galaxy. This is known as inflation.

3–20 minutes
Gravity and the other forces began to pull things together. Quarks and gluons joined to form the nuclei of the smallest atoms, hydrogen. Then hydrogen nuclei joined to make helium nuclei.

300,000 years
The first atoms formed and made gases.

One million years
After one million years or so, the gases began to curdle like sour milk into long strands called filaments with vast dark holes called voids in between.

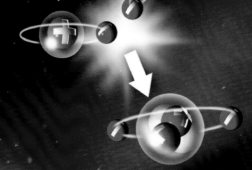

Galaxies are flying out and away from each other in all directions. This means the Universe must be expanding rapidly, so in the past it must have been much smaller. Indeed, it is now thought that long ago—about 13.5 billion years ago—the Universe was tinier than an atom. That was when it burst into being in what is often called the Big Bang. After the Big Bang, the Universe began swelling with such force and speed that astronomers are not sure if it will ever stop.

2,726 °C	253.15 °C	−270 °C
300,000 years	1 billion years	Today (13.7 billion years)

OLD AND YOUNG

When astronomers observe galaxies 13 billion light-years away, it is as if they are staring into ancient history. But the galaxies they are seeing are (relatively) very young. The oldest stars we can see are quite close to us, in globular clusters, which are groups of a few million stars within the Milky Way. Stars in the NGC 6397 cluster are 13.4 billion years old.

SCIENTISTS HAVE WORKED OUT THAT THE BIG BANG WAS ACTUALLY MORE LIKE A DEEP HUM OR THE ROAR OF A JET PLANE THAN A BANG.

Today

The Sun is almost halfway through its life today, but new stars and planets are forming all the time throughout the Universe.

4.567 billion years

The Solar System was born—the Earth and other planets were formed from a ring of dust around the Sun.

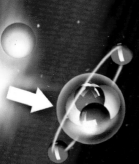

0.5–1 billion years

The filaments gradually clumped into clouds. Eventually, these clouds formed stars and galaxies.

Body SCIENCE

Take a top-to-toe tour of the human anatomy, from amazing microscopic views to X-rays of the body in action.

◄ A scanning electron microscope (SEM) reveals a clot of red and white blood cells in a blood vessel.

Building
THE BODY

The body is made up of 12 different, interlinking systems—each one performs a particular task, but they are all dependent on each other. Some, such as the circulatory system, spread throughout the body. Others, such as the digestive system, are mainly in one place.

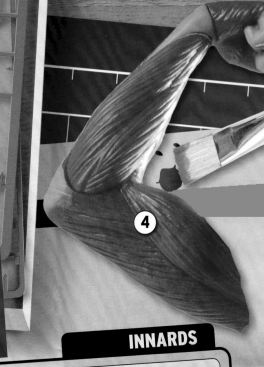

4

INNARDS

1  The **digestive system** breaks down food into chemicals that the body can absorb and use for fuel and materials, and then removes the rest as waste. It includes the stomach, intestines, and anus.

2 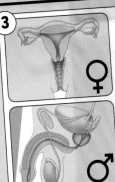 The **urinary system** removes excess water as urine. It also gets rid of impurities in the blood. It includes the kidneys and bladder.

3  The **reproductive system** consists of the sex organs that enable humans to have children. Males have a penis, scrotum, and testicles. Females have a uterus, cervix, vagina, fallopian tubes, and ovaries.

FRAMEWORK AND WEATHERPROOFING

4  The **muscular system** is made up of three types of muscle—skeletal, smooth, and heart. It circulates blood around the body and enables it to move.

5  The **skeletal system** consists of bone, cartilage, and ligaments. It supports the body, protects the major organs, and also provides an anchor for the muscles.

6 The **integumentary system**—the skin—protects the body and helps to keep it at the correct temperature. The system is also the largest sense receptor, responding to touch, pressure, heat, and cold.

WIRING AND CONTROL

7 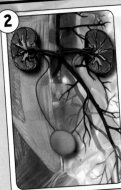 The **nervous system** contains the brain and the nerves. The brain receives electrical signals from the body via nerves and quickly sends back a response.

8 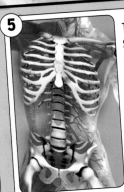 The **endocrine system** controls body processes. It releases floods of chemical messages called hormones into the blood from glands around the body.

6

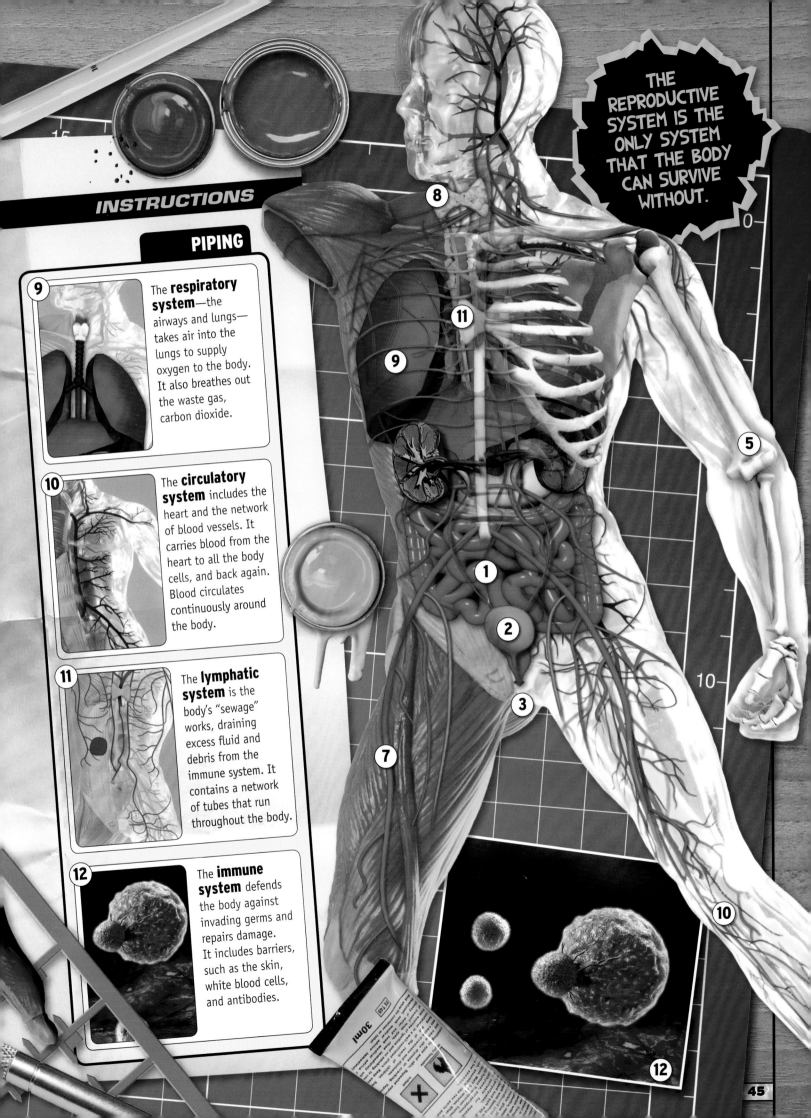

THE REPRODUCTIVE SYSTEM IS THE ONLY SYSTEM THAT THE BODY CAN SURVIVE WITHOUT.

PIPING

9 The **respiratory system**—the airways and lungs—takes air into the lungs to supply oxygen to the body. It also breathes out the waste gas, carbon dioxide.

10 The **circulatory system** includes the heart and the network of blood vessels. It carries blood from the heart to all the body cells, and back again. Blood circulates continuously around the body.

11 The **lymphatic system** is the body's "sewage" works, draining excess fluid and debris from the immune system. It contains a network of tubes that run throughout the body.

12 The **immune system** defends the body against invading germs and repairs damage. It includes barriers, such as the skin, white blood cells, and antibodies.

WILD
Landscape

Powerful microscopes have revealed the surface of the body to be surprisingly varied. Close-up, skin looks like rough terrain and hair grows on it like a forest. The skin is such an important organ that it receives more than one third of the body's blood supply.

Hair-raising

Humans are one of the few land mammals to have almost bare skin, so we wear clothes to keep warm. This bare skin, however, helps to keep the body cool. The 100,000 hairs on our heads grow faster than anything else on the body—and under a microscope they look like bumpy tree trunks.

Scalp hairs grow 2–3 mm each week. Each hair grows for three to five years before it falls out, and a new hair starts to grow.

Although just 2 mm thick, skin is made of various layers.

Mighty overcoat

The skin is the biggest organ in the body and has many important functions. It's waterproof and germproof, insulates the body from the cold and lets out excess heat, responds to touch, and gives the body nourishment by soaking up vitamin D from sunlight.

Shedding skin

To stay effective, skin has to be continually renewed. New cells push up from the dermis to provide the outer layer of protective dead cells in the epidermis. The body loses 40,000 of these dead cells every minute. In a human's lifetime, nearly 100 lb (50 kg) of skin is lost.

ROLLED OUT FLAT, YOUR SKIN WOULD COVER 21 SQ FT (2 SQ M). IT WEIGHS 9 LB (4 KG).

▶ The nail plate—the visible part of the nail—is made of a hard, transparent type of keratin.

Nailing it

Just like hair, nails are made from a tough material called keratin, created when certain cells die and harden. Fingernails grow about 1.5 in (3.5 cm) a year—so, uncut, they could grow 10 ft (3 m) or more in a lifetime. The middle fingernail grows fastest and the thumbnail grows slowest.

The outer layer of the skin, or **epidermis**, is a tough coating of overlapping layers of dead skin cells.

Underneath, in the **dermis**, there's a thicker layer containing glands, nerve endings, and touch sensors.

Under that, there's a blanket of fat, called "**subcutaneous fat**," to keep the body warm.

The dermis and fat layers are well supplied with **blood**.

▶ As old skin cells die, they leave a hard protein called keratin on the outside of the skin. Keratin gives the skin a tough, protective outer coat, which eventually flakes off.

GROWING SKIN

Artificial skin can be grown in laboratories. It is used to treat people who have suffered severe burns or skin diseases, as well as for testing the effects of drugs and cosmetics.

▶ Each piece of artificial skin is usually grown from a tiny piece of human skin.

CELLuLAR Cosmos

The body is made up of 100 trillion microscopic parcels called cells. They come in many shapes and sizes as soft cases of chemicals, each with its own personal set of life instructions in the form of DNA.

SCIENTISTS ESTIMATE THAT ONLY FIVE PERCENT OF THE BODY'S CELLS BELONG TO THE BODY—THE REST ARE BACTERIA.

SOME TYPES OF CELL AUTOMATICALLY DIE WHEN THEY BECOME DAMAGED.

2

1

3

THE SMALLEST CELLS ARE RED BLOOD CELLS AT ONLY 0.0075 MM ACROSS.

THE CELL ZOO

There are more than 200 different kinds of body cell, such as fat cells and skin cells, each with its own special task. The smallest cells are granules in the brain, and the longest are nerve cells that run through the spinal cord from the brain to the toes.

BLOOD CELLS
carry oxygen around the body.

MUSCLE CELLS
contract to enable the body to move.

NERVE CELLS
carry messages between the brain and the body.

BONE CELLS
make bone harden as it forms.

SPERM CELLS
carry the male's genes to the egg.

OVUM CELLS
contain the female genes, ready for fertilization.

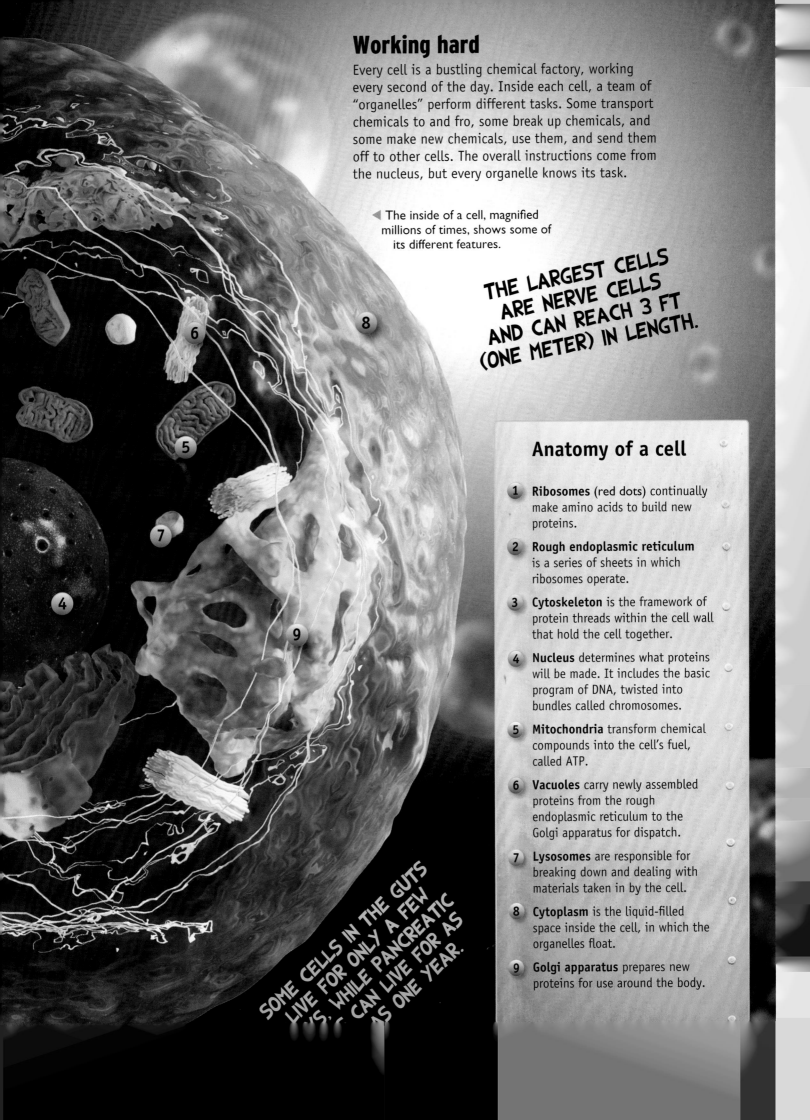

Working hard

Every cell is a bustling chemical factory, working every second of the day. Inside each cell, a team of "organelles" perform different tasks. Some transport chemicals to and fro, some break up chemicals, and some make new chemicals, use them, and send them off to other cells. The overall instructions come from the nucleus, but every organelle knows its task.

◀ The inside of a cell, magnified millions of times, shows some of its different features.

THE LARGEST CELLS ARE NERVE CELLS AND CAN REACH 3 FT (ONE METER) IN LENGTH.

SOME CELLS IN THE GUTS LIVE FOR ONLY A FEW DAY'S, WHILE PANCREATIC CELL CAN LIVE FOR AS LONG AS ONE YEAR.

Anatomy of a cell

1. **Ribosomes** (red dots) continually make amino acids to build new proteins.

2. **Rough endoplasmic reticulum** is a series of sheets in which ribosomes operate.

3. **Cytoskeleton** is the framework of protein threads within the cell wall that hold the cell together.

4. **Nucleus** determines what proteins will be made. It includes the basic program of DNA, twisted into bundles called chromosomes.

5. **Mitochondria** transform chemical compounds into the cell's fuel, called ATP.

6. **Vacuoles** carry newly assembled proteins from the rough endoplasmic reticulum to the Golgi apparatus for dispatch.

7. **Lysosomes** are responsible for breaking down and dealing with materials taken in by the cell.

8. **Cytoplasm** is the liquid-filled space inside the cell, in which the organelles float.

9. **Golgi apparatus** prepares new proteins for use around the body.

CHEMICAL Plant

The body is made from a mixture of water and organic chemicals, and contains more than half the known chemical elements in the Universe. Every part of the body is involved in changing one chemical to another.

You're wet

The body is more than 60 percent water, found both in cells and body fluids such as blood and lymph. Without water for chemicals to dissolve in, vital reactions could not take place.

You're fat

Much of the body is simply fat. "Essential fat" is needed for particular body tasks—making up 3–5 percent of men's bodies and 8–12 percent of women's. "Storage fat" is fat built up as adipose tissue to give the body an energy reserve. Pads of fat also help to keep out the cold and act as shock absorbers.

▲ Adipose cells are packed with lipids (fat), which store emergency energy reserves.

You're strong

Chemicals called proteins make up about 20 percent of the body. Some proteins are building materials—every cell and tissue is part-protein, including muscles, bones, tendons, hair, nails, and skin. Other proteins make chemical reactions happen (enzymes), send chemical messages (hormones), fight infection (antibodies), or carry oxygen in the blood (hemoglobin).

▷ Blue and red fluorescent dyes show up the protein in throat tissue.

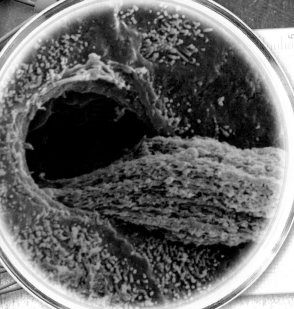

You're sweet

Carbohydrates provide fuel, either circulating in the blood ready for action as simple sugars, or stored as glycogen in the liver and the muscles.

◄ The uterine gland in a pregnant woman's womb secretes glycogen to give the egg energy to grow.

You're made to plan

Nucleic acids are the body's programmers. Deoxyribonucleic acid (DNA) in every cell, passed on from your parents, stores the instructions that tell the body not only how to grow, but also what to do throughout life.

► A sample of DNA that has been extracted from body cells.

You're a mineral mine

Bones are partly made of the minerals calcium and phosphorus. Calcium and sodium in the blood, and phosphorus, potassium, and magnesium in the cells, are essential for chemical processes. Iron is crucial to hemoglobin, which carries oxygen in the blood. Traces of other minerals are also vital, including cobalt, copper, iodine, manganese, and zinc.

► The calcium in cheese (magnified here) strengthens bones.

You're a gas

The body contains gases, such as oxygen, carbon dioxide, nitrogen oxide, hydrogen, carbon monoxide, and methanethiol. Some are dissolved in fluids and others are bubbles of gas in the lungs or gut.

BODY CHEMICALS

About 99 percent of the mass of the human body is made up of just six elements:

CHEMICAL	%	FOUND
Oxygen	65%	Liquids and tissues, bones, proteins
Carbon	18%	Everywhere
Hydrogen	10%	Liquids and tissues, bones, proteins
Nitrogen	3%	Liquids and tissues, bones, proteins
Calcium	1.5%	Bones, lungs, kidney, liver, thyroid, brain, muscles, heart
Phosphorus	1%	Bones, urine

VITAL Juice

Blood is the body's multitasking transport system. It not only delivers oxygen from the lungs to every body cell, it also carries food to fuel and maintain the cells, and washes away waste to the liver, kidneys, and lungs for disposal. Blood rushes immune cells into action to guard against infection, and even helps to spread body heat.

▼ Scabs are the body's way of protecting a wound from infection.

Plugging a leak

When you cut yourself and bleed from the damaged blood vessels, platelets instantly gather. As they do, they send out an alarm in the form of "clotting factors." These draw in other platelets and encourage them to clump together to make fibers or "fibrin" that plug the leak. The fibrin dries out to form a scab, protecting the wound until it has healed.

▲ Blood cells and fibrin (yellow) rush to a wound to form a clot. This is called coagulation.

Fresh Frozen Plasma (CPD-A1)
129169J 6

O RhPOSITIVE

COMPLEX MIXTURE

Blood looks red in color, but it is mostly made up of a clear, yellowish fluid called plasma. The color red comes from the red blood cells that are swept along by it. Plasma also contains giant white cells called leucocytes and little lumps called platelets.

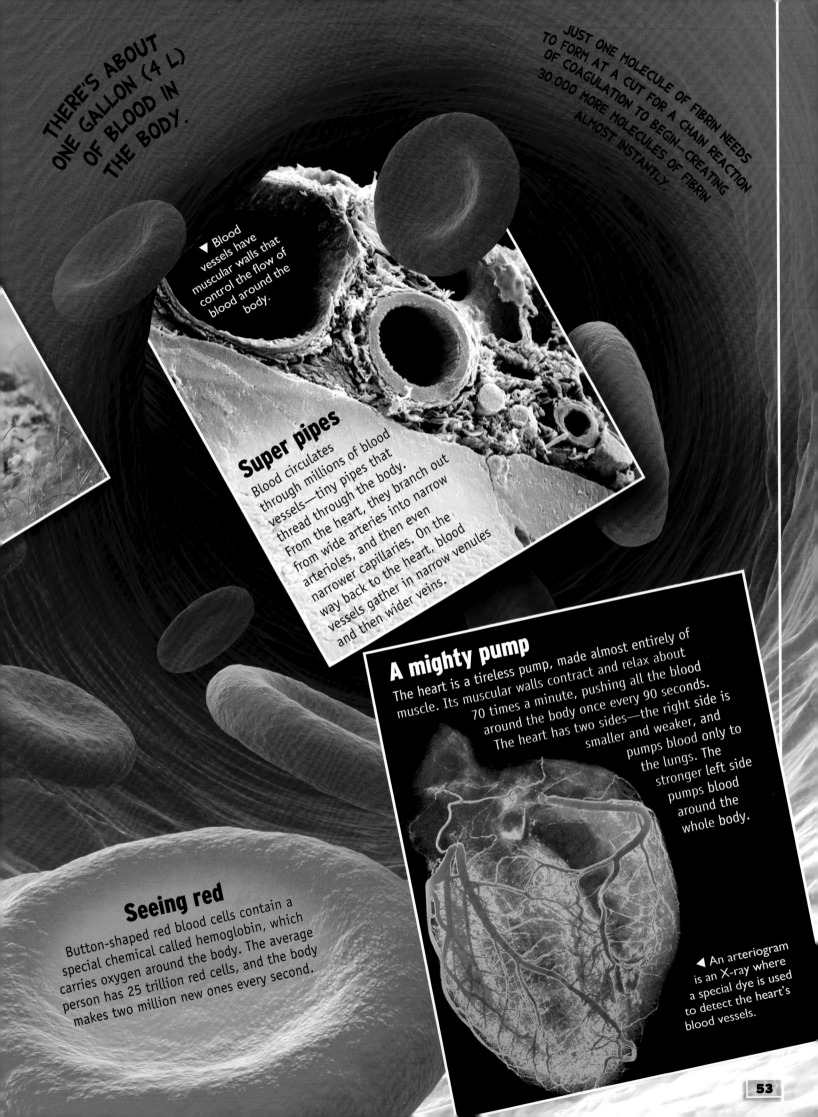

THERE'S ABOUT ONE GALLON (4 L) OF BLOOD IN THE BODY.

JUST ONE MOLECULE OF FIBRIN NEEDS TO FORM AT A CUT FOR A CHAIN REACTION OF COAGULATION TO BEGIN—CREATING 30,000 MORE MOLECULES OF FIBRIN ALMOST INSTANTLY.

▼ Blood vessels have muscular walls that control the flow of blood around the body.

Super pipes

Blood circulates through millions of blood vessels—tiny pipes that thread through the body. From the heart, they branch out from wide arteries into narrow arterioles, and then even narrower capillaries. On the way back to the heart, blood vessels gather in narrow venules and then wider veins.

A mighty pump

The heart is a tireless pump, made almost entirely of muscle. Its muscular walls contract and relax about 70 times a minute, pushing all the blood around the body once every 90 seconds. The heart has two sides—the right side is smaller and weaker, and pumps blood only to the lungs. The stronger left side pumps blood around the whole body.

◄ An arteriogram is an X-ray where a special dye is used to detect the heart's blood vessels.

Seeing red

Button-shaped red blood cells contain a special chemical called hemoglobin, which carries oxygen around the body. The average person has 25 trillion red cells, and the body makes two million new ones every second.

The body cannot survive for long without the continuous input of energy from food. Energy drives all the body's chemical reactions, which release heat energy for warmth and muscle energy for movement.

◄ A thermogram detects heat. Red shows the hottest parts and blue the coldest. The head and chest are the warmest parts of the body.

▼ Some cells only contain one mitochondrion, but others contain thousands.

A trillion fires
Tiny bursts of energy are constantly released inside each of the trillions of body cells in a process called cellular respiration. In each cell, microscopic "furnaces" called mitochondria use oxygen to break down glucose molecules and release energy. This process generates heat.

STORED ENERGY IS PACKED INTO MILLIONS OF TINY MOLECULES CALLED ATP (ADENOSINE TRIPHOSPHATE). ATP IS LIKE A COILED SPRING, READY TO UNWIND AND RELEASE ITS ENERGY.

Hot bodies
For body processes to function well, the body must remain at the perfect temperature—98.6°F (37°C). This is warmer than the outside world, so the body continually generates heat by moving the muscles and triggering chemical reactions in the liver.

ENERGY FOOD

Energy comes from carbohydrates in food, including sugar and starch. Fats in food provide energy, too, but this is stored rather than used immediately. Energy-rich molecules are either delivered to every body cell as glucose in the blood, or temporarily held in the liver as glycogen.

▽ When people play sports, the body sweats to release heat energy.

Stay cool

If the body becomes too hot, the hypothalamus (the brain's "thermostat") tells the body to lose heat by sweating through the skin's pores. Sweating not only takes warm water out of the body, but also cools the skin as the moisture evaporates. The hypothalamus also boosts the supply of blood to the skin to take heat away from the body's core.

Brrrrrrrr...

If the body becomes too cold, the hypothalamus generates heat by boosting cell activity and making the muscles move rapidly in shivers. It also cuts heat loss by restricting the supply of blood to the skin to keep warmth in the body's core.

DURING A MATCH, A TOP TENNIS PLAYER USES ENOUGH ENERGY TO BOIL A KETTLE EVERY MINUTE.

In 2005, Lewis Gordon Pugh broke the world record for the farthest-north, long-distance swim, by swimming one kilometer through water in cracks between the North Pole ice.

ROUGH SKIN

When the body is cold, hairs on the skin may stand on end, creating "goose bumps." This traps a layer of warm air next to the skin, making the body feel warmer.

Human COMPUTER

The brain contains more than 100 billion nerve cells, or neurons. Each neuron is connected to as many as 25,000 other neurons—creating trillions of routes for signals to buzz around the body. This enables us to think and learn, jump and sit, and laugh and cry—everything that makes us human.

RECEIVING SIGNALS
The cerebral cortex is the wrinkled layer of interconnected nerve cells around the outside of the brain. It is made up of different structures, each with individual functions. Many sense signals are received and responded to here.

The demanding brain
The brain makes up less than two percent of the body's weight, yet demands more than 20 percent of its blood supply. Deprived of the oxygen blood carries for even a few moments, brain cells quickly die. If the blood supply is cut off entirely, the brain loses consciousness in ten seconds and death occurs within a few minutes.

◀ Blood floods into the brain continuously through large arteries to give it energy for thinking.

PREFRONTAL CORTEX
is involved with memory, solving problems, and judgment.

A brain of two halves
The brain is split into two halves or hemispheres, linked by a bundle of nerves. The left half controls the right side of the body and the right half controls the left side of the body. It is believed that the left side deals with logical and analytical thinking, while the right side expresses emotion and creativity.

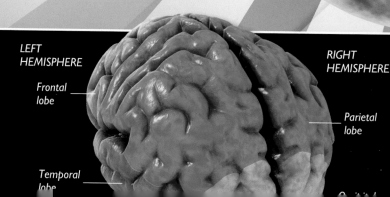

LEFT HEMISPHERE

RIGHT HEMISPHERE

Frontal lobe

Parietal lobe

Temporal lobe

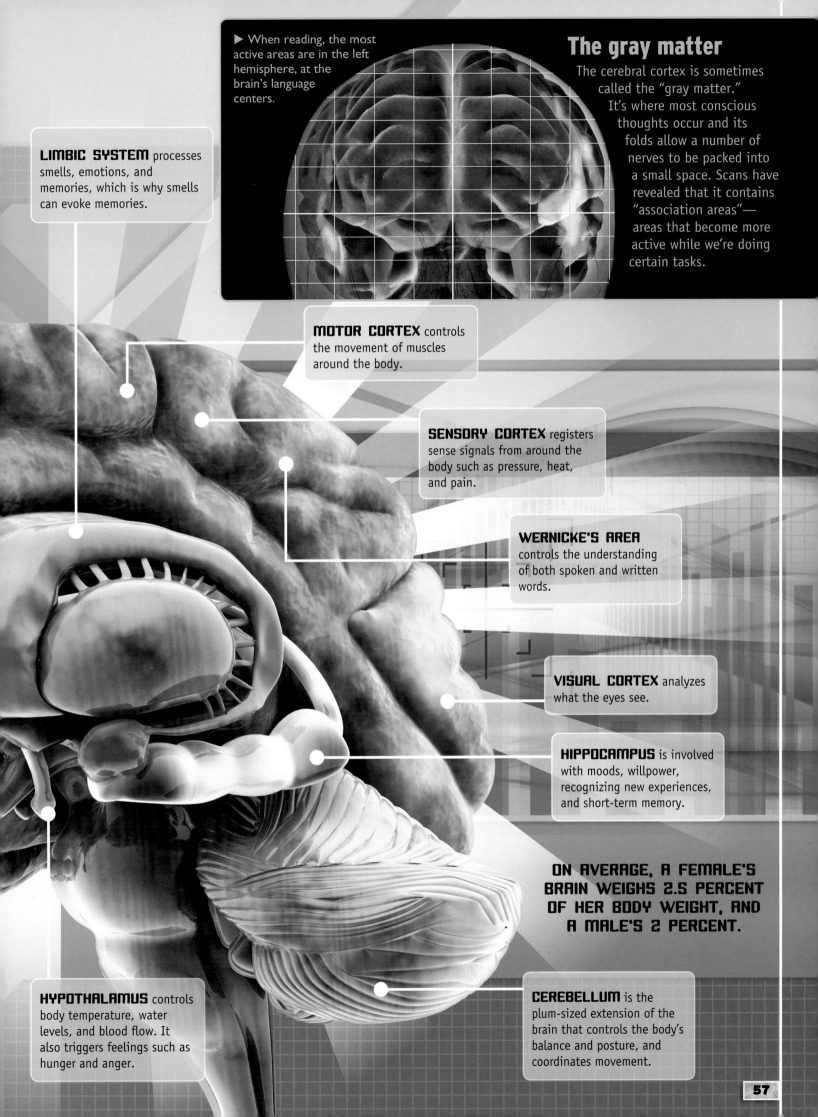

▶ When reading, the most active areas are in the left hemisphere, at the brain's language centers.

The gray matter

The cerebral cortex is sometimes called the "gray matter." It's where most conscious thoughts occur and its folds allow a number of nerves to be packed into a small space. Scans have revealed that it contains "association areas"— areas that become more active while we're doing certain tasks.

LIMBIC SYSTEM processes smells, emotions, and memories, which is why smells can evoke memories.

MOTOR CORTEX controls the movement of muscles around the body.

SENSORY CORTEX registers sense signals from around the body such as pressure, heat, and pain.

WERNICKE'S AREA controls the understanding of both spoken and written words.

VISUAL CORTEX analyzes what the eyes see.

HIPPOCAMPUS is involved with moods, willpower, recognizing new experiences, and short-term memory.

ON AVERAGE, A FEMALE'S BRAIN WEIGHS 2.5 PERCENT OF HER BODY WEIGHT, AND A MALE'S 2 PERCENT.

HYPOTHALAMUS controls body temperature, water levels, and blood flow. It also triggers feelings such as hunger and anger.

CEREBELLUM is the plum-sized extension of the brain that controls the body's balance and posture, and coordinates movement.

Body SIGNALING

Nerves make up the body's communication network. They carry instant messages from the brain to every part of the body—and stream back a constant flow of data to tell the brain what's going on both inside the body and in the outside world.

Body network

The central nervous system is made up of the brain and the spinal cord—the nerves in the spine. It is responsible for collecting information fed in through nerves from all over the body, processing data, and sending out responses. The nerves of the peripheral nervous system branch out from the central nervous system to every limb and body part.

Bundle of nerves

The brain stem, spinal cord, and branches of the peripheral nervous system are made of long bundles of nerve fibers called nerves. These bundles are made from the axons (tails) of nerve cells, bound together like the wires in a telephone cable. Signals can travel at up to 395 ft (120 m) per second.

▶ Nerve fibers are bundled together and insulated by a sheath of fatty myelin to keep the signal strong.

SCIENTISTS LEARNED HOW HUMAN NERVES WORK BY STUDYING THE NERVES OF SQUID.

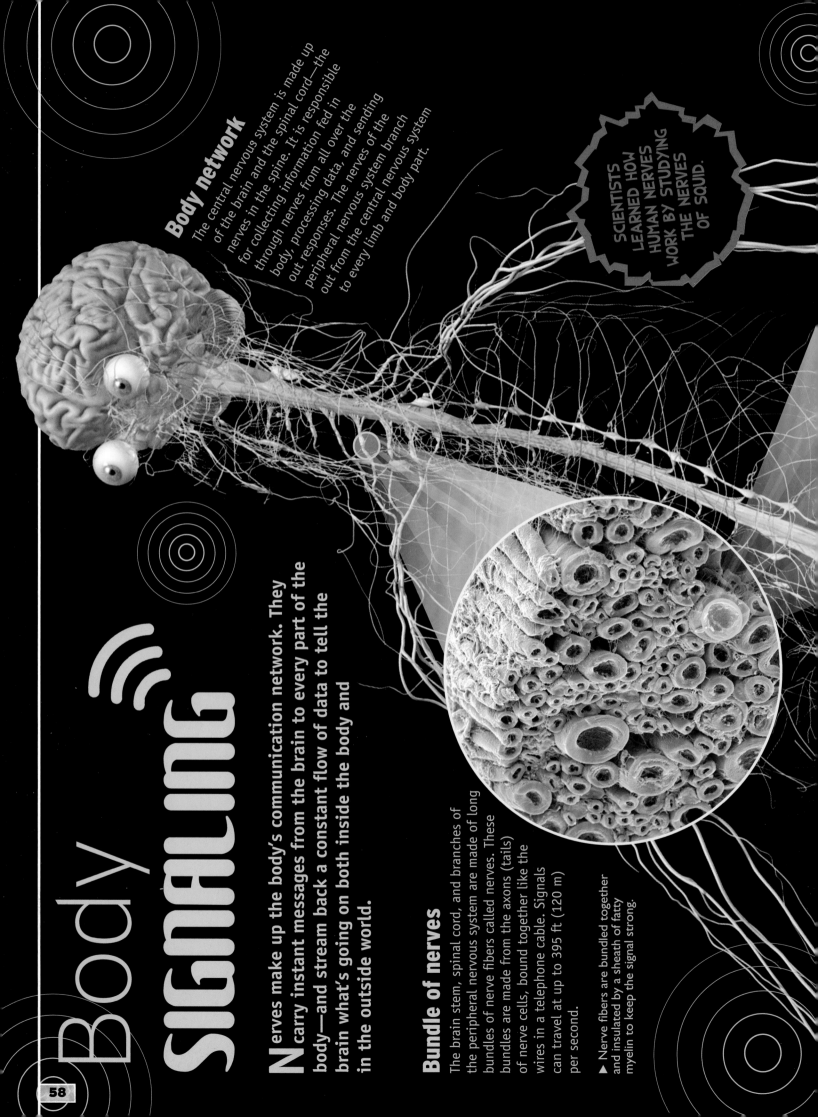

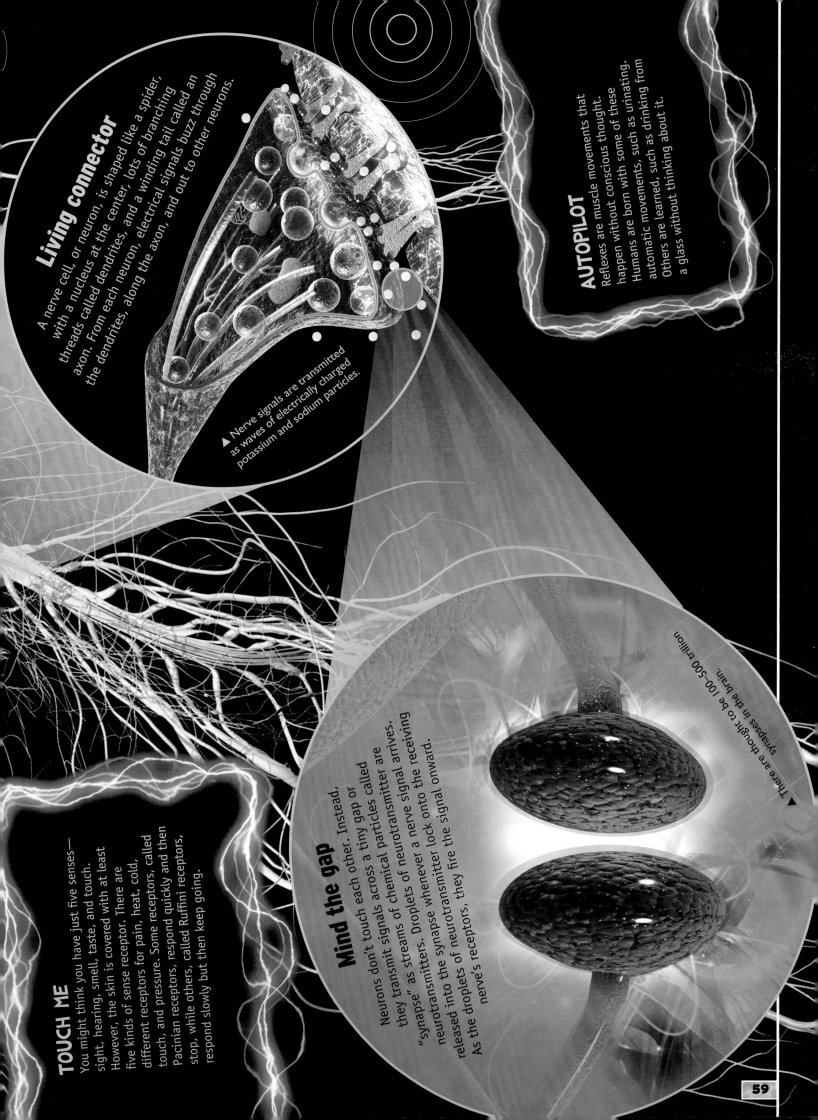

Living connector

A nerve cell, or neuron, is shaped like a spider—with a nucleus at the center. lots of branching threads called dendrites, and a winding tail called an axon. From each neuron, electrical signals buzz through the dendrites, along the axon, and out to other neurons.

▲ Nerve signals are transmitted as waves of electrically charged potassium and sodium particles.

AUTOPILOT

Reflexes are muscle movements that happen without conscious thought. Humans are born with some of these automatic movements, such as urinating. Others are learned, such as drinking from a glass without thinking about it.

TOUCH ME

You might think you have just five senses—sight, hearing, smell, taste, and touch. However, the skin is covered with at least five kinds of sense receptor. There are different receptors for pain, heat, cold, touch, and pressure. Some receptors, called Pacinian receptors, respond quickly and then stop, while others, called Ruffini receptors, respond slowly but then keep going.

Mind the gap

Neurons don't touch each other. Instead, they transmit signals across a tiny gap called a "synapse" as streams of chemical particles are neurotransmitters lock onto the receiving nerve's receptors, they fire the signal onward. As the droplets of neurotransmitter arrives. Droplets of neurotransmitter released into the synapse whenever a nerve signal are transmit signals across a tiny gap or "synapse."

▲ There are thought to be 100–500 trillion synapses in the brain.

EYE OPENER

1 -
2 -
3 -
4 -
5 -
6 -
7 -
8 -
9 -
10 -

YOUR AWESOME EYES COMBINE THE PICTURE QUALITY OF THE BEST DIGITAL CAMERAS WITH A VERSATILITY THAT NO CAMERA CAN MATCH. THEY CAN FOCUS BOTH ON A SPECK OF DUST INCHES AWAY AND A GALAXY FAR ACROSS THE UNIVERSE, AND WORK IN BOTH STARLIGHT AND SUNLIGHT.

20/70

20/50

Black hole

The dark "pupil" is a porthole that lets light into the eye. It looks black because the eye is so dark inside. When light gets very dim, the fringe or "iris" around it can open wide to let more light in.

▼ The pattern of fibers in the iris is unique to each human, so it can be used to identify individuals, just like fingerprints.

▼ A damaged cornea can cause blurred vision. To restore normal eyesight, surgeons lift the top layer of the cornea and trim it minutely with a laser.

Stay sharp

The cornea is the transparent window at the front of the eye that gives the main focusing power. Light rays pass through the cornea and are refracted (bent) before hitting the lens. The lens adjusts the focus to give a sharp picture, whether you are looking at something close-up or far away. Each adjustment takes barely one fiftieth of a second.

Movie time

The inside of the eyeball is like a mini cinema. The cornea and lens project an image onto the back of the eye, called the retina. Although the image is just a few millimeters across inside the eye, you see it at its real size.

THE EYES CONSTANTLY SCAN THE SCENE YOU ARE LOOKING AT IN INCREDIBLY RAPID MOVEMENTS TO BUILD UP A PICTURE AND PICK OUT KEY DETAILS.

2.50

▲ When the muscles surrounding the lens contract, the lens becomes thicker and can focus on close-up objects.

▶ There are only seven colors in the rainbow, but the eye's cones can distinguish ten million colors!

Taking the picture

The retina acts like the photocells in a camera—150 million rods detect if it's dark or light, and even work in very low light, while eight million cones detect colors and work best in daylight.

Highway to the brain

It's actually the brain that "sees," not the eyes, using the visual cortex. When light hits the retina, the rods and cones send nerve signals down the optic nerve to create a picture in the brain.

▶ Signals from the right side of each retina go to the right of the visual cortex; those from the left of each retina go to the left of the visual cortex.

NEW Life

The human body can create a new version of itself. It starts when two single, microscopically tiny cells—a male's sperm cell and a female's egg cell—join. From this combined cell a new life begins, as a baby slowly grows inside the female's womb for the nine months of pregnancy.

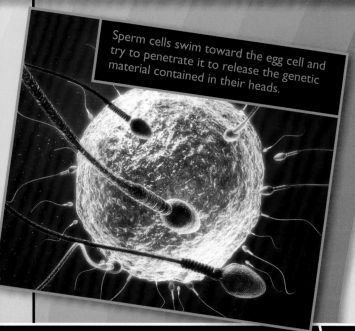

Sperm cells swim toward the egg cell and try to penetrate it to release the genetic material contained in their heads.

AFTER ONLY ONE WEEK, THE EMBRYO CONTAINS HUNDREDS OF CELLS.

Fertilized egg to embryo

As soon as the sperm and egg join successfully, the egg is fertilized, and the new life is "conceived." The egg immediately begins to divide rapidly, making seemingly identical copies of itself to create an embryo. As the cells multiply, differences appear, and layers that will become skin and organs develop.

Day 1

Millions try, but in most cases, only one sperm cell will succeed and fertilize the egg cell.

Day 6

The ball of cells attaches to the lining of the female's womb.

Day 40

In the beginning

The sperm and egg are special not because they have something extra, but because they have something missing. Unlike other body cells, they have only one set of 23 chromosomes, not the usual two. The sperm must add its 23 chromosomes to the egg's 23 chromosomes to make the full complement of 46 and start a new life. This happens during sexual intercourse, when the male's sperm swim into the female's womb to reach the egg.

IF TWO EGGS ARE RELEASED AT THE SAME TIME AND ARE BOTH FERTILIZED, NON-IDENTICAL TWINS DEVELOP.

The fertilized egg divides to form a small bundle of cells.

Embryo to fetus

After about 40 days, the embryo, though barely as big as a pea, has developed some recognizable features, such as a nose, mouth, and ears. Dark spots show where the eyes will grow. A heart beats rapidly inside, and a brain, muscles, and bones start to grow. After nine weeks, the embryo has become so babylike (though with a giant head) that it is described as a fetus, not an embryo.

At this early stage, the embryo looks like a tadpole.

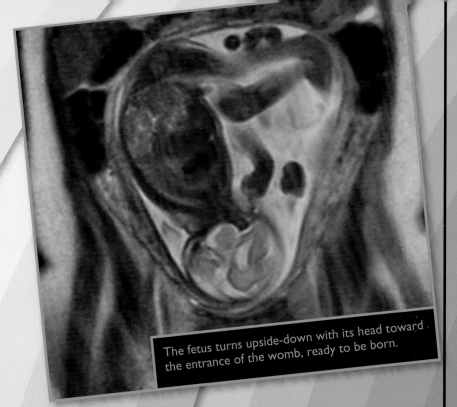

The fetus turns upside-down with its head toward the entrance of the womb, ready to be born.

Growing strong

At the halfway stage, the fetus looks like a curled-up baby, only smaller and less defined. It's only about the size of an adult's hand, so still has some way to grow, but it begins to move around and may even kick its developing legs inside the mother's womb. Research suggests the baby may even be able to hear things outside its mother's body.

Time for birth

Finally, after about 37 weeks, the fetus is fully developed. Birth begins when the mother goes into "labor." Firstly, the womb muscles contract and burst the bag of fluid that surrounds the baby. Secondly, the muscles around the womb's neck contract and relax rhythmically to push the baby out through the birth canal.

The embryo is now about 5 mm long and buds for the arms and legs start to develop.

Day 133
The fetus is now about 6.5 in (16 cm) long and fine, downy hair covers its body.

Day 266
The fetus is about 14 in (36 cm) long and has a firm grip.

An ultrasound scanner reveals the baby growing inside the womb.

THE YOUNGEST BABY TO BE BORN AND SURVIVE WAS ONLY 21 WEEKS OLD.

GROWTH Factor

The rate at which the body grows depends on age and gender—babies and teenagers grow rapidly, and males become taller than females. Body proportions also develop with age—a baby's legs only make up one quarter of its length, but by adulthood the legs equal half of the body's height.

Big head

A newborn baby's head is already three-quarters of its adult size because it contains the brain. There are two gaps called fontanelles between the bones of a baby's skull, where there is only membrane (a "skin" of thin tissue), not bone. This allows the skull to flex, so there is room for the brain to grow even more. The gaps close and the bones join together after about 18 months.

BABIES HAVE A MUCH STRONGER SENSE OF SMELL THAN ADULTS.

Time to grow

Children grow quickly because the brain is continually sending out a "grow-faster" chemical. This growth hormone is secreted by the pituitary gland in the center of the brain. It tells cells to make protein and break down fat for energy. Too much growth hormone can cause a condition called gigantism, or acromegaly where the body grows too big and in the wrong places.

6 months–1 year

A baby begins to grow teeth—the upper and lower incisors come first.

1–4 years

Toddlers start to talk from one year old and can read simple words from four years old.

9–13 years

◄ For the first nine months or more, babies can only move on their hands and knees.

◄ Toddlers only gradually develop the strength and balance to walk upright.

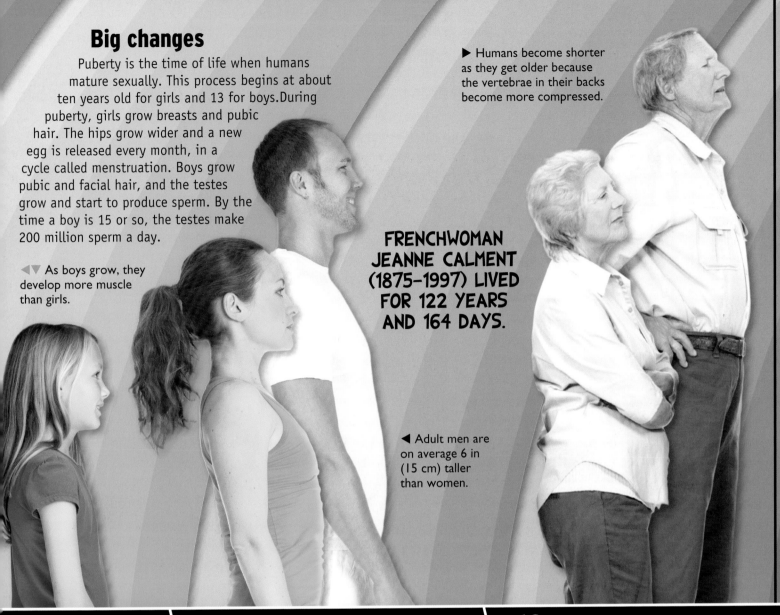

Big changes

Puberty is the time of life when humans mature sexually. This process begins at about ten years old for girls and 13 for boys. During puberty, girls grow breasts and pubic hair. The hips grow wider and a new egg is released every month, in a cycle called menstruation. Boys grow pubic and facial hair, and the testes grow and start to produce sperm. By the time a boy is 15 or so, the testes make 200 million sperm a day.

◀▼ As boys grow, they develop more muscle than girls.

▶ Humans become shorter as they get older because the vertebrae in their backs become more compressed.

FRENCHWOMAN JEANNE CALMENT (1875–1997) LIVED FOR 122 YEARS AND 164 DAYS.

◀ Adult men are on average 6 in (15 cm) taller than women.

During adolescence a boy grows about 3.75 in (9.5 cm) a year and a girl 3.35 in (8.5 cm).

20+ years

Early adulthood is from 20 to 39 years and "middle age" is from 40 to 59 years.

60+ years

In old age, eyesight and hearing often weaken.

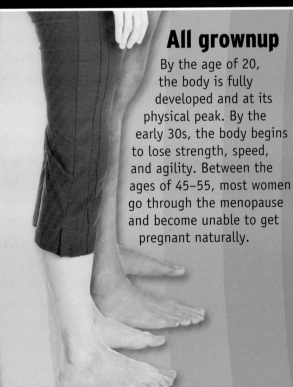

All grownup

By the age of 20, the body is fully developed and at its physical peak. By the early 30s, the body begins to lose strength, speed, and agility. Between the ages of 45–55, most women go through the menopause and become unable to get pregnant naturally.

Old age

As the body grows older, it stops renewing itself so well—the muscles weaken, bones become more brittle, joints stiffen, and the skin starts to slacken and wrinkle. The hair may eventually turn gray as pigment cells stop working.

MUSCLE Power

Every move the body makes needs muscles, from lifting a finger to jumping in the air—even for sitting still. Without muscles, the body would slump like a sack of potatoes. Muscles are amazing little motors that work instantly, whenever they are needed, by constantly contracting and relaxing.

IF ALL THE MUSCLES IN THE BODY PULLED TOGETHER, THEY COULD LIFT A BUS.

Running on air

Ideally, muscles work aerobically—the cells get enough oxygen from glucose to release energy. However, if a person is unfit or has worked the muscles too hard, the cells may burn glucose "anaerobically"—without oxygen. This uses up glucose rapidly, making the body tired and leaving a buildup of lactic acid, which makes the muscles sore. To draw in the extra oxygen needed to burn this lactic acid, you pant when you stop running.

The walls of the heart are made of cardiac muscle.

Outside and in

The body has two kinds of muscle—voluntary muscles that are under conscious control and involuntary muscles that work automatically. Voluntary muscles cover the skeleton and allow the body to move. Involuntary muscles control bodily functions, such as the heartbeat.

Power stripes

Muscles get their power from bundles of fibers that contract and relax. Inside each fiber are alternating, interlocking stripes or "filaments" of actin and myosin. When the brain tells a muscle to contract, little buds on each myosin filament twist, pulling on the actin filaments and making the muscle shorter. Each time a muscle contracts, another muscle fiber needs to shorten in the opposite direction to pull it back to its original length.

▶ Muscles work in pairs of actin and myosin filaments because they can only shorten themselves.

THE STRONGEST MUSCLES ARE THE MASSETER MUSCLES, WHICH CONTROL THE JAW'S BITING MOVEMENT.

▲ The body has several layers of muscle. Most are attached to bones with tough fibers called tendons.

Muscle building

During exercise, the muscles grow larger. At first, the fibers simply grow fatter. With regular exercise, the body grows new muscle fibers, which means they become stronger. The blood supply improves, too, so the muscles can work longer without tiring.

▶ Fibers in the voluntary muscles move the bones.

On demand

There are 640 voluntary muscles on the skeleton. The brain can only consciously control combinations that work together, rather than individual muscles. The longest is the sartorius muscle at the front of the thigh, while the biggest is the gluteus maximus in the buttocks.

STRONG Structure

Bones give the body a strong, rigid, light framework. Bone can stand being squeezed twice as much as granite and stretched four times as much as concrete. Yet it's so light that bone accounts for barely 14 percent of the body's weight.

A lasting framework

The skeleton is made of 206 bones. As living tissue, the bones are constantly replenished with new cells that grow in the bone's center, called the marrow. The skeleton is the only body part that survives long after death.

THE HAND AND WRIST HAVE ABOUT 30 SMALL JOINTS.

Living bones

Bones are packed with living cells called osteocytes. Each osteocyte sits in a little pocket called a lacuna, and is constantly washed in blood. Some, called osteoblasts, make new bone. Others, called osteoclasts, break down the old, worn-out bone. The soft spongy center or "marrow" of bone produces new blood cells.

The tiniest bone is in **the ear**. It's called the stirrup bone and is only 3 mm long.

▲ Inside osteoblast cells, lumps of calcium salts crystallize to make hard bone.

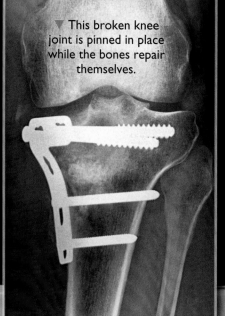

▼ This broken knee joint is pinned in place while the bones repair themselves.

Broken bones

Bones are strong, but they can break or "fracture." Most fractures heal—the body stems any bleeding, then gradually fills the gap with osteoblasts, which weave new bone across the break. The break may need to be straightened and the bone held in place with pins or a plaster cast to ensure it repairs in the right way.

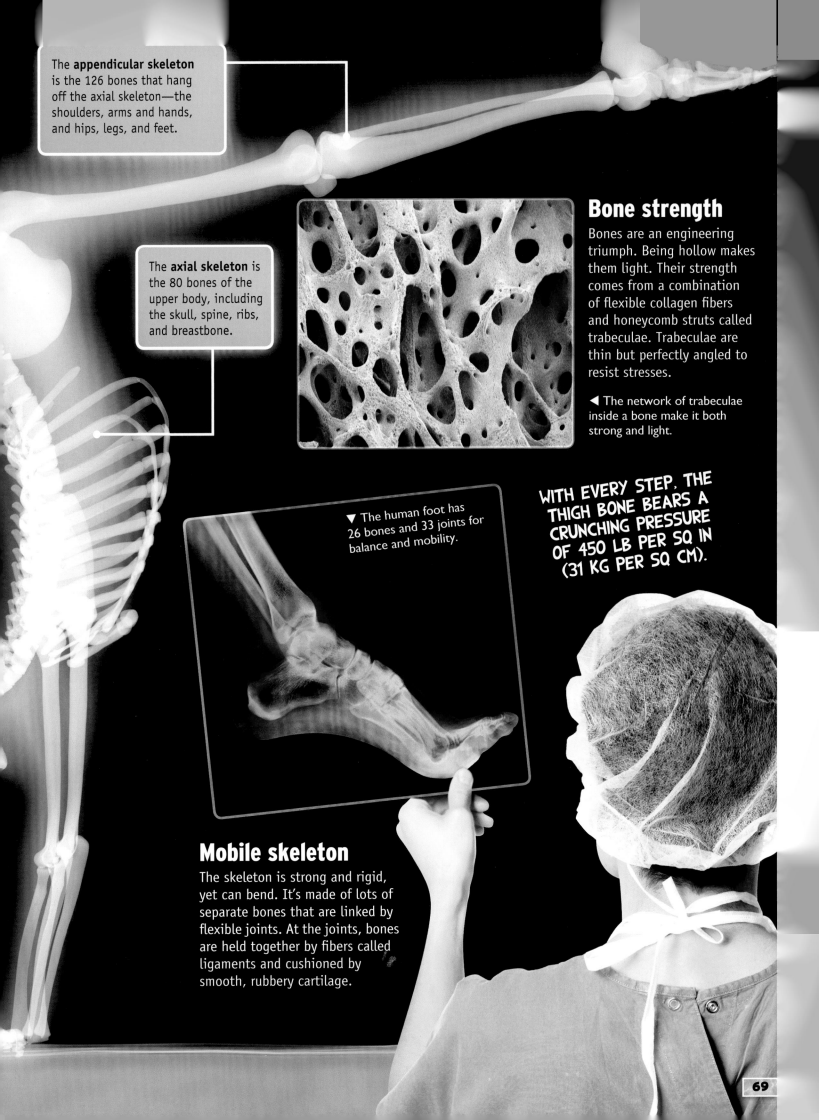

The **appendicular skeleton** is the 126 bones that hang off the axial skeleton—the shoulders, arms and hands, and hips, legs, and feet.

The **axial skeleton** is the 80 bones of the upper body, including the skull, spine, ribs, and breastbone.

Bone strength

Bones are an engineering triumph. Being hollow makes them light. Their strength comes from a combination of flexible collagen fibers and honeycomb struts called trabeculae. Trabeculae are thin but perfectly angled to resist stresses.

◄ The network of trabeculae inside a bone make it both strong and light.

▼ The human foot has 26 bones and 33 joints for balance and mobility.

WITH EVERY STEP, THE THIGH BONE BEARS A CRUNCHING PRESSURE OF 450 LB PER SQ IN (31 KG PER SQ CM).

Mobile skeleton

The skeleton is strong and rigid, yet can bend. It's made of lots of separate bones that are linked by flexible joints. At the joints, bones are held together by fibers called ligaments and cushioned by smooth, rubbery cartilage.

ALIEN INVADERS

You might think you're clean, but you're actually a zoo of microscopic bugs. Living inside your guts are up to 1,000 different species of bacteria—and a similar number are encamped on your skin. Then there are fungi and viruses, mosquitoes, fleas, bedbugs, blackflies, botflies, lice, leeches, ticks, mites, and worms...

Very lice

The head louse (*plural* lice) is a tiny insect that has made human hair its only home for thousands of years. Lice are just big enough to see with the naked eye. They cannot fly, and spend all their lives crawling through their host's hair sucking tiny amounts of blood from the scalp.

Mite have

Your feet, wrists, genitals, and the roots of your hairs are home to a little bug—the follicle mite. Mites are related to spiders, but they are so small, even as adults (less than 0.25 mm long), that you can't see them with the naked eye.

These tiny mites live in the roots of human eyelashes.

The head louse spends its entire life in human hair.

Got you taped

In some parts of the world, people who have eaten uncooked meat end up with flat, ribbonlike tapeworms living in their gut. These worms settle in and feed off the food the infected person eats, soon making their host ill. They are so flat and the human guts are so long that they can grow to more than 30 ft (9 m) in length!

▲ The head of a tapeworm has suckers for gripping the inside of the gut.

Coli wobbles

About 0.1 percent of the bacteria living in the gut belongs to the strain *Escherichia coli*. Most *E coli* are harmless, but occasionally they can make you ill with food poisoning. They enter the body on unwashed vegetables or in uncooked meat, then multiply and release floods of toxins in the intestines.

▼ Under UV light, bacteria can be seen on the hands.

▲ E coli bacteria live in your gut and supply you with vitamins K2 and B1.

Skin bugs

A powerful microscope reveals your skin is absolutely crawling with tiny bacteria. Many are Actinobacteria, which are also common in soil. Although there are many billions of bacteria living on your skin, they are so small, their combined volume is no bigger than a pea.

MILLIONS ARE COMING!

BODY DEFENDERS!

THE BODY OFTEN COMES UNDER ATTACK FROM DISEASE-CAUSING BACTERIA, VIRUSES, AND OTHER GERMS. TO DEFEND AGAINST THESE ONSLAUGHTS, THE BODY IS ARMED WITH AN AMAZING SERIES OF BIOLOGICAL WEAPONS, KNOWN AS... THE IMMUNE SYSTEM.

Bacteria cause diseases such as whooping cough, tetanus, and typhoid.

THE VILLAINS

Germs cause illness when they invade or "infect" the body and multiply.

Viruses are tiny and cause diseases such as colds, flu, mumps, rabies, and AIDS.

Sometimes, germs beat the outer defenses and get inside the body to start their nasty work.

Germs make you feel ill with the toxins they release. Plus, the body's battle against these intruders can cause fever, aching joints, and inflammation. It's time for the inner defenses to get ready...

OUTER DEFENSE

Like a fortress, the body has lots of barriers and booby traps to stop germs getting in. The first barrier is the skin.

When germs sneak in, they get bogged down in slimy mucus in the nose and lungs—and blasted out with a sneeze or cough. The stomach vomits germs out!

FIRST INNER DEFENSE

Floods of little "complement" proteins mob the intruding germs.

They send out an alarm to the body, which causes soreness and inflammation.

PHAGOCYTES

Troops of "special forces" are called in—the phagocytes. There are three types of phagocyte—granulocytes, dendritic cells, and macrophages.

MACROPHAGE

GRANULOCYTE

DENDRITIC CELL

Repair and Rebuild

The body is remarkably good at shielding itself against harm and repairing any damage. Sometimes, though, it needs medical help. Vaccines arm the body's immune system against future infections, antibiotic drugs kill many disease-causing bacteria, and surgery corrects defects.

► This titanium knee joint (red) replaced a knee destroyed by bone disease.

New joints

Bones are tough, but can be damaged, especially at the joints. With the aid of special materials such as titanium, surgeons can remove a damaged joint and replace it with an artificial one that lasts for ten years. By using a computer to visualize the replacement, it is always a perfect match.

▼ Scottish firefighter Ian Reid, who lost his hand in an accident, has a bionic replacement that can grip as tightly as a real hand.

Bionic bodies

Artificial hands and limbs respond to nerve signals directly from the brain. Therefore a person only has to think to control the tiny electric motors that make a bionic, or prosthetic, hand move. Bionics are used to replace lost or irreversibly damaged hands or limbs. In the future, soldiers may have extra bionics to give them "super powers."

ADD-ON POWERED LIMBS COULD ENABLE A SOLDIER TO RUN UP A HILL CARRYING MORE THAN 650 LB (300 KG).

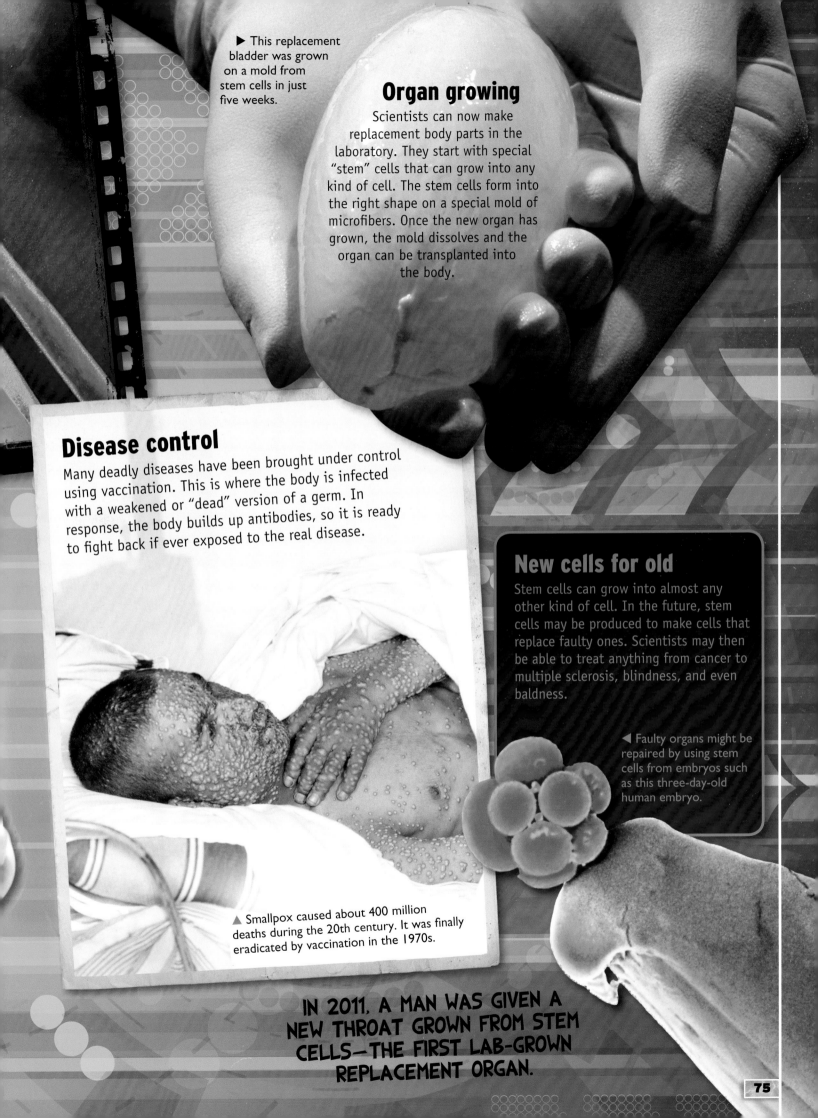

▶ This replacement bladder was grown on a mold from stem cells in just five weeks.

Organ growing

Scientists can now make replacement body parts in the laboratory. They start with special "stem" cells that can grow into any kind of cell. The stem cells form into the right shape on a special mold of microfibers. Once the new organ has grown, the mold dissolves and the organ can be transplanted into the body.

Disease control

Many deadly diseases have been brought under control using vaccination. This is where the body is infected with a weakened or "dead" version of a germ. In response, the body builds up antibodies, so it is ready to fight back if ever exposed to the real disease.

New cells for old

Stem cells can grow into almost any other kind of cell. In the future, stem cells may be produced to make cells that replace faulty ones. Scientists may then be able to treat anything from cancer to multiple sclerosis, blindness, and even baldness.

◀ Faulty organs might be repaired by using stem cells from embryos such as this three-day-old human embryo.

▲ Smallpox caused about 400 million deaths during the 20th century. It was finally eradicated by vaccination in the 1970s.

IN 2011, A MAN WAS GIVEN A NEW THROAT GROWN FROM STEM CELLS—THE FIRST LAB-GROWN REPLACEMENT ORGAN.

CHEMICAL Messengers

How does the body know when to grow and by how much? How does it cope with stress? How does it keep thousands of substances in the right balance? The complex task of controlling the body is managed by an extraordinary system of chemicals called hormones.

Stop & Go

Hormones work automatically using clever "feedback" systems. The liver supplies the blood with the energy chemical glucose. If glucose levels rise too high, the pancreas releases the hormone insulin, which feeds back to the liver, triggering it to stop supplying glucose.

▲ Islets of Langerhans cells in the pancreas release hormones to control sugar levels in the blood.

▶ Thyroglobulin (shown in orange) makes thyroid hormones to control the body's energy usage.

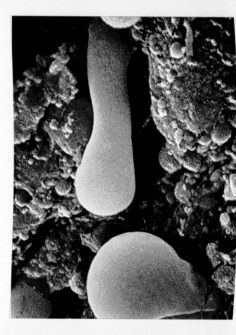

Hormones and glands

Hormones are chemicals that have particular effects on certain cells. "Endocrine" glands release tiny drops of hormone into the blood to spread around the body. Each gland releases its own type of hormone, and each hormone has a special task.

THE PITUITARY GLAND WEIGHS LESS THAN ONE GRAM, BUT IT IS ONE OF THE MOST IMPORTANT ORGANS IN THE BODY.

Grow-faster chemicals

The thyroid gland in the neck and pituitary gland in the brain are no bigger than cherries, but supply vital hormones to make sure the body grows normally. The three thyroid hormones control how fast cells burn energy. The pituitary gland makes the growth hormone, which controls how fast cells grow and multiply.

▼ Too much growth hormone can make the body grow unusually big. Sultan Kösen has the largest handspan in the world at 12 in (30.5 cm) wide.

▼ During extreme activities, such as bungee jumping, the body releases hormones to prepare for "fight or flight."

Adrenaline rush

A sudden scare prepares the body for danger, as it triggers a flood of the hormones adrenaline and noradrenaline. As the hormones rush into the blood, they make the heartbeat faster and stronger. This boosts the blood supply to the muscles to help you run or fight. The blood supply to the skin is restricted, making it go pale and cold. The eyes widen, giving better vision.

Time for change

At a certain age, known as puberty, sex hormones start to be released into the body. A female's ovaries make estrogen and progesterone, which control the menstrual cycle. A male's testes make testosterone, which promotes the production of sperm and creates characteristics such as a deep voice and bigger muscles.

▼ When blood is evaporated, the sex hormone testosterone is left behind as crystals.

ARTIFICALLY MADE STEROID HORMONES CAN BE USED IN INHALERS TO REDUCE THE EFFECTS OF ASTHMA.

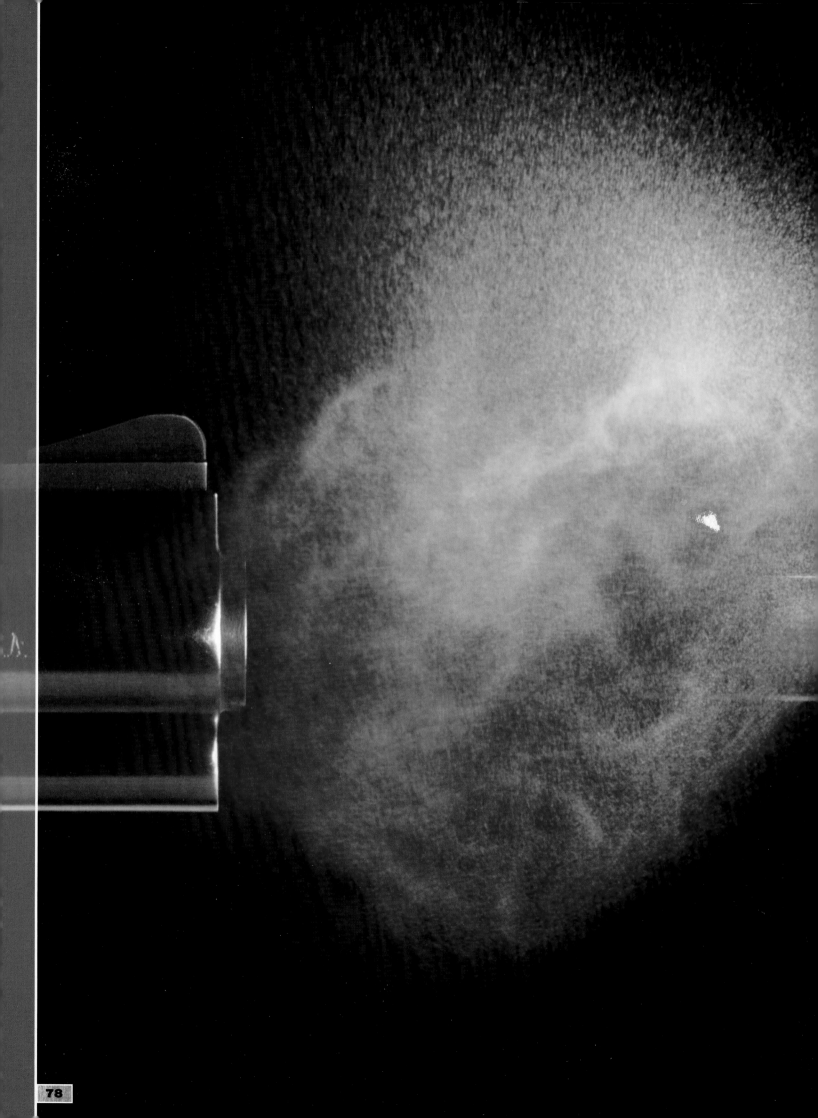

wild SCIENCE

Find out about extreme reactions and deadly materials. From highly corrosive acid to explosions inside stars, this is where science goes off with a bang.

◄ A high-speed photograph shows the explosive power of a bullet leaving the muzzle of a gun.

CRAZY Matter

Under normal conditions, such as those that exist on Earth, matter exists in three phases—solid, liquid, and gas. These phases can transform from one to another by changing the temperature and pressure. Matter can also exist in other more exotic phases, but only under the most extreme conditions.

◄ Inside a plasma globe, a high-voltage electrode turns gases into glowing plasma.

See-through solid

Unlike most solids, glass is amorphous—it does not have a crystal structure. With no crystal surfaces to interfere with the passage of light, glass is transparent. Some people believe that solid glass flows very slowly, like a liquid, but this is just a myth. Glass is a true solid because it has a definite shape and volume.

3.6 million °F
(2 million °C)

2,700°F
(1,500°C)

Pulsing plasma

Plasma, the fourth state of matter, is made of electrically charged atoms and electrons. In nature, plasma is found in extremely high-energy situations such as lightning bolts and stars. Man-made plasmas are used in street lighting and neon signs. Plasma technology can produce bright light from very little electricity.

▲ When glass is melted, it forms a thick, rubbery liquid that can be shaped.

Low-energy gas

Bose-Einstein condensate is a fifth phase of matter named after the two mathematicians who proposed its existence. Scientists prepare a condensate by cooling a dilute gas to within a thousandth of a degree from absolute zero (-459.67°F, -273.15°C). At this very low temperature, the atoms in the gas are at their lowest possible energy state and behave in strange ways.

LIGHT TRAVELING THROUGH A BOSE-EINSTEIN CONDENSATE IS SLOWED TO ABOUT 37 MPH (60 KM/H) AND MAY EVEN STOP ALTOGETHER.

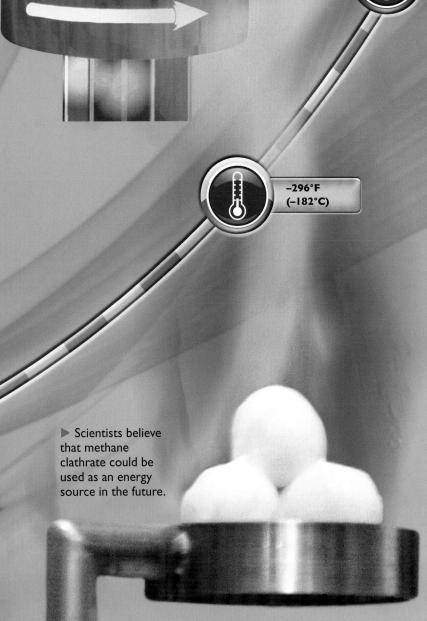

◀ Lasers are used to cool the atoms of gas to make a Bose-Einstein condensate.

Glass container

Laser beam

−459.67°F (−273.15°C)

−296°F (−182°C)

Dry ice

When carbon dioxide gas freezes at -109.3°F (-78.5°C), it is known as "dry ice" because it does not melt into a liquid. Instead, it sublimes—turns from a solid to a gas without going through the liquid phase. Liquid carbon dioxide can only exist under conditions of more than five times normal atmospheric pressure.

-109.3°F (-78.5°C)

▶ Scientists believe that methane clathrate could be used as an energy source in the future.

▲ Dry ice is often used to refrigerate frozen goods for transportation. It freezes quickly and doesn't leave messy liquid behind.

Ice that burns

Methane is a highly flammable gas that solidifies at -296°F (-182°C). However, it can become part of solid water ice at the higher temperatures found in Arctic permafrost or beneath the seabed. Tiny bubbles of methane become trapped between crystals of frozen water to form a substance known as methane clathrate, or fire ice. If you set fire to it, the methane burns while the ice melts.

In the air

We live at the bottom of the atmosphere, surrounded by a mixture of gases called air. As air, these gases are essential to support life. Individually, however, gases such as oxygen and hydrogen reveal a savage and unforgiving nature.

The big H

The first element in the periodic table, hydrogen is the simplest and lightest. Air contains only a tiny amount of hydrogen—0.000055 percent! Hydrogen is lighter than air, so it was used to fill passenger airships in the early 20th century. Unfortunately, hydrogen has another property —it is highly flammable. After several fatal disasters, hydrogen airships were abandoned.

1
H
Hydrogen
1.01

▲ Filled with flammable hydrogen, the Hindenburg airship burst into flames in 1937, killing 36 passengers and crew.

Life-giving oxygen

Oxygen gas makes up 21 percent of air and without it, life would not exist. Living organisms depend on oxygen because it helps the body to convert food into energy. As one of the most reactive elements, it is often found as part of a chemical compound. Its reaction can be gradual—when a layer of oxide slowly forms on the surface of metal. Or it can be extremely rapid and energetic—when an entire building burns ferociously.

Safe or not?

Nitrogen is the most abundant gas in air, making up 78 percent. An inert gas, it does not react easily with other elements. However, in a process called fixation, nitrogen combines with other substances to make compounds including nitrates. These compounds are used by plants to convert energy into food, to help them grow. Scientists discovered how to produce synthetic nitrogen compounds in the 1880s. These are now produced on an industrial scale to make both fertilizer and explosives.

▲ A nitrogen-based explosive, such as TNT, was used to demolish this high-rise building.

Glowing gas

Neon makes up only 0.0018 percent of air. Neon is a noble gas—it does not react with other elements. However, it does react to electricity. When an electrical current is passed through a gas discharge tube containing neon, the noble gas turns into brightly glowing plasma. It is used to make cities fluoresce with colored light.

To extinguish fire, firefighters douse the flames with water to remove the heat, so the fire can no longer burn.

▲ Neon signs light up New York City, U.S. Neon tubes can be any shape or size and neon gas itself gives off an orange-red light.

10		
	Ne	
	Neon	
	20.18	

8		
	O	
	Oxygen	
	16.00	

Toxic pollutant

A less abundant form of oxygen called ozone has three oxygen atoms instead of the more usual two, making it even more reactive. High in the atmosphere, ozone forms a layer that protects Earth's surface from the Sun's harmful ultraviolet rays—making it beneficial. However, when ozone occurs near Earth's surface it attacks the respiratory system. It is a harmful pollutant—as smog.

▶ Ozone is one of the toxic ingredients in photochemical air pollution, formed by toxic surfacery photochemical smog.

7		
	N	
	Nitrogen	
	14.01	

ACTIVE Metals

Most of the elements in the periodic table are metals, and many are safe to handle. An aluminum or iron pan, for example, can be heated on the stove or washed in water without a reaction occuring. Other metals, such as sodium and magnesium, react to air, water, and heat with violent chemical fury.

CESIUM IS A PALE-GOLDEN METAL THAT EXPLODES IF IT COMES INTO CONTACT WITH ICE.

GONE IN A FLASH

Francium is an unstable metal that decays so rapidly, it almost doesn't exist. Scientists estimate that there is only about one ounce (28 g) of francium in Earth's crust. Any amount of this metal big enough to be visible immediately vaporizes in the heat produced by its decay. The largest mass of francium that scientists have ever assembled weighed a mere 300 million billionths of an ounce (0.0000000000000000016 g).

▲ When sodium reacts with water, it produces a bright yellow-orange flame.

11
Na
Sodium
23.00

Sodium sizzle

A silver-colored metal, sodium is soft enough to be cut with a table knife. But drop a piece of sodium into water and it reacts furiously, fizzing and dashing around the surface. The exothermic reaction produces heat as well as hydrogen gas. The heat quickly ignites the hydrogen, causing an explosion.

▲ This lump of rock contains a few scattered atoms of francium.

87
Fr
Francium
223.00

Potassium perils

Only small amounts of potassium and water are needed to produce a reaction that gives off enough heat to ignite the hydrogen released. Powdered potassium ignites spontaneously when exposed to air, so it must be stored in mineral oil. If potassium is exposed to air for a long period, its surface becomes coated with a layer of pressure-sensitive superoxide that may explode at the slightest touch.

19
K
Potassium
39.10

▼ A distinctive purple flame indicates the presence of potassium vapor.

12
Mg
Magnesium
24.31

▲ Magnesium burns with an intense white light.

Burning bright

Although magnesium is a highly reactive element, on contact with air, it forms a less-reactive oxide layer. This enables it to be stored and handled with safety. Magnesium ignites very easily. It burns so brightly that it was once used by photographers to provide the "flash" for their cameras.

IMMERFORT

Dangerous decay

Radium reacts fiercely with water, but that is nothing compared to its other dangers. Discovered by Nobel Prize winner Marie Curie (1867–1934), radium is a heavy, unstable element that slowly decays. This decay produces large amounts of radioactive energy. Long-term exposure leads to diseases such as cancer, tumors, and leukemia.

88
Ra
Radium
226.03

▲ Radium generates so much energy that it glows in the dark. It was once used to paint clock faces, making them luminous.

▶ Marie Curie carried out radium experiments without any protection. She later died of aplastic anemia caused by exposure to radioactivity.

Hazardous HALOGENS

Dangerous, highly reactive elements are lurking in every room of your home and on every shelf in your local store. No need to panic! The products are completely safe—when used correctly. But if you don't respect the halogens, proceed at your peril...

CHLORINE

Poisonous to all forms of life, green-colored chlorine gas is the only element to have ever been used as a weapon—when it was released onto battlefields during World War I (1914–1918). When breathed in, it reacted with water in the lungs to produce hydrochloric acid, which dissolved lung tissue. However, chlorine's killer nature also works as a lifesaver. Used in disinfectants and at water purification plants, it kills dangerous microorganisms before they can do serious harm.

Deadly iodine

Iodine is a dark, shiny solid. Minute amounts are essential for a healthy diet and occur naturally in many foods, such as strawberries. When dissolved in alcohol, iodine is used as an antiseptic and disinfectant; it was also used in the manufacture of photographic film. However, large amounts are poisonous and iodine vapor is toxic, causing breathing problems.

▲ Iodine turns from a solid into a poisonous violet-colored gas at room temperature.

| 53 |
| I |
| Iodine |
| 126.90 |

| 9 |
| F |
| Fluorine |
| 18.998 |

Fierce fluorine

Poisonous and dangerously reactive, fluorine gas must be handled with care. It is so unstable that on contact with water, it spontaneously burns with a bright flame. However, fluorine is part of useful products, too. It is one of the main components of refrigerants used in household fridges and freezers. Surprisingly, fluoroplastics—plastics containing fluorine—are some of the most stable man-made substances, widely used for electrical insulation.

199.99

17 Cl
Chlorine
35.45

Bad bromine
Although it is now considered too dangerous to be used in pesticides, bromine is still added to disinfectants for hot tubs and spa pools. Bromine has an unusual property —it interferes with combustion reactions— making it perfect for fire-retardant materials.

▶ Some halogen bulbs contain bromine. They produce brighter light, use less energy, and last longer than normal lightbulbs.

▼ Sodium metal burns and glows when added to chlorine gas.

35 Br
Bromine
79.90

▼ At room temperature, bromine is a dark-brown poisonous liquid that rapidly evaporates into an orange gas.

Tiny amounts of chemicals containing fluorine, known as fluorides, are added to drinking water and toothpaste to make our teeth stronger and more resistant to decay.

LETHAL Liquids

Acids are savage solutions that produce hydrogen ions when dissolved in water, conduct an electrical current, and taste slightly sour. Strong acids are corrosive chemicals, powerful enough to dissolve metal and stone. Weak acids are irritants, causing blisters on contact with skin.

DISSOLVING GLASS
Hydrofluoric acid is highly corrosive and must be stored in plastic containers because it dissolves most materials, including glass and metal. This trait is put to good use, however, as hydrofluoric acid is used to etch words and images onto glass. Extreme caution and care must be taken when using hydrofluoric acid; as well as causing severe burns to exposed skin, it is also deadly poisonous.

Emergency crews require special training and equipment to deal with exposure to acids and other hazardous materials.

RISKY SPILLS
A highly dangerous, colorless liquid, hydrochloric acid is produced by bubbling hydrogen chloride gas through water. A strong acid, it is widely used in the manufacture of plastics and household cleaning agents. Its fumes are irritating to the lungs and contact with the skin causes chemical burns. With more than 20 million tons produced and transported annually, accidental spillages sometimes occur.

DISSOLVING GOLD

Gold became known as the royal metal not only because of its rarity and beauty, but also because it could not be dissolved or tarnished by acid. That is until aqua regia, a mixture of hydrochloric acid and nitric acid, was developed. Aqua regia is used in gold mining to dissolve the metal out of gold-bearing rock. The mixture of acids and dissolved gold is then chemically treated to obtain the pure gold.

Gold in concentrated hydrochloric acid

Gold in concentrated nitric acid

Gold in aqua regia

| 79 Au |
| Gold |
| 196.97 |

◀ The brownish tinge in the right-hand tube shows that gold has dissolved in the "royal water."

▼ Karst landscapes, such as the Shillin Stone Forest in Yunnan, China, form naturally from years of carbonic acid exposure.

SHAPING THE LAND

Rainwater absorbs minute amounts of carbon dioxide as it falls through the atmosphere, turning it into weak carbonic acid. Although harmless to plants and animals, the acid passes through small cracks in rocks. Over time, this dissolves the limestone rock, shaping it into peaks and caverns.

Pollution!

When fossil fuels such as coal are burned, they release sulfur dioxide gas into the atmosphere. This gas reacts with water vapor to produce weak sulfuric acid, which falls to Earth as rain. Acid rain is strong enough to kill trees and poison wildlife in lakes and streams.

▶ Acid rain damages stone statues and buildings.

TOP 10

TOXIC ROCKS

Earth's crust contains many valuable and useful minerals, but some of them can also be extremely harmful to living things—and the dangers are far from obvious. Unlike poisonous animals, toxic minerals do not carry a warning about the dangers they represent.

1 THALLIUM

A soft, silvery metal, thallium is used in the electronics and glass industries. Chemicals containing thallium were once widely used as insecticides and rat poison, but they were banned for being too dangerous. It caused damage to the internal organs and nervous system, as well as death.

81 **Tl**
Thallium
204.38

2 ARSENIC

Arsenic was once used to preserve wood and in agricultural products. But any substance containing arsenic is deadly to all living things, apart from a few unusual bacteria. Short-term contact causes sickness and diarrhea. Long-term exposure causes multiple organ failure and death.

33 **As**
Arsenic
74.92

3 BERYLLIUM

This strong, lightweight metal has a high melting point and is ideal for many industrial applications, such as the manufacture of aircraft and computers. Unfortunately beryllium has major drawbacks—it is rare, expensive, and toxic. It can cause a pneumonialike illness, as well as skin diseases.

4 **Be**
Beryllium
9.01

4 PHOSPHORUS

...osphorus is essential to life ...cause it adds strength to bones ...nd teeth. But it is far from ...iendly. Chemicals containing ...osphorus are among the ...adliest poisons ever made. ...fter a short period, joint pain is ...xperienced. Longer exposure leads ...o weak bones and kidney damage.

Cd 48 Cadmium 112.41

5 CADMIUM

This highly toxic metal is rare in Earth's crust, but is widely used to make rechargeable batteries because it doesn't easily corrode. If inhaled, it can damage the lungs. If consumed, it irritates the stomach, causing vomiting and diarrhea. Long-term effects include kidney disease and fragile bones.

7 ASBESTOS

A naturally occuring mineral, asbestos was once widely used for building insulation because it is incombustible. However, asbestos was outlawed in many countries around the world in the 1980s when it was discovered that inhaling asbestos dust caused deadly lung diseases.

10 ANTIMONY

This silvery metal is usually found combined with sulfur as kohl—a black substance that is easily crushed to form a slightly greasy powder. The ancient Egyptians used kohl as an eye cosmetic, not realizing that even small doses of this toxic metal can cause headaches and nausea.

Sb 51 Sb Antimony 121.75

9 CINNABAR

An important ore of mercury, cinnabar is often found near recent volcanic activity. This soft mineral can be ground up to make a rich red-colored pigment called vermillion. It can also be heated to produce the highly toxic element, mercury. Contact can cause shaking, nerve damage, and death.

P 15 P Phosphorus 30.97

6 CERUSSITE

This innocent-looking mineral is easily converted into "white lead," a substance that was once used in paints and cosmetics to give them opacity. Unfortunately, lead is extremely poisonous, especially to children, and is now considered too dangerous to be used in household products.

Se 34 Se Selenium 78.96

8 SELENIUM

The human body needs minute quantities of selenium and it is found in some foods, such as nuts and fish. Larger doses are toxic. Minor symptoms of selenium poisoning include bad breath, fever, and hair loss. Serious effects include nerve damage, organ problems, and even death.

SUPER CARBON

ONE ELEMENT CAN TRANSFORM ITSELF INTO DIFFERENT FORMS, EACH WITH UNIQUE AND AMAZING PROPERTIES. IS IT IRON? IS IT CALCIUM? NO, IT'S CARBON! DEPENDING ON HOW THE CARBON ATOMS ARE ARRANGED, IT CAN EXIST AS DIAMOND, THE HARDEST KNOWN SUBSTANCE, OR AS GRAPHITE AND CHARCOAL, WHICH ARE SOFT AND POWDERY.

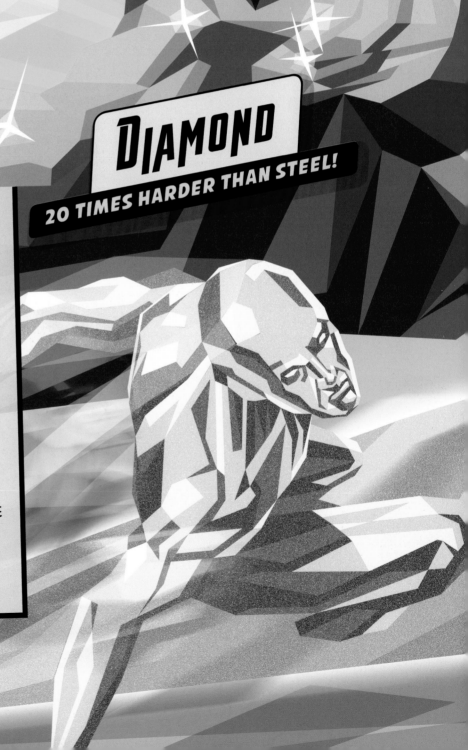

DIAMOND
20 TIMES HARDER THAN STEEL!

INDESTRUCTIBLE AND SPARKLING

DEEP BENEATH EARTH'S SURFACE, HEAT AND EXTREME PRESSURE TRANSFORM CARBON INTO **DIAMOND**! WITH CARBON ATOMS LOCKED IN AN IMMOVABLE LATTICE, DIAMOND'S TRANSPARENT CRYSTALS ARE HARDER THAN ANY OTHER KNOWN NATURAL SUBSTANCE. BLASTED TO EARTH'S SURFACE BY VOLCANIC EXPLOSIONS, ITS UNIQUE PROPERTIES MAKE DIAMOND THE ULTIMATE ALLOTROPE (FORM) OF CARBON. DIAMOND CAN CUT THROUGH ANYTHING, ONLY MELTS AT A SUPERHOT 6,420°F (3,550°C), REFLECTS ALL FORMS OF LIGHT, BLOCKS ELECTRICITY, AND SURVIVES EXTREME PHYSICAL, CHEMICAL, OR RADIOACTIVE FORCES. PLUS DIAMOND FORMS BEAUTIFUL, GLITTERING GEMSTONES THAT PEOPLE WILL PAY MILLIONS TO GET THEIR HANDS ON!

BUCKYBALL
IMMUNE TO SEVERE IMPACT!

STABLE AND VERSATILE

BURSTING ONTO THE SCENE IN 1985, ALL-ROUNDER BUCKYBALL—FULL NAME, **BUCKMINSTERFULLERENE**—IS THE RESULT OF A SCIENTIFIC EXPERIMENT GONE RIGHT! ITS HOLLOW CAGELIKE STRUCTURE OF 60 CARBON ATOMS ALLOWS IT TO CAPTURE AND CARRY OTHER ATOMS. DEPENDABLE BUCKYBALL WILL NOT REACT WITH ANY CHEMICAL OR DISSOLVE IN WATER. LIGHT AND STRONG, BUCKYBALL IS A HEAT CONDUCTOR, AN ELECTRICAL INSULATOR, AND STOPS LIGHT IN ITS TRACKS.

GRAPHITE
WITHSTANDS EXTREME TEMPERATURES OF SPACE!

THE FUTURE IS STRONGER, HARDER, AND LIGHTER

ONLY ONE ATOM THICK, 300 TIMES STRONGER THAN STEEL, HARDER THEN DIAMOND, TRANSPARENT, SUPERFLEXIBLE, AND AN EXCELLENT CONDUCTOR OF HEAT AND ELECTRICITY... WHAT IS THIS MAN-MADE SUPERMATERIAL? **GRAPHENE**! DISCOVERED IN 2004, ITS CARBON ATOMS ARE ARRANGED IN A FLAT HONEYCOMB STRUCTURE, GIVING IT THE STRONGEST BONDS KNOWN TO SCIENCE.

SLIPPERY AND SOFT

CRUSHED AND HEATED UNDERGROUND, CARBON-RICH ROCKS MUTATE INTO METAMORPHIC ROCK AND **GRAPHITE** IS BORN! ITS CARBON ATOMS FORM SHEETS THAT SLIDE OVER EACH OTHER WITH EASE. THIS SLIPPERY PROPERTY MAKES IT A PERFECT LUBRICANT FOR FREEING SURFACES TRAPPED TOGETHER BY FRICTION. AN INCREDIBLE HEAT SHIELD, GRAPHITE RESISTS SCORCHING TEMPERATURES OF 5,400°F (3,000°C). GRAPHITE IS USED AROUND THE WORLD EVERY DAY—AS THE SOFT "LEAD" IN PENCILS.

COOL Cryogenics

Matter—solids, liquids, and gases—can be heated to millions of degrees, but cannot be cooled below -459.67°F (-273.15°C). This temperature is absolute zero and as substances approach it, they stop acting as they normally do and exhibit strange properties.

▼ Aluminum foil covers *Ariane 5*'s fuel tanks to protect the fuel from external heat build up.

Powerful combination

Inside a typical liquid-propellant rocket, such as *Ariane 5*, liquid oxygen below -297°F (-183°C) and liquid hydrogen below -423°F (-253°C) are kept in separate tanks. At liftoff, they are fed into a reaction chamber where they ignite, producing enormous amounts of heat and thrust to power the rocket into space.

▲ Human cells, such as egg and sperm cells, are stored in liquid nitrogen to preserve them until they are needed.

Cold storage

Extreme cold has the same effect on living tissue as extreme heat —it kills, but with an important difference. Heat destroys living structures, whereas cold preserves them. Medical researchers preserve specimens in liquid nitrogen because slow freezing can damage the tissues. Liquid nitrogen reaches temperatures of -320.33°F (-195.74°C) so rapidly that water in the cells cannot form crystals. Some scientists believe that it is possible to preserve entire human bodies. Known as cryonics, more than 100 people have been stored this way, but no one has been revived.

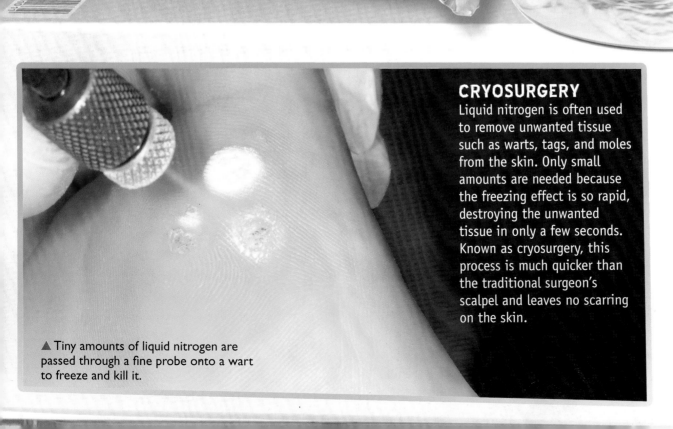

▼ A soccer player uses a cryogenic cylinder before a game to reduce any swelling caused by injury.

Freezing therapy

Some athletes use low-temperature cryogenic chambers to recover from injury. Wearing nothing but socks, gloves, earmuffs, and a bathing suit—to protect against frostbite—they spend up to three minutes in a small room or container cooled by liquid nitrogen, at temperatures of about -256°F (-160°C). The low temperature causes the body to release endorphins, which speed recovery. It also numbs the body's nerves, providing immediate pain relief and reducing any swelling.

WHEN COOLED TO -455°F (-270°C), HELIUM BECOMES A SUPERFLUID THAT FLOWS UPHILL.

COOL IMAGE

Liquid helium is a vital part of Magnetic Resonance Imaging (MRI) scanners. It cools the superconductive magnets inside, allowing an electric current to flow through them without any resistance. This creates a magnetic field that helps doctors to build accurate and detailed images of inside the human body.

▼ MRI scanners use magnetic fields and radio waves to produce images of soft body tissues, such as a fetus.

CRYOSURGERY

Liquid nitrogen is often used to remove unwanted tissue such as warts, tags, and moles from the skin. Only small amounts are needed because the freezing effect is so rapid, destroying the unwanted tissue in only a few seconds. Known as cryosurgery, this process is much quicker than the traditional surgeon's scalpel and leaves no scarring on the skin.

▲ Tiny amounts of liquid nitrogen are passed through a fine probe onto a wart to freeze and kill it.

Under PRESSURE

Pressure is measured in pascals and normal atmospheric pressure on Earth is about 101 kPa (14.7 psi). We understand the characteristics that substances possess and the way in which they behave at normal pressure. When put under greater pressure, the same substances often behave in sudden and unexpected ways.

Dollar bill on a surface

1 Pa	Gentle breeze
10 Pa	Popping corn
2 kPa	Water boiling at room temperature
2.6 kPa	Atmospheric pressure for Earth at sea level
101 kPa	Air pressure in a car tire
250 kPa	Impact of a punch
350 kPa	An average human bite
1.1 mPa	
30 mPa	

30 mPa

Deep-sea dive

The increased pressure, even during a fairly shallow dive, forces extra gas into a diver's blood. If the diver surfaces too quickly, bubbles of nitrogen may form in the blood. This causes dizziness and a painful and potentially fatal condition known as "the bends." At greater depths, the pressure has a crushing effect on the whole body.

These polystyrene cups were identical until one was taken to a depth of about 9,850 ft (3,000 m). The pressure at this depth—equivalent to 300 atmospheres—compressed the cup to a fraction of its original size.

◄ Water jet cutters are safer for firefighters because they can make holes for the main jet of water without getting too close to the flames.

Chamber pressure of a gun firing

Bottom of the Mariana Trench, 7 mi (11 km) below sea level

70 mPa

110 mPa

690 mPa

2 gPa

Water jet cutter

690 mPa

Under enough pressure, water can cut through concrete, metal, and solid rock. A water jet cutter uses high-speed electric pumps to produce a narrow jet of water driven by pressures up to 690 mPa (100,000 psi)—almost 7,000 times atmospheric pressure. The jet can cut to depths of 18 in (45 cm) and can be as narrow as 0.076 mm—about the width of a human hair.

Meteorite impact

2 gPa

When a 300,000-ton, iron meteorite smashed into Arizona 50,000 years ago, it did more than produce a spectacular crater. The pressure created by the sudden impact was so great, it transformed the minerals in the surrounding rocks.

◄ The crater measures 600 ft (183 m) in depth and 3,900 ft (1,200 m) in diameter.

▼ The liquid metal inside Jupiter can conduct heat and electricity.

Making metallic hydrogen

200 gPa

Scientists believe that the gravity of Jupiter creates so much pressure that hydrogen starts to behave like a metal. To make metallic hydrogen in a laboratory, scientists must achieve pressures of more than 2 million times atmospheric pressure.

1
H
Hydrogen
1.01

The Planck Pressure—only ever reached shortly after the Big Bang or in a black hole

200 gPa   360 gPa 4.6×10^{113} Pa

Crude Crackdown

Crude oil is like black gold—a chemical treasure containing hundreds of useful substances. After oil has been extracted from the ground, it is subjected to harsh treatment to obtain the maximum by-products from this precious commodity.

The ingredients

Crude oil comes from the ground. It is formed from the remains of animals and plants. Over millions of years, these remains are covered in layers of mud and rock, creating great heat and pressure. These conditions turn the remains into crude oil, a mixture of hydrocarbons.

FRACTIONING COLUMN

77°F (25°C)

FRACTIONS DECREASE IN DENSITY AND BOILING POINT

FRACTIONS INCREASE IN DENSITY AND BOILING POINT

CRUDE OIL

660°F (350°C)

The breakdown

The mixture is separated by heating the oil inside tall metal towers. This process is called fractional distillation, popularly known as "cracking." Near the top of the tower, the first substances to be released are liquid petroleum gases. Lower down, kerosene and heating oil evaporate and condense for collection. At the bottom of the tower, solids such as wax and asphalt are gathered.

BURNING OIL

HOME | NEWS | CONTACT

Crude oil is flammable and oil-well fires can occur through human accidents or natural events such as lightning strikes. Due to the enormous fuel supply, the jets of flames are difficult to extinguish. Firefighters detonate explosives to create a shockwave that pushes the burning fuel and oxygen away from the unburned fuel—like blowing out a huge candle!

Along with gases such as methane and pentane, **BUTANE** is mainly used as a fuel for cooking stoves.

BUTANE

GASOLINE

Liquid **NAPTHA** is mainly converted to gasoline, but is also used as an industrial cleaning agent.

GASOLINE for cars and small trucks is by far the most precious product obtained from crude oil.

Jets are the only engines that can burn **KEROSENE** efficiently. It is also used in heating stoves.

We rely on **DIESEL** engines in trains and large trucks to move goods over land.

LUBRICATING OIL

Engines and other machines require a thin coating of **LUBRICATING OIL** to keep parts moving smoothly.

Ships have special engines that burn **FUEL OIL**. It is also used for home-heating furnaces.

BITUMEN is used on roads and roofs.

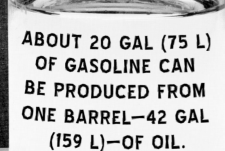
BITUMEN

ABOUT 20 GAL (75 L) OF GASOLINE CAN BE PRODUCED FROM ONE BARREL—42 GAL (159 L)—OF OIL.

Top 10 global oil reserves

COUNTRY	BARRELS (IN BILLIONS)
Venezuela	297
Saudi Arabia	265
Iran	151
Iraq	143
Kuwait	102
United Arab Emirates	98
Russia	79
Libya	47
Kazakhstan	40
Nigeria	37

BURNING Issue

A small spark is all it takes to start a fire. Traditionally sparks were created by striking a piece of steel against a hard rock such as flint to produce microscopic pieces of burning metal. Nowadays, most sparks are electric, made of minute clouds of glowing plasma.

▼ Matches use the heat produced by friction to initiate a reaction between two chemicals—in the match head and on the side of the box. The flame produced ignites the wooden stem.

Combustion occurs when a substance reacts with oxygen to produce large amounts of heat. Only gases actually burn. Solids and liquids must be heated until they vaporize before they will catch fire. Some substances spontaneously burst into flames, but most fires need an ignition source.

Invisible danger

Flashovers usually occur in confined spaces when a small fire produces enough heat to vaporize inflammable materials. This creates lighter-than-air gases that become concentrated in the upper part of a room. Even though there are flames below, the gases do not ignite because there isn't enough oxygen. That is, until a window breaks or someone opens a door. The fresh supply of oxygen that enters the room causes flames to flash upward and across the ceiling, instantly turning the whole room into a raging inferno.

▶ Firefighters battle a flashover by directing jets of water at the ceiling.

ON EARTH

Oxygen boost

An ordinary flame, such as a burning match, is known as a diffusion flame. The oxygen required for combustion diffuses from the air into the flame. The heat and intensity of the flame is limited by the supply of oxygen. A much fiercer, hotter flame is obtained by injecting pure oxygen. A gas-torch, which mixes oxygen with the inflammable gas acetylene, produces a flame with a temperature of about 6,300°F (3,500°C). The flame is so hot, it can easily cut through steel.

PAPER WILL SPONTANEOUSLY BURST INTO FLAME IF IT IS HEATED TO A TEMPERATURE OF ABOUT 454°F (234°C).

Spontaneous combustion

Elements such as potassium and phosphorus are pyrophoric in their pure form—they react so strongly with oxygen in the air that they burst into flame. Although rarely encountered in everyday life, pyrophoric substances can be found in haystacks and compost heaps, causing them to suddenly burst into flame with no external cause.

▼ When bacteria in a haystack decomposes, it produces heat, which becomes trapped. The temperature of the hay eventually rises above its ignition point, causing it to spontaneously combust.

Gravity vs. Zero gravity

On Earth, flames stretch upward and taper to a point. The yellow part of the flame is made up of tiny glowing particles of soot that rise through convection, and against the force of gravity. In a zero-gravity environment (in space), flames are spherical, produce less soot, and are less yellow in color.

Making a BANG

Bulky and smoky, gunpowder is limited as an explosive. A gunpowder explosion is an example of very rapid combustion, with a speed of up to about 1,300 ft/s (400 m/s). High explosives, which were first developed in the 19th century, do not combust—they detonate, producing a shockwave that travels at speeds of up to 29,550 ft/s (9,000 m/s).

Gaining by graining

To make gunpowder, powdered charcoal, sulfur, and potassium nitrate are mixed with water to form a thick paste, which is then rolled into thin sheets. Before the paste dries, the sheets are cut into tiny fragments called grains. Graining the gunpowder has three advantages. Equal-sized grains are easier to measure accurately. Small grains have a larger surface area, so they burn much faster than a solid lump. Finally, small spaces between the grains in a pile ensure that there is enough air for each grain to burn efficiently.

Magic mixture

The secret of making gunpowder was discovered in China 1,000 years ago when a mixture of charcoal, sulfur, and potassium nitrate proved to have powerful and explosive qualities. The newly discovered gunpowder was soon put to use—packed into bamboo tubes to make simple rockets and bombs.

Rainclouds often formed over battlefields, so people in the 19th century tried to use gunpowder explosions to make it rain during droughts.

Rocket launcher

A firework rocket is lifted into the air by a propellant. When the fuse burns into the rocket tube, it ignites the propellant, which launches the rocket upward. When the propellant has burned through, it ignites an explosive charge that scatters colored stars into the sky.

▲ Chrysanthemum fireworks produce stars in a perfect sphere. The brightness increases as it spreads across the sky.

◄ A trained bee sits inside a specially designed cassette.

SNIFFER BEES

Honeybees can be trained to recognize a particular scent, such as gunpowder. Trained bees are placed inside small machines rigged with digital cameras. When the bees detect the odor, they extend their proboscis, or tongue, ready for a food reward. The machine then reports the presence of explosives to a human operator.

Smoke of battle

Gunpowder weapons, such as cannon and muskets, made it almost impossible to see the enemy after the first few minutes of battle. Gunpowder produces thick smoke when it burns—and with hundreds of cannon and thousands of muskets all firing at once, battlefields soon became shrouded in smoke that reduced visibility to a few yards. The 19th-century invention of so-called "smokeless" powder, a type of high explosive, went a long way to solving this problem.

▲ A musket produced clouds of dense smoke with each shot.

Explosive MINDS

Throughout history, scientists have devised methods and formulas to make bigger and better bangs, often making use of ordinary substances such as cotton, sawdust, and air.

BIG BANG

In 1847 Italian chemist Ascanio Sobrero (1812–1888) announced his discovery of nitroglycerine, a high explosive that detonated with devastating results if subject to even the smallest physical shock. It was not safe to handle until years later when it was tamed by Alfred Nobel.

False claim

English scholar Roger Bacon (c. 1214–1294) is sometimes credited with the invention of gunpowder. Although he describes a gunpowder explosion in one of his books and he spread word of its existence, Bacon did not invent it. It is most likely that he learned about gunpowder from the Chinese in Central Asia.

CHRISTIAN SCHOENBEIN

SOFT BUT DEADLY

The first high explosive was made from cotton wool. German-Swiss chemist Christian Schoenbein (1799–1868) treated cotton fibers with nitric acid to produce an explosive that was much more powerful than gunpowder. Although known as guncotton, it was too powerful to be used as a propellant in cannon and firearms.

ROGER BACON

ASCANIO SOBRERO

THE DYNAMITE KID

Swedish chemist and industrialist Alfred Nobel (1833–1896) was a fellow student of Ascanio Sobrero. He became obsessed with making nitroglycerine safer after his brother Emil was killed by an accidental explosion. Nobel discovered that absorbent clay or sawdust enabled nitroglycerine to be formed into small sticks that could be handled and transported without the danger of detonation. This new, safe explosive was named dynamite.

DYNAMITE

DYNAMITE

ALFRED NOBEL

HERMANN SPRENGEL

Kaboom!

Hermann Sprengel (1834–1906) invented "safe" explosives by only mixing the components—highly reactive fuels and substances containing oxygen—immediately before use. In 1885, the U.S. Army Corps of Engineers used 140 tons of this mixture to blow apart rocks at Hell Gate, near New York Harbor—one of the most powerful preatomic explosions.

Trinity tester

The atomic bomb was developed by the top-secret Manhattan Project during World War II (1939–1945). Working under the direction of Robert Oppenheimer (1904–1967), a team of scientists completed the first successful atomic explosion in July 1945, code-named the Trinity test.

Cool explosive

German engineering professor Carl Linde (1842–1934) was a pioneer of industrial refrigeration. In 1895 Linde liquefied air at a temperature of -319°F (-195°C). He then obtained liquid oxygen (LOX) by boiling away the nitrogen. When mixed with charcoal, LOX made a powerful explosive, which was widely used for coal mining until the 1950s.

CARL LINDE

ROBERT OPPENHEIMER

SPEEDING Bullets

When a gun is fired, a propellant inside the bullet burns. This generates gas, which shoots the bullet down the barrel at about 1,000 ft/s (300 m/s). At this speed, the bullet has a lot of momentum and kinetic energy. On impact, the bullet's energy is transferred to its target—with devastating results.

Shotgun blast

A shotgun shell contains up to 500 spherical metal pellets, known as shot. Inside the shell, the shot is held in a plastic cup, separated from the propellant by lightweight wadding. When the gun is fired, expanding gases push the shell along the barrel. At the end of the barrel, the wadding and cup fall away and the shot begins to spread out.

I Wadding and shot leave barrel.

2 Propellant gases billow and disperse.

3 Plastic shot cup falls away.

4 Shot separates from wadding.

SLOW AND STEADY

One early attempt to produce a high-velocity antitank gun involved first slowing down the bullet. The WWII sPzB 41 gun fired a bullet that was larger than the muzzle of the gun. As the bullet traveled along the tapered barrel, it slowed down as it was squeezed to the right size. The expanding gases behind it developed high pressure and the bullet left the barrel with a much higher velocity— up to 4,600 ft/s (1,400 m/s).

▼ The squeeze gun had a range of about 1,600 ft (500 m).

Tank targets

Tank guns fire metal arrows, called penetrators, to pierce the 12-in (30-cm) armor of enemy tanks. The penetrators are enclosed in a lightweight plastic sheath that falls away when the penetrator leaves the muzzle at speeds of about 6,000 ft/s (1,800 m/s).

▲ A soldier loading armor-piercing penetrator ammunition onto a tank.

6

▶ This bulletproof glass has a layer of plastic between two layers of glass. The plastic makes this glass 100 times stronger than glass alone.

Stopping a bullet

Bulletproofing isn't possible—we can only provide protection against certain types of bullet. Modern body armor uses superstrong plastics such as Kevlar. A Kevlar vest will stop low-velocity handgun bullets. To stop high-velocity rounds, additional protection such as hardened ceramic plates are necessary. Some body armors also use gels that cause the kinetic energy of a bullet to spread out.

SHOCKING Power

Electricity is an invisible force that provides power for much of the world. An electric current is produced as electrons flow through a wire or jump through the air. When we see a spark, it's actually the air being turned into plasma by the power of electricity.

SHOCKING TOUCH

The shock you sometimes feel when you touch metal actually takes place a fraction of a second beforehand. Electricity normally travels through conductors such as metals, but not through insulators such as glass and air. However, electricity can jump between two conductors across a gap of insulating air—the higher the voltage, the greater the distance it can jump.

▲ A purple spark of static electricity jumps across the gap between two metal spheres.

Caged safety

English scientist Michael Faraday (1791–1867) proved that if you surround yourself with a conducting network, such as a metal cage, electrical discharges will travel along the bars, leaving you unharmed—as long as you don't touch the sides! Faraday cages are used to protect electrical equipment from lightning strikes.

▶ Touching the metal sphere of a Van de Graaff generator discharges a small amount of electricity, causing hair to stand on end.

▲ Safely inside a Faraday cage, this lab worker survived a 2 million-volt spark.

Megavolts

Invented by American electrical engineer Nikola Tesla (1856–1943), a Tesla coil can discharge sparks of million-volt electricity more than 10 ft (3 m) long. The highest voltages, up to 1.5 million volts, are produced at the upper part of the apparatus, which is shaped like a doughnut to maximize its surface area. Once used in radio transmission and to provide high voltages for neon lighting, the Tesla coil has now been replaced by modern electronics.

SHOCKPROOF

Maintenance crews are able to safely work on power lines that carry more than 100,000 volts of electricity. The helicopter that carries workers to a power line must be bonded to the line using a special metal rod. This makes electricity flow around the helicopter. From this point, the helicopter cannot touch anything else otherwise the workers onboard would be instantly electrocuted. The workers are then free to fix the line problems without any immediate danger.

▼ An Australian inventor used a Tesla coil to create this sparkling display around himself.

Hair-raising invention

Invented by American physicist Robert Van de Graaff (1901–1967), a Van de Graaff generator is a simple device for producing high-voltage electricity. Inside the hollow metal sphere, a moving belt causes an electrical charge to build up. When this sphere is touched by a conductor, the electricity is discharged. Large Van de Graaff generators are used to produce the extremely high voltages needed by atom-smashing linear accelerators.

RADIATION Hazard

When unstable elements decay into other elements, they produce dangerous amounts of radioactivity. There are three types of radiation—alpha, beta, and gamma. Alpha and beta radiation consist of fragments of atoms, called subatomic particles, traveling at high speed. Gamma radiation is the most energetic form of light.

Beta beams

Beta rays are composed of minute specks of matter—electrons, the smallest of all stable particles—traveling at about 90 percent of the speed of light. These electrons, known as beta particles, can damage human tissue. But with little penetrating power, they can be easily blocked by 0.2 in (5 mm) of aluminum.

▶ Beta radiation is used by machines to control the thickness of materials such as plastic. If the plastic becomes too thick, it absorbs more radiation, which is detected by the Geiger counter. This prompts the rollers to move closer together.

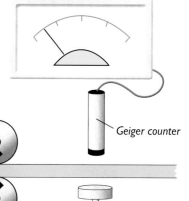

Geiger counter

Plastic sheeting

Rollers

Source of beta radiation

Slow and steady

Alpha rays are composed of alpha particles, which are about 8,000 times bigger and heavier than beta particles and travel much more slowly at about 10,000 mi/s (16,000 km/s). Alpha particles are damaging to living tissue, but are so large and slow, they cannot penetrate the skin. They can be stopped by only a sheet of paper.

▲ A detector is worn by people who work with radiation on a daily basis.

BETA β

ALPHA α

ALUMIN

▶ The blue light is called Cerenkov radiation. It occurs in water because the charged particles are moving faster than the speed of light in water.

Paper

▶ Customs officers use gamma-ray scanners to see the shapes of cargo inside trucks.

Piercing light

Gamma rays travel through matter almost as easily as ordinary light travels through glass—only blocked by lead that is several inches thick. When gamma rays pass through the human body, the high energy they carry causes tremendous damage. High doses cause radiation burns and rapid death; lower doses kill more slowly through cancer and other radiation-induced diseases.

GAMMA γ   LEAD

Nuclear electricity

A nuclear power station harnesses the energy produced by the decay of highly unstable elements, such as plutonium, and uses it to generate electricity. Although alpha, beta, and gamma rays are invisible, the level of radioactivity inside a nuclear power station is enough to make ordinary water glow with a blue light.

DISASTERS

CHERNOBYL, UKRAINE, APRIL 1986

In the evening of April 25, engineers began an experiment to see whether the cooling system could function if the electricity supply were to fail. This caused the reactor to overheat, fuel to explode, and fires to break out. The reactor was not protected by a concrete shell, so radioactive debris escaped into the atmosphere, carried for hundreds of miles by the wind.

▼ Found two years after the disaster, the quince fruit on the right has mutated to a much larger size.

FUKUSHIMA, JAPAN, MARCH 2011

When a tsunami struck the coast of Japan on March 11, it damaged the cooling system at the Fukushima nuclear power station. Without this, the nuclear fuel overheated and caught fire, releasing large amounts of radiation and radioactive material into the atmosphere. The radiation levels were so high that the authorities evacuated the entire area within 12 mi (19 km) of Fukushima.

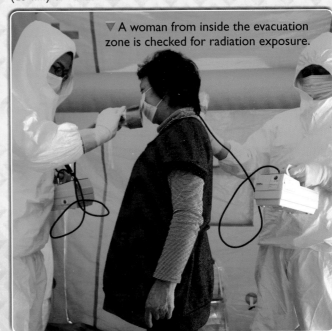

▼ A woman from inside the evacuation zone is checked for radiation exposure.

Star BIRTH

Stars are made from atoms of the two lightest elements, hydrogen and helium, drawn together by gravity. The actual moments of star birth are hidden by thick clouds of dust, but nothing can conceal the spectacular surroundings of these explosive events.

① The Eagle nebula

Not-so empty space

The vast reaches of space between the stars are not completely empty. Each cubic inch (16 cu cm) of space contains about 16 atoms—usually hydrogen, sometimes helium, and occasionally another element. These atoms are not evenly spread because they tend to clump together in clouds. The biggest of these clouds are known as Giant Molecular Clouds (GMCs), and this is where many new stars are born.

Compressed gas

When a Giant Molecular Cloud reaches a large enough size, at least 1,000 times the mass of the Sun, it undergoes gravitational collapse—the cloud implodes and breaks up. Vast amounts of energy are released, creating shockwaves that compress and heat the fragments of the cloud to such an extent that nuclear fusion begins. The central region of each fragment becomes the core of a new star.

② Pleiades star cluster

③ Orion nebula

Nebulous evidence

After a Giant Molecular Cloud has collapsed and produced stars, the remains can be seen as a bright nebula in the night sky. The young stars blast radiation into space—creating delicate glowing shapes that will eventually disappear after a few million years.

2 **3**

6

5

Scientists estimate that 95 percent of all the stars there will ever be have already been born.

Announcing arrival

Young stars announce their presence by blasting twin, high-speed jets of material out in space. Dust and gas that fall toward the surface of a new star are swirled around and then ejected in long streams above the star's poles. The shockwave from these jets travels at more than 187 mi/s (300 km/s). As it smashes into surrounding gases, it causes them to glow brightly.

4 Planetary formation

New planets

When a new star blazes into existence, its gravity may pull dust and gas into a swirling protoplanetary disk around the star. After many collisions over time, the dust and gas clump together to form small planetesimals, which eventually combine to form planets. Astronomers have so far discovered more than 1,000 planets that orbit around stars other than the Sun.

5 Stellar jets

6 Bok globule

Starry globules

Bok globules—small, dense clouds of dust and gas that block light—were discovered last century by the astronomer Bart Bok (1906–1983). Astronomers believe that new stars can be formed inside Bok globules when dust and gas contract under the gravity of the clouds.

Extreme UNIVERSE

From a storm more than twice the size of Earth, to colliding galaxies and the fiery birth of a star—this tour of the Universe is guaranteed to make you feel tiny.

◀ The Orion Nebula is one of the nearest to Earth. It measures about 30 light-years across and contains 2,000 times more matter than is found in the Sun.

The Big Bang Theory

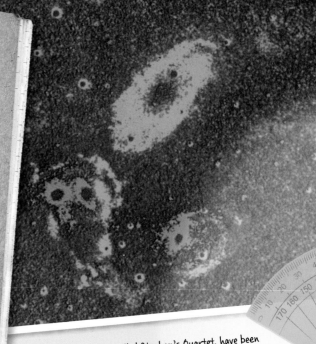

▲ These four galaxies, called Stephan's Quartet, have been colored to show their red shifts. The three red galaxies are further away and traveling faster than the closer, bluer galaxy.

The Universe is unimaginably big. It contains all the matter and energy we know about, and scientists are learning more all the time. The Big Bang Theory describes how the Universe began and expanded rapidly into the Universe that exists today.

The Universe began with an enormous outpouring of energy from a microscopic point called a singularity.

WHERE DID THE UNIVERSE COME FROM?

HOW DO WE KNOW THE UNIVERSE IS EXPANDING?

As distant galaxies move away from Earth, the light waves they give off are stretched out behind them, making them look red in color. This effect, called red shift, was first discovered by Austrian mathematician Christian Doppler in 1842. Edwin Hubble then showed that a galaxy's red shift is proportional to its distance from Earth. The further away a galaxy is, the greater its red shift and the faster it must be moving away from Earth. Massive red shifts reveal that the most distant objects in the Universe are flying away from Earth at astonishing speeds—often approaching the speed of light.

Can we see after-effects of the Big Bang?

Spacecraft have mapped the afterglow of the Big Bang, an echo of energy called the Cosmic Microwave Background that can still be detected today. Ripples in this energy led to the stars and galaxies that we see today. The Cosmic Background Explorer (COBE) spacecraft made the first map of it in the early 1990s. The most detailed map yet was made in 2010 by the Planck spacecraft.

Scientists think the Universe was once smaller than a single atom. This tiny point is called a singularity. Then about 13.8 billion years ago, it burst out in all directions as a superhot fireball. This huge outburst is called the Big Bang. As the new Universe expanded, it cooled and some of its energy began to condense into the first particles of matter.

MEGA COMICS

MULTIVERSE 117

IS OUR UNIVERSE ALL ALONE?

YOU ARE HERE

OUR VAST UNIVERSE MIGHT BE JUST ONE OF MANY UNIVERSES IN A MULTIVERSE!

▼ The Planck spacecraft produced this map of radiation left over from the Universe when it was just 380,000 years old.

SCIENTISTS THINK THE MATTER WE CAN SEE FORMS ONLY 4 PERCENT OF THE UNIVERSE. THE REST IS DARK MATTER AND DARK ENERGY.

THE MULTIVERSE

A few years ago the Big Bang was thought to be the beginning of everything—time, space, energy, and matter. Scientists are now coming up with theories that, if correct, suggest that the Big Bang wasn't the beginning of everything, but just the beginning of our Universe—one of many. The theory of many universes is called the multiverse, but it has yet to be proven.

▲ This cluster of galaxies, called Abell 2744, is 3.5 million light-years away from us, so we see it as it looked 3.5 million years ago.

How far back can scientists look?

Scientists use modern telescopes to look back in time at distant galaxies—if a galaxy is one million light-years away from Earth, it will take one million years for the light waves to reach Earth. Therefore what we see is light that is one million years old! Astronomers have discovered galaxies that are 13 billion years old and gas clouds that are 12 billion years old, made up of the simplest elements—hydrogen and helium. They can work out the age of distant objects by analyzing light from them to find their red shift.

GALAXY

Gallery

Stars travel through space in giant groups called galaxies. There are billions of galaxies, each containing billions of stars. Galaxies are so vast and far apart that their sizes and the distances between them have to be measured in light-years—the distance light travels in a year.

Spiral

Elliptical

Irregular

Shape up

Galaxies are divided into three main groups according to their shape. About three-quarters of all galaxies are spiral shaped. They have a center called a hub and long, curved arms. If the center is rectangular, the galaxy is called a barred spiral. The next most common, called elliptical galaxies, are round or oval in shape and contain few new stars. Irregular galaxies have no definite shape and form when two galaxies collide.

Andromeda Galaxy

Hubble Ultra Deep Field

Our neighbor

One of the largest galaxies in the Universe is a spiral galaxy called Andromeda. Although it's about 2.5 million light-years away from Earth, it's so big that it can be seen with the naked eye. Andromeda is surrounded by more than a dozen dwarf galaxies that line up in a strange way—scientists can't yet explain why.

Teeming with galaxies

In 2004, the Hubble Space Telescope took a photograph of one tiny spot in space. The image was found to contain 10,000 of the most distant galaxies ever seen. Based on this, scientists worked out that the Universe could contain as many as 500 billion galaxies. Light from these galaxies travels across the Universe for about 13 billion years to reach Earth.

Eagle Nebula

Cloud of creation

Nebulae are vast clouds of gas and dust within galaxies. They glow brightly, either because they are hot or because they are lit up by nearby stars. Dark nebulae are clouds of dust that block light coming from stars behind them. Inside nebulae are all the elements needed to form new stars, so some act as nurseries where new stars are born. The Eagle Nebula is 75 light-years across and has several star-forming regions within it.

THERE ARE MORE THAN 7,000 KNOWN NEBULAE IN THE UNIVERSE.

Collision course

Occasionally, two galaxies collide. As the galaxies move through each other, the energy from the crash sends streams of gas and stars flying out into space. Sometimes, the two galaxies merge to form a new galaxy. The Milky Way is on a collision course with the Andromeda Galaxy, but the impact won't occur for 4 billion years. The Antennae Galaxies violently smashed into each other a few billion years ago, causing stars to be ripped from each galaxy to form an arc between them.

Antennae Galaxies

A LIGHT-YEAR IS EQUIVALENT TO NEARLY 6 TRILLION MI (9.5 TRILLION KM).

THE MILKY WAY

When you look into the night sky, the stars you see belong to our galaxy, the Milky Way. A barred spiral galaxy, it measures 100,000 light-years across and 1,000–7,000 light-years thick. Inside its clouds of gas and dust are more than 100 billion stars.

WHAT SHAPE?

From Earth, the Milky Way looks like a bright hazy band across the sky. This shows that the Milky Way is a flat, disk-shaped galaxy. All other galaxies of this shape are spirals, so scientists worked out that the Milky Way is a spiral galaxy.

▲ Earth is situated in one of the vast arms of stars curling out from the middle of the Milky Way.

FRIED EGGS

From the side, the Milky Way looks like a thin disk with a central bulge, sometimes described as looking like two fried eggs back-to-back. The bulge contains old stars and the disk contains younger stars. Dust clouds form a dark line that runs through the middle of the disk. The Sun is in the bulge, about two-thirds of the way out from the galaxy's center.

▲ A galaxy's spinning motion flattens it into a disk shape with a large ball of stars in the middle.

STICK TOGETHER

The Milky Way (left) and Andromeda (right) travel through space with a cluster of galaxies called the Local Group. Held together by gravity, this group contains more than 50 galaxies. Some of the largest clusters, such as the Coma, contain more than 1,000 galaxies. The Local Group and 100 other clusters make up the Virgo supercluster. There are millions of other superclusters throughout the Universe.

◄ The Local Group of galaxies is about 10 million light-years across.

▼ The disk of the Milky Way galaxy stretches across the whole sky, seen here from Dorset, U.K.

▼ The blue-white star, Kappa Cassiopeiae, is surrounded by a red bow shock of glowing gas.

Speed shock

As stars speed through space, particles flying off them smash into the dust and gas that float between the stars. If a star is traveling fast enough, the gas and dust collide so violently that they light up. A bright streak, called a bow shock, appears around the star and shows up most clearly at infrared wavelengths.

The Hipparcos satellite spent four Years positions in space measuring the of 118,000 stars.

How far?

The distances between stars are immense. Apart from the Sun, the closest star to Earth— Proxima Centauri—is 4 light-years away. Astronomers have spent centuries measuring the positions of thousands of stars with greater precision. This is called astrometry. The Hipparcos satellite was the first spacecraft designed for precision astrometry.

Star clusters

Scientists know that stars are born in groups, or clusters, because they can see new stars forming close together. Large clusters contain as many as one million stars. Some clusters stay together for billions of years, while others drift apart after a few million years. Some stars are so close together that they orbit each other. Two orbiting stars are called a binary star.

Glow show

At the center of a star, the temperature and pressure are so great that hydrogen nuclei fuse together, forming helium nuclei. This reaction releases energy, which travels from the core to the star's surface— causing it to glow—before radiating into space.

A STAR is Born

Each star twinkling in the night sky is actually a massive ball of searing-hot gas with a nuclear reactor in its core spewing out energy. The largest stars in the Universe are monsters, more than 1,500 times the size of our star, the Sun.

Convection zone

Radiative zone

Core

Photosphere

A star like the Sun has a superhot core with a temperature of 27 million°F (15 million°C.)

Hot colors

Blue stars are the hottest type of star. Their surface temperature is more than 40,000°F (22,000°C). Blue-white stars are almost as hot. One called Rigel has a temperature of 21,000°F (12,000°C). Orange-red stars are the coolest, and may be as cool as 3,100°F (1,700°C). Betelgeuse is a red star with a surface temperature of 5,500°F (3,000°C).

▲ The color of light given out by stars tells astronomers how hot they are.

Type of star	Surface temperature
O	Over 44,540°F (24,730°C)
B	19,340–44,540°F (10,730–24,730°C)
A	13,040–19,340°F (7,225–10,730°C)
F	10,340–13,040°F (5,725–7,225°C)
G	8,540–10,340°F (4,725–5,725°C)
K	5,840–8,540°F (3,225–4,725°C)
M	Less than 5,840°F (3,225°C)

PRETTY PATTERNS

People have divided the night sky into familiar patterns, or constellations, after patterns of stars for thousands of years. They named the patterns, or constellations. Different cultures chose different names. Ursa Major, mythical figures and creatures. Ursa Major, the Great Bear, was seen as the leg of a bull by the ancient Egyptians and a mythical parrot by the Mayans. Today, the sky is divided into 88 internationally recognized constellations.

▲ The constellations range in size from the tiny Lyra to the giant Ursa Major.

Northern Hemisphere

Cancer, Leo, Ursa Major, Corona Borealis, Gemini, Ursa Minor, Hercules, Auriga, Pole Star, Cepheus, Lyra, Orion, Andromeda, Cassiopeia, Cygnus, Taurus, Perseus, Pegasus

Making stars

1. A supernova triggers the collapse of a giant cloud of gas, dust, and ice.
2. As the cloud collapses, it starts to spin.
3. The spinning motion forms a disk.
4. A star forms in the middle and planets form in the disk.

▲ The first stars appeared about 100 million years after the Big Bang.

Star DEATH

Although stars appear to be constant and unchanging from century to century, they don't last forever. All the time they are shining, stars are using up fuel. When this fuel runs out, the stars die, causing some of the most extreme explosions in the Universe.

1. Red giant

When a star runs out of fuel, it swells to hundreds of times its original size, forming a red giant. The expanding outer layers of the star cool, making it look red. In about 5 billion years, the Sun will become a red giant, huge enough to swallow Mercury and Venus. The largest red giants are called red supergiants, and are up to 1,500 times bigger than the Sun.

Red giants are stars that have used up all the hydrogen in their core.

THE RED GIANT SUN WILL BE
UP TO 200 TIMES BIGGER
THAN THE SUN TODAY.

2. White dwarf

A red giant's core eventually loses its grip on its outer layers, which drift into space. The layers form a huge shell of gas called a planetary nebula with a white dwarf, a tiny remnant of the original star, in the middle. A white dwarf cannot produce enough heat to survive, so gradually cools and dies.

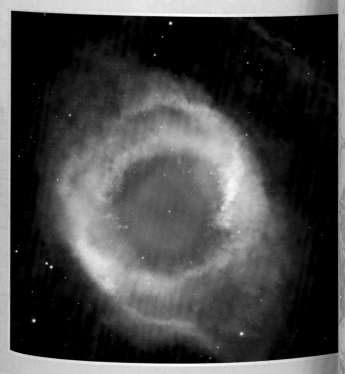

▲ A giant ring of gas, a planetary nebula, surrounds a dying star.

3. Supernova

The most massive stars end their days in a violent explosion called a supernova. The star's core collapses so fast that it blasts the outer layers away. Gas rushes outward in all directions, making a glowing shell. A tiny, hot star is left in the center of the shell. A supernova can shine more brightly than a whole galaxy. After a few weeks, it fades and disappears.

4. Neutron star

After a supernova, the core that is left behind collapses to form a dense object called a neutron star. A typical neutron star is more massive than the Sun, but so dense that it is 60,000 times smaller than the Sun. A Boeing 747 squashed to the same density as a neutron star would be the size of a grain of sand!

▲ A quasar is a black hole surrounded by a disk. It is the brightest object in the Universe.

▼ A supernova blasts out gas into space in all directions.

▼ A neutron star is made of neutrons, particles of matter with no electrical charge that are normally found in atomic nuclei.

5. Black hole

A massive star continues to collapse beyond the neutron star stage, becoming a black hole. This region in space becomes so dense with such powerful gravity that nothing, not even light, can escape. It sucks in nearby stars and nebulae. Most galaxies have a supermassive black hole at their center. The black hole at the center of the Milky Way is as massive as 4.3 million Suns.

the Sky

Some of the energy given out by stars and galaxies is blocked by Earth's atmosphere, so doesn't reach telescopes on the surface. To study this energy, telescopes and other instruments are launched into space and stay active for ten years or more.

SPECTRUM STUDY

Most of the electromagnetic spectrum does not pass through Earth's atmosphere—if any gets through, it is distorted by the atmosphere. Visible light and some radio waves reach the ground. Gamma rays, X-rays, most ultraviolet light, most infrared rays, and long radio waves can only be studied by instruments in space.

▼ Chandra studies X-rays coming from the hottest parts of the Universe.

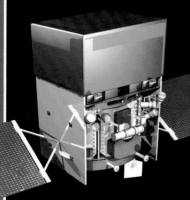

▲ Fermi is a scientific satellite carrying a telescope that scans the Universe for gamma rays.

High-energy explorer

The Fermi Gamma-ray Space Telescope was launched in 2008 to study high-energy rays from space. These rays come from strange objects such as massive black holes and pulsars. Pulsars are spinning neutron stars that send out beams of energy. Fermi discovered new pulsars and saw high-energy explosions called gamma-ray bursts. It is designed to work in space for up to ten years.

X-ray search

The Chandra X-ray Observatory has been searching for X-rays in space since 1999. At 45 ft (14 m) long, it was the biggest satellite ever launched by a Space Shuttle. Chandra has discovered X-rays coming from black holes and pulsars. It also found new stars that had never been seen before. Some of the objects it studies are so far away that light and X-rays from them have taken 10 billion years to reach our Solar System.

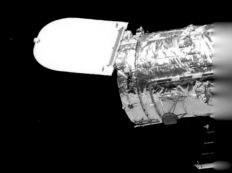

ELECTROMAGNETIC ENERGY

GAMMA RAY　　　　**X-RAY**　　　　**ULTRAVIOLET**

The Big Four

Between 1990 and 2003, NASA's Great Observatories Program launched four powerful space telescopes. Each one studied a different part of the electromagnetic spectrum. The Hubble Space Telescope was first, working mainly with visible light. It made many major discoveries, including capturing the moment Shoemaker-Levy 9 comet collided with Jupiter in 1994. It was followed by the Compton Gamma Ray Observatory and then the Chandra X-ray Observatory. The last was the Spitzer Space Telescope, working at infrared wavelengths.

Herschel's discoveries

In 2009, the European Space Agency launched the Herschel Space Observatory. It made important discoveries about the process of star formation and the evolution of galaxies. It found enough water vapor around one young star to fill thousands of oceans, leading scientists to believe that water-covered planets may be common in the Universe. Its mission ended in 2013 when the liquid helium that cooled the telescope ran out.

▼ The Spitzer infrared space telescope had to be super-cold to work. Liquid helium chilled it to −449°F (−267°C).

▲ The 7,300-lb (3,300-kg) Herschel Space Telescope was designed to study the coldest and dustiest objects in space.

▼ The Hubble Space Telescope has been taking spectacular photographs of stars and galaxies since 1990.

Future launch

The James Webb Space Telescope is being built as a successor to the Hubble Space Telescope and will be launched in 2018. It will work mainly at infrared wavelengths, studying the history of our Universe, from the Big Bang to the evolution of the Solar System.

▲ The James Webb Space Telescope will search for new planetary systems that are forming now.

VISIBLE   **INFRARED**   **MICROWAVE**   **RADIO**

EXPLORING
the Universe

The Universe is so vast that most of it is too far away to reach with spacecraft. Instead, scientists use powerful telescopes to explore and observe galaxies, distant planets, and outer space objects. The largest telescopes are the most effective, creating detailed images.

STAR STUDIES

Until the 20th century, astronomers studied only the light given out by stars and galaxies. However, this is just a fraction of the radiation they emit. By studying stars at other wavelengths—such as radio, X-ray, ultraviolet, and infrared—astronomers receive more information about what's happening inside stars and galaxies, and in the space around them.

▼ The five HESS telescopes have found many new gamma ray sources in the Milky Way.

Spotting gamma rays

The High Energy Stereoscopic System (HESS) looks for gamma rays in a clever way. Earth's atmosphere blocks gamma rays from space, but as the rays dive into the atmosphere and collide with atoms, they produce flashes of light called Cerenkov radiation. Five HESS telescopes in Namibia, Africa, look at the sky from different angles to spot this telltale light.

Observatory up high

Earth's atmosphere bends starlight and causes stars to twinkle, which makes it difficult for optical telescopes to produce sharp images. One answer is to build telescopes, such as the W.M. Keck Observatory, on mountaintops where they are above most of the atmosphere. The dark skies, low humidity, and high altitude at the summit of Mauna Kea in Hawaii make it an ideal location for astronomical telescopes.

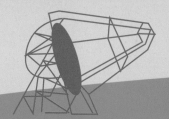

ELECTROMAGNETIC ENERGY

GAMMA RAY   **X-RAY**   **ULTRAVIOLET**

◄ The orange areas are clouds of hot gas on either side of a galaxy. They are invisible to ordinary telescopes, but radio telescopes reveal them.

Building the SKA

While optical telescopes use light to create images, radio telescopes use radio waves. To study radiation in the most remote parts of the Universe, astronomers need an enormous radio telescope—so they are building the biggest yet. The Square Kilometre Array (SKA) will combine radio signals from thousands of smaller antennae over an area of 0.4 sq mi (one square kilometer).

CARMA

The Combined Array for Research in Millimeter-wave Astronomy (CARMA) is a group of telescopes that study radio waves given out by cold gas and dust in space. The information collected by the 23 telescopes is combined to form detailed images. The Array has been built 7,200 ft (2,200 m) up in the Inyo Mountains, California, U.S., where the thin, dry air is perfect for receiving radio waves from space.

▼ The CARMA telescopes study the clouds of gas and dust in other galaxies where new stars are born.

▼ The summit of Mauna Kea is home to a dozen astronomical telescopes.

▼ The Square Kilometre Array is being built across two sites in Australia and South Africa.

VISIBLE **INFRARED** **MICROWAVE** **RADIO**

EXOPLANET
Lottery

KEPLER 22b

For centuries, astronomers believed that other stars in the Universe had their own planets—just like the Sun in the Solar System—but they could not prove it. Then in 1992 the first "extrasolar planet," or exoplanet, was discovered. Several thousand exoplanets have now been found.

KEPLER 62e

SUPER-EARTH

The first exoplanets to be found were bigger than Jupiter. As technology improved, smaller exoplanets could be detected. Exoplanets that are bigger than Earth but smaller than gas giants are called super-Earths. The first super-Earth orbiting a Sunlike star, called 55 Cancri e, was found in 2004. Kepler-22b, a super-Earth discovered in 2011, is bigger than Earth but smaller than Neptune.

HABITABLE WORLDS

The list of habitable planets is growing and recent discoveries include Kepler-62e. Known as Goldilocks planets, they lie within their star's Habitable Zone, or Goldilocks Zone—just the right distance from the star for life to exist. Scientists believe that 40 billion stars in our galaxy are similar to the Sun and there may be 8.8 billion Earth-sized planets. There is a chance that these planets may harbor life and could be colonized by humans in the distant future.

PLANET-HUNTING SPACECRAFT

▶ The Kepler spacecraft has been hunting for planets since 2009. Its mission is expected to last until 2016.

Many of the exoplanets found so far were named after the spacecraft that discovered them, called Kepler. The number in the planet's name identifies the star and the letter identifies the planet. For example, Kepler-22b is the second planet orbiting a star called Kepler-22. The Kepler spacecraft monitors more than 100,000 stars simultaneously, detecting tiny changes in brightness due to planets that are orbiting them.

KEPLER 20f

TOO HOT FOR LIFE

The first Earth-sized exoplanet orbiting a Sunlike star was discovered in 2011. The planet, called Kepler-20e, is a little smaller than Earth. It orbits too close to its star to have liquid water on its surface. Another planet in the same system, Kepler-20f, orbits a bit further away from the star, but its surface temperature is still too high for liquid water to exist.

KEPLER 20e

LUCKY DIP

Exoplanets are so far away that the only way to find them is to look for their effect on their host star. As a planet passes in front of a star, the star's brightness dips a little. Spacecraft can measure this dip and detect the planet.

▼ A planet passing in front of a star dims the brightness by just 0.01 percent.

WANTED!

SIZZLING SUN

EXTREMELY DANGEROUS

The Sun is the nearest star to Earth and provides just the right amount of light and warmth to sustain life.

It looks like a small, yellow disk, but it's actually a gigantic ball of superhot gases—a form of matter called plasma. Magnetic storms and violent outbursts of energy rage across its surface.

DISTINGUISHING FEATURES

1 Iron at a temperature of 18 million°F (10 million°C) or more gives out radiation. This causes explosions called solar flares on the Sun's surface.

2 Helium emits radiation that shows what's happening in the Sun's chromosphere, which is 1,240 mi (2,000 km) below the surface.

3 This ultraviolet image shows activity in the Sun's chromosphere and corona (outer atmosphere).

4 Radiation from iron at one million°F (600,000°C) reveals activity in the Sun's outer atmosphere called the corona.

5 A magnetic map of the Sun shows up details of its magnetic field.

6 Radiation from iron at 11 million°F (6 million°C) shows how solar flares affect the corona.

7 A visible light image of the Sun shows a layer called the photosphere—the surface that we can see.

8 This map of the Sun, called a dopplergram, shows gas rising to the surface and sinking again.

9 Magnetically active regions of the corona are revealed by iron at 4.5 million°F (2.5 million°C).

10 Radiation from iron at up to 36 million°F (20 million°C) shows hot regions of the corona.

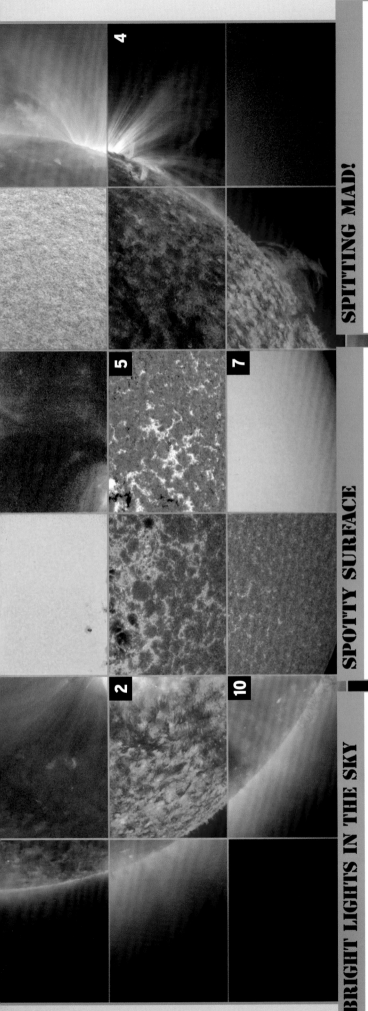

4

5

7

2

10

SPITTING MAD!

The surface of the Sun throws out long, curling tongues of gas, called prominences. They usually form in about a day and last for several weeks. The biggest loop ever recorded was 500,000 mi (800,000 km) long. Usually, the gas falls back onto the Sun, but sometimes it is thrown out into space—and could reach Earth.

▲ Prominences are loops of cooler hydrogen gas that are held in place by the Sun's magnetic field.

SPOTTY SURFACE

Dark spots called sunspots often appear on the Sun's surface. They last for a week or two and then disappear again. They are caused by regions of intense magnetism, which stop hot gas rising to the surface. They look dark because they are cooler than the rest of the Sun. Sunspot activity rises and falls on an 11-year cycle.

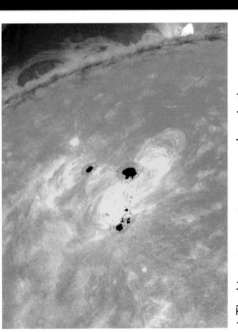

▲ The biggest sunspots are more than six times the size of Earth.

BRIGHT LIGHTS IN THE SKY

A shimmering glow called an aurora often appears in the sky near Earth's North and South poles. It's caused by a stream of particles called the solar wind that flies out of the Sun at up to 500 mi/sec (800 km/sec). The particles dive into the atmosphere near the poles and collide with gas atoms, which give out light and create the aurora.

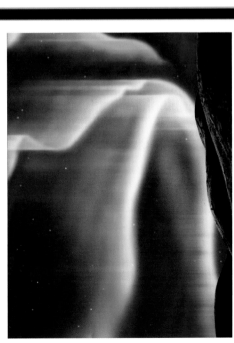

▲ The Northern Lights occur in the Arctic region. The Southern Lights appear over the Antarctic.

SOLAR System

Earth—the only planet in the Universe known to harbor life.

Mars—the red planet is named after the Roman god of war.

Uranus—the first planet to be discovered in modern times by using a telescope.

Sun—the superhot star at the center of the Solar System.

The Solar System is the Sun and everything that surrounds it, from planets to asteroids. Measuring about 4 light-years across, the vast system of planets, moons, and other bodies is held together by gravity.

THE ROUND TRIP

The planets travel in elliptical orbits in the same direction as the Sun rotates. They also rotate in the same direction as the Sun, with the exception of Venus and Uranus. Venus rotates in the opposite direction to the other planets. Uranus lies on its side. Their differing rotation was probably caused by massive collisions with other bodies while the planets were forming.

ASTRONOMICAL UNITS

Earth orbits the Sun at a distance of nearly 93 million mi (150 million km), also known as 1 Astronomical Unit. The outermost planet, Neptune, orbits at a distance of 30 Astronomical Units from the Sun. The immense force of the Sun's gravity reaches out to a distance of about 2 light-years, or more than 126,000 Astronomical Units.

▶ The four planets closest to the Sun are small and rocky. The four planets furthest from the Sun are gas giants.

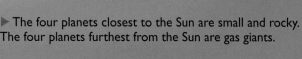

134

Mercury—the innermost planet of the Solar System, which is also the smallest.

Jupiter—the Solar System's largest planet and the first of the four gas giants.

Venus—the second planet from the Sun and the closest planet to Earth.

Neptune—the eighth Solar System planet and the most distant from the Sun.

Saturn—the second largest planet in the Solar System is well known for the rings that encircle it.

SOLAR SYSTEM DISCOVERIES

1610 Galileo Galilei discovered Jupiter's four biggest moons, now known as the Galilean moons. He also found Saturn's rings, but didn't know what they were.

1655 Giovanni Domenico Cassini discovered Jupiter's storm, the Great Red Spot. Christiaan Huygens discovered Titan, Saturn's largest moon.

1781 The planet Uranus was discovered by William Herschel.

1846 The planet Neptune was discovered by Urbain Le Verrier and Johann Gottfried Galle.

1930 Pluto was discovered by Clyde Tombaugh and named the Solar System's ninth planet.

1958 The Explorer 1 satellite discovered layers of charged particles, called the Van Allen radiation belt, around Earth.

1972 The Mariner 9 spacecraft discovered dry riverbeds, the Solar System's biggest volcano—Olympus Mons—and giant canyons on Mars.

1992 The Kuiper Belt, a region of icy bodies beyond the furthest planet, is discovered.

2005 The dwarf planet Eris was discovered. The Huygens mini-probe landed on Saturn's moon, Titan, and sent back the first photographs of its surface.

WANDERING STARS

People have studied the Solar System for thousands of years. Before telescopes were invented, astronomers could see six planets—Earth, Mercury, Venus, Mars, Jupiter, and Saturn. They were called planets from Greek words meaning "wandering stars" because of the way they move across the sky.

135

The ROCKIES

The four planets closest to the Sun are made of rock and each has an iron core. They have the same internal structure as Earth—made of metals and silicate rock—so they are known as terrestrial (Earthlike) planets.

Hothouse world

Slightly smaller than Earth, Venus is hidden under a thick atmosphere of carbon dioxide and sulfuric acid clouds. This atmosphere traps heat from the Sun, making Venus the Solar System's hottest planet. Its surface is covered with hundreds of volcanoes and the surface pressure on Venus is 92 times that on Earth. Venus is visible from Earth near the Sun just before sunrise and after sunset, so it is also known as the morning star or evening star.

Scorched rock

Mercury is the closest planet to the Sun, but it is not the hottest because it lacks a thick atmosphere, which would trap the heat. The smallest planet, it has a dusty surface and is covered with craters. One side of Mercury is roasted by the Sun, while the other side is frozen. This gives Mercury the greatest difference in night and day temperatures, from −280°F to 800°F (−173°C to 427°C).

Venus
Diameter: 7,521 mi (12,104 km)
Distance from the Sun: 67 million mi (108 million km)
Time to spin once: 243 days
Time to orbit the Sun: 225 days
Average temperature: 867°F (464°C)
Moons: 0

Mercury
Diameter: 3,030 mi (4,876 km)
Distance from the Sun: 36 million mi (58 million km)
Time to spin once: 59 days
Time to orbit the Sun: 88 days
Average temperature: 332°F (167°C)
Moons: 0

Home planet

Earth is the biggest of the terrestrial planets. It is the only planet known to have liquid water on its surface. The water, warmth from the Sun, and oxygen-rich atmosphere provide ideal conditions for sustaining life. Earth's surface is a thin crust of rock, on top of a layer of rock called the mantle. Below the mantle, in the middle of the planet, there is a core made of solid iron, with liquid iron around it.

The red planet

Mars is half the size of Earth and surrounded by a thin carbon dioxide atmosphere. It once had oceans and rivers, but they have now disappeared. The water probably evaporated into the thin atmosphere. The only water on Mars today is in the form of ice in its polar caps and under the surface. The red color of Mars comes from iron oxide, the same substance that makes rust look red.

Mars
Diameter: 4,212 mi (6,779 km)
Distance from the Sun:
142 million mi (228 million km)
Time to spin once: 24.6 hours
Time to orbit the Sun: 687 days
Average temperature: −85°F (−65°C)
Moons: 2

Earth
Diameter: 7,916 mi (12,742 km)
Distance from the Sun:
93 million mi (150 million km)
Time to spin once: 23.9 hours
Time to orbit the Sun: 365.2 days
Average temperature: 59°F (15°C)
Moons: 1

TRANSITS OF VENUS
Venus is closer to the Sun than Earth. Occasionally, Venus passes directly between the Sun and Earth. The distant planet looks like a small, black dot crossing the bright disk of the Sun. Hundreds of years ago, scientists used these transits of Venus to calculate the size of the Solar System. The last transit was in June 2012, and there will not be another until 2117.

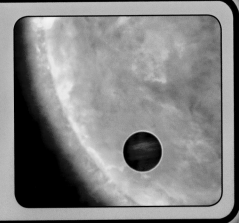

EARTH'S MOON

Dominating the night sky, the Moon travels through space with Earth, making one orbit of the planet every 27 days. Apart from Earth, it is the only other space object that people have set foot on—but we still have a lot to learn about it.

▼ The protoplanet that crashed into Earth is called Theia, after an ancient Greek goddess. It was completely destroyed.

▼ The Sun's atmosphere becomes visible when the Moon blots out the Sun during a total solar eclipse.

CRASH! BANG!

The Moon is thought to have formed when Earth collided with a Mars-sized protoplanet, causing material to be blasted out of Earth's surface. Some of the rock thrown out began to orbit around Earth. Eventually it came together to form the Moon. This giant collision happened about 4.5 billion years ago. It is the biggest impact in Earth's history.

INCREDIBLE ECLIPSES

As the Moon orbits Earth, and Earth orbits the Sun, all three occasionally line up. If the Moon passes between Earth and the Sun, the result is a solar eclipse. The Moon blots out part or all of the Sun, leaving a ring of light. If Earth passes between the Sun and Moon, the result is a lunar eclipse. Light from the Sun leaks around Earth through its atmosphere, turning the Moon red.

...p caves to protect themselves from solar radiation.

The Moon is slowly drifting away from Earth at a rate of 1.48 in (3.78 cm) a year. When the Moon formed, it was only 14,000 mi (22,500 km) away and a day on Earth was only five hours long. As the Moon receded, it made Earth spin more slowly, resulting in the 24-hour day that we have now. The Moon is now 238,850 mi (384,400 km) from Earth.

LUNAR COLONIES

Moon-bases have been the stuff of science fiction for decades, but several countries are now talking about sending astronauts to the Moon for the first time since the last Apollo mission in 1972. Instead of living on the surface, they could set up home in large tunnels and caves that have been discovered by space probes. Living underground would protect astronauts from dangerous solar radiation.

▲ The distance between Earth and the Moon is measured by firing a laser at reflectors left on the Moon by the Apollo astronauts.

▼ A supermoon can look up to 15 percent bigger and 20 percent brighter than usual.

ISO 64

WATER ON THE MOON

Some scientists think there could be water on the Moon. It could exist as ice in the permanent shadow of craters near the poles. In 2009, India's Chandrayaan-1 probe found more than 40 permanently dark craters near the Moon's north pole. In the same year, NASA's LCROSS probe crashed a rocket into the Moon's surface and analysed the plume of material thrown up. It found evidence of water.

▼ The LCROSS space probe follows its Centaur rocket on a collision course with the Moon as it searches for water.

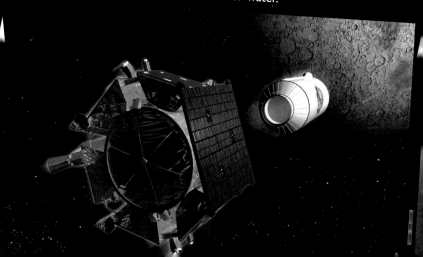

GIANT MOON

A supermoon occurs when the Moon's elliptical orbit causes it to come close to Earth. If it is closer to Earth at full Moon, the whole disk of the Moon looks bigger and brighter. It can happen during a new Moon too, but the Moon is then in shadow and invisible.

MEGA STUDIOS PRESENTS

LIFE ON MARS

As Mars is the most Earthlike planet in the Solar System, it has always been the focus of the search for life. However, the first spacecraft to visit Mars found a dry, dusty world with no signs of life. Scientists haven't given up and the search is still on.

ASTRONAUTS ON MARS

Plans for manned space missions to Mars have been made since the 1950s, but astronauts have not yet set foot on the red planet. However, Russia, America, China, and several privately funded spaceflight organizations have announced plans to send astronauts to Mars before 2040. A space voyage to Mars would be a daunting prospect because the first Martian explorers could be away from Earth for 2–3 years.

WILD WEATHER

Mars has a thinner atmosphere than Earth, so it's colder. The nighttime temperature near the poles can plunge to −195°F (−125°C). Near the equator, rovers have recorded temperatures higher than 86°F (30°C). Near the polar ice caps, snowstorms occur in winter and duststorms take place during summer.

▲ This dust storm on the surface of Mars was spotted by the Mars Reconnaissance Orbiter spacecraft in 2006.

TERRAFORMING MARS

Making a planet more Earthlike is called "terraforming." Some scientists think it might be possible to change Mars into a planet that humans could live on without having to wear spacesuits. Melting the ice caps to release carbon dioxide, or sending large amounts of ammonia or methane from Earth to Mars would give Mars a thicker, warmer atmosphere. Then green plants could be grown, adding oxygen through the process of photosynthesis.

◄ In the distant future, a terraformed Mars might look like Earth, with water and green plants.

ROCK LIFE

In 1996, scientists announced that they had found evidence of past life on Mars in a meteorite. The meteorite, called ALH 84001, was collected in Antarctica in 1984 and contained microscopic fossils. However, other scientists argued that the structures were more likely the result of non-biological processes. Tests failed to settle the matter.

▼ Wormlike structures in the ALH 84001 Martian meteorite could be fossilized bacteria that once lived on Mars.

THE SEARCH FOR LIFE

Orbiting spacecraft, landers, and rovers have been searching for signs of life on Mars since the Mariner 9 mission in 1971. The red planet may have supported life in the past because Mars was once warmer and wetter. However, no evidence of past or present life has been found so far.

▼ The Curiosity rover has been exploring Mars since August 2012. One of its tasks is to find out if its landing site might have supported life in the past.

GAS Giants

Beyond Mars there are four giant planets known as the Jovian planets, after Jupiter. They are almost entirely made of gas, with rocky centers surrounded by liquid. Astronauts will never set foot on them because they don't have a solid surface, but spacecraft have been sent to explore them in detail.

Giant of giants

Jupiter is the largest planet in the Solar System—2.5 times the mass of all the other planets added together. It is made mainly of hydrogen and helium—the same elements as stars—so if it were 70 times more massive, it would have become a star. Underneath its atmosphere, the gas is under so much pressure that it changes to liquid. Deeper still, it behaves like metal. At the center of the planet, there is a solid core made of rock.

Jupiter
Diameter: 86,881 mi (139,822 km)
Distance from the Sun:
484 million mi (779 million km)
Time to spin once: 9.9 hours
Time to orbit the Sun: 11.9 years
Average temperature: -166°F (-110°C)
Moons: 67

JUPITER'S GREAT RED SPOT
IS A HURRICANE-LIKE
STORM THAT'S 2.5 TIMES
BIGGER THAN EARTH.

Furthest away

The outermost planet in the Solar System, Neptune's chemical makeup is similar to that of Uranus. Its blue color is caused by methane gas in its atmosphere. Enormous, dark, Earth-sized storms have appeared in its atmosphere from time to time, but disappear after a few years. The fastest winds in the Solar System have been detected on Neptune, with a top speed of 1,500 mph (2,400 km/h).

Neptune
Diameter: 30,598 mi (49,243 km)
Distance from the Sun:
2,793 million mi (4,495 million km)
Time to spin once: 16.1 hours
Time to orbit the Sun: 163 years
Average temperature: -328°F (-200°C)
Moons: 14

Ringed planet

The Solar System's second-largest planet, Saturn, is famous for its bright rings made of water-ice. The other three gas giants have rings too, but they're thin, dark, and dusty. Like Jupiter, Saturn is made mostly of hydrogen and helium. Superfast winds and heat rising from the planet's interior cause hazy yellow bands in its atmosphere.

Saturn
Diameter: 74,998 mi (120,698 km)
Distance from the Sun:
891 million mi (1,434 million km)
Time to spin once: 10.7 hours
Time to orbit the Sun: 29.4 years
Average temperature: -220°F (-140°C)
Moons: 62

Tilted spin

In addition to hydrogen and helium, Uranus contains water, ammonia, and methane gas. Methane in its atmosphere gives the planet its blue-green color. As it orbits the Sun, tilted on its side, one pole receives continuous sunlight for 42 years, and then the other pole faces the Sun for the next 42 years.

Uranus
Diameter: 31,518 mi (50,724 km)
Distance from the Sun:
1,785 million mi (2,873 million km)
Time to spin once: 17.2 hours
Time to orbit the Sun: 83.7 years
Average temperature: -320°F (-195°C)
Moons: 27

MANY *Moons*

More than 160 moons orbit the planets in the Solar System. As technology improves, more moons are discovered. The number of known moons has nearly doubled since 2003. Most of them are tiny worlds orbiting the gas giants, but the biggest, Jupiter's moon Ganymede, is bigger than Mercury.

TITAN, DENSE WITH RIVERS OF METHANE

One of Saturn's moons, Titan, is the only moon with a dense atmosphere and the only body in the Solar System, apart from Earth, to have liquid on its surface. The Cassini spacecraft dropped the *Huygens* probe on Titan. It photographed the surface, but the rivers and lakes it found aren't filled with water—they're full of liquid methane.

SHEPHERD MOONS, DUSTY AND CRATERED

Some of Saturn's rings have defined edges because moons are orbiting nearby or inside gaps between the rings. They are called shepherd moons because their gravity keeps the ring particles together like a shepherd herds a flock of sheep. Any particles that stray out of the ring are either deflected back into the ring or attracted onto the moon by its gravity.

EUROPA, WATERY WITH A THICK, ICY SURFACE

One of Jupiter's moons, Europa, is covered with ice that might be floating on a water ocean up to 60 mi (100 km) deep. It is thought that this ocean could harbor life. To protect it from bacterial contamination, the Galileo space probe that explored Jupiter and its moons was deliberately sent into Jupiter's atmosphere to burn up.

TRITON, WITH BURSTS OF LIQUID NITROGEN

Many moons that orbit the outer planets are asteroids that were captured by the planets. One sign of this is if the moon orbits in the opposite direction to other moons—Triton, Neptune's largest moon, does this. Triton is so cold that it has ice volcanoes shooting out a mixture of liquid nitrogen, methane, and dust.

MIRANDA, ICY WITH CRACKS AND CANYONS

Uranus' small moon, Miranda, is covered with a strange patchwork pattern of canyons, grooves, and cracks. It may be that this tiny world was smashed apart by a collision long ago and then the parts came together again in orbit. Scientists think its surface is made mostly of ice.

GANYMEDE, WITH A THICK LAYER OF ICE

Jupiter's moon Ganymede is the biggest moon in the Solar System, larger than Mercury. It is thought to be covered with a deep layer of ice up to 500 mi (800 km) thick. Discovered in 1610, Ganymede and three other large moons of Jupiter were the first moons ever seen orbiting another planet.

DWARFS in Space

Countless millions of small worlds made of rock and ice orbit the Sun between the planets and far beyond them. Some of these worlds are nearly as big as planets, so they are called dwarf planets. Many of them are found in the Kuiper Belt.

EX-PLANET

In 1930, U.S. astronomer Clyde Tombaugh discovered the Solar System's ninth planet, Pluto. In 2005, another distant planet, named Eris, was found. At first, it was hailed as the Solar System's tenth planet. When astronomers realized that many more of these small worlds are likely to be discovered, they decided to call them dwarf planets.

▲ The New Horizons space probe will fly past Pluto in 2015 and then carry on into the Kuiper Belt.

COMPARING THE BELTS

The Kuiper Belt is like the Asteroid Belt but further away and far bigger. It lies beyond Neptune's orbit, is about twice the size of the Solar System, and consists of lots of cometlike objects. The Asteroid Belt extends from Mars to Jupiter. Although, the Kuiper Belt is 20 times wider then the Asteroid Belt and 200 times more massive, it is so far away that we can see very little of it.

▼ The Kuiper Belt is a disk-shaped region that extends from Neptune's orbit to 4.6 billion mi (7.4 billion km) from the Sun.

Kuiper Belt

Asteroid Belt

EGG PLANET

Dwarf planet Haumea has a reddish spot on its surface. Calculations based on the way it reflects light suggest that Haumea has a stretched elliptical shape, with its length twice as long as its width. Its strange shape may be caused by its fast rotation—it spins once every four hours, possibly due to a collision with something in the past.

▲ Haumea is very dense, so it probably contains more rock and less ice than other Kuiper Belt objects.

▲ Eris was discovered in 2005 and named as a dwarf planet on September 13, 2006.

WARRIOR PRINCESS

Dwarf planet Eris orbits the Sun three times further out than Pluto and has a tiny moon called Dysnomia. It was first named after a television series, *Xena: Warrior Princess*. Later, it was given its official name of Eris, after the Greek god of strife, chaos, and discord.

▼ The dwarf planet Ceres may have a deep layer of ice under its thin, dusty crust.

▲ Makemake is so small and far away that, even through the most powerful telescope, it is a tiny, blurred image.

FAR, FAR AWAY

The dwarf planet Makemake was discovered on March 31, 2005, by astronomers at the Palomar Observatory in the U.S. It was named after a god worshipped by the Easter Island people, because it was discovered at Easter. It is so far away that it takes nearly 310 years to orbit the Sun.

THE BIGGEST ASTEROID

At 590 mi (950 km) across, Ceres is the biggest asteroid in the Asteroid Belt. When it was discovered in 1801, it was thought to be a comet. When smaller similar objects were found, the word "asteroid" was invented to describe them. Finally, when Pluto was reclassified as a dwarf planet, Ceres became a dwarf planet too. The Dawn probe, launched in 2007, visited the giant asteroid Vesta in 2011, on the way to explore Ceres.

TO THE EXTREMES

▼ Io's volcanic activity is driven by heat caused by the gravitational pull of Jupiter and its other moons.

The Solar System is a place of extremes and strange phenomena. Sulfur-spewing volcanoes, comet storms, and mysterious glows in a planet's atmosphere continually surprise and amaze scientists. The more they study the Solar System, the more surprises they find.

VOLCANO WORLD

Io, one of Jupiter's moons, is the most geologically active object in the Solar System. This tiny world is covered with hundreds of active volcanoes. The yellow, orange, and black colors on its surface are sulfur at different temperatures. White patches are sulfur dioxide frost. Active volcanoes are found in only two other places in the Solar System—Earth and Enceladus, one of Saturn's moons.

Aurorae are named after the Roman goddess of the dawn.

Polar lights

The poles of Jupiter and Saturn are sometimes lit up by shimmering rings of light called aurorae, fuelled by particles flying off their moons. In images taken by the Hubble Space Telescope, the aurorae appear blue because of the ultraviolet camera, but they are actually red and purple. The color comes from excited hydrogen molecules.

▲ Saturn's aurorae shimmer and glow up to 600 mi (1,000 km) above its clouds.

РОССИЯ **24**
ПРЯМОЙ ЭФИР

я область

ергей Ламзин
меститель директора астрономического
ститута им. Штенберга МГУ

МВД РФ

Near-Earth Objects

Countless comets and asteroids fly through the Solar System. Occasionally, their orbits are affected by the gravitational pull of other planets and moons, bringing them close to Earth. Some near-Earth Objects pose a danger to Earth, so thousands of orbits are closely monitored. Small, stony asteroids hit Earth every year, but major impacts only occur every few thousand years.

◀ On February 13, 2013, a near-Earth asteroid dived into our atmosphere and exploded over Chelyabink in Russia.

EXTREME TEMPERATURES

Temperatures in the Solar System range from 27 million°F (15 million°C) at the center of the Sun to just a few degrees above absolute zero (−459°F or −273°C) in the Oort Cloud on the outermost fringes of the Solar System.

"A sungrazing comet called Ikeya-Seki came within 280,000 mi (450,000 km) of the Sun in 1965 and survived!"

▲ A long-tailed sungrazing comet (left) sweeps past the Sun, seen by the SOHO space probe.

Icy storm

In December 2011, a comet storm began in space. In ten days, 25 comets, known as sungrazers, were seen diving into the Sun. Recorded by the Solar and Heliospheric Observatory (SOHO) space probe, a comet storm like this had never been seen before. Since its launch in 1995, SOHO has discovered more than 2,400 comets while monitoring the Sun.

INDEX

◄ When explosives are set off, by applying heat or friction, they instantly produce intense heat and a large volume of expanding gas.

INDEX

Entries in **bold** refer to main subject entries; entries in *italics* refer to illustrations.

ACKNOWLEDGMENTS

The publishers would like to thank the following sources for the use of their photographs:

KEY
A/AL=Alamy, B=Bridgeman, CO=Corbis, D=Dreamstime, F=Fotolia, FLPA=Frank Lane Picture Agency, GI=Getty Images, GW=Glow Images, IS=istockphoto.com, MP=Minden Pictures, N=Newscom, NG=National Geographic Creative, NPL=Nature Picture Library, P=Photoshot, PL=Photolibrary, R=Reuters, RF=Rex Features, S=Shutterstock, SJC=Stuart Jackson-Carter, SPL=Science Photo Library, SS=Superstock, TF=Topfoto

t=top, a=above, b=bottom/below, c=center, l=left, r=right, f=far, m=main, bg=background

FRONT COVER VOLKER STEGER/SPL, SPINE MichaelTaylor/S, BACK COVER Andrea Danti/S, Pavel Vakhrushev/S, Mark Scott/S, Sebastian Kaulitzki/S, Tony Hallas/NASA, PRELIMS 1 F, 2–3 RTimages/S, 4 Dmitri Melnik/S, 5 SNEHIT/S, iurii/S

INCREDIBLE SCIENCE 6–7 A 8–9 David Scharf/SPL 8(tl) Pedro Nogueira/S, (tr) NASA-JPL, (bl) Lane V. Erickson/S, (b, l–r) Top Photo Group/RF 9(tl) Pedro Nogueira/S, (bl) James Balog/Aurora Photos/Corbis, (r, t–b) oku/S, David Arts/S, Dmitri Melnik/S, Sergey Kamshylin/S, Andrey Burmakin/S, (frame) Phase4Photography/S 10–11(m) NASA/GI, (b) Joseph C Dovala/P 10(l) Edward Kinsman/SPL, (c) Abel Tumik/S, (b, panel) Matthias Pahl/S, (b, chain) Henry Nowick/S, (r) Phase4Photography/S 11(l) E.R.Degginger/SPL, (r, t–b) Melli/S, Vakhrushev Pavel/S, Arsgera/S, ArtmannWitte/S 12–13(bg) lolloj/S 12(m) GI, (t) Eye of Science/SPL, (bl) Nicemonkey/S, (br) Lawrence Berkeley National Laboratory/SPL 13(tl) NASA/SPL, (tr) RF, (bm) Innespace Productions/SEABREACHER, (bl) Dmitri Mihhailov/S, (br) Gwoeii/S 14–5(bg) dinadesign/S, (frame) ivn3da/S, (c) adziohiciek/S, (ice cubes) Alex Staroseltsev/S 14(tr) NASA/Science Faction/Corbis, (bl) Vitaly Raduntsev/S, (br) SPL 15(tl) Patrick Landmann/SPL, (tr) Ria Novosti/SPL, (tr, frame) Hintau Aliaksei, (bl) Diego Barucco/S, (br) Yva Momatiuk & John Eastcott/GI 16–7(bg) Zinatova Olga/S, (c) Gordan/S, (b) Sergey Mironov/S, (t) NASA-JPL 16(l) Edward Kinsman/SPL, (r) Jean-Luc & Françoise Ziegler/P 17(t) NASA-GSFC, (bl) NASA-JPL, (br) NASA/WMAP Science Team/SPL 18–9(bg, wood) Ford Photography/S, (bg, book) Valentin Agapov/S, (doodles) Bukhavets Mikhail/S, (masking tape) Studio DMM Photography, Designs & Art/S, (frames) Phase4Photography/S 18(t) NASA-MSFC, (b) NASA-JPL 19(tr) Viktar Malyshchyts/S, (r) happydancing/S 20–1(m) Tony Craddock/SPL 20(b) J.C. Revy, ISM/SPL 21 Volker Springel/Max Planck Institute for Astrophysics/SPL 22–3(bg) Kheng Guan Toh/S, (atoms) Johan Swanepoel/S, (molecules) Serdar Duran/S 22(l) Steve Gschmeissner/SPL, (tr) David McCarthy/SPL, (br) Susumu Nishinaga/SPL 23(t) Dr Gary Gaugler/SPL, (cl) Dr Linda Stannard, UCT/SPL, (cr) Omikron/SPL, (b) Jan Kaliciak/S 24(t) Eye of science/SPL, (c) Ower and Syred/SPL, (b) SPL 25(tl) Jan Hinsch/SPL, (tr) Susumu Nishinaga/SPL, (bl) Steve Gschmeissner/

SPL, (br) Astrid & Hanns-Frieder Michler/SPL 26(bg) argus/S, (m) Thierry Berrod, Mona Lisa Production/SPL, (b) Bristish Museum/Munoz-Yague/SPL 27(m) Stephen & Donna O'Meara/SPL, (tl) Jochen Tack/P, (tr) Augusto Cabral/S, (bl) Smit/S 28–9(m) Anakaopress/Look at sciences/SPL 28(b) optimarc/S 29(t) Stephen Alvarez/GI, (c) Carsten Peter/GI, (b) Jeff Rotman/ NPL 30–9(t) shelbysupercars.com, (b) David J. Cross/P 30 GI 31 NASA/SPL 32(bg, pink) Panos Karapanagiotis/S, (bg, writing) Inga Nielsen/S, (tl) National Library of Medicine/SPL, (tr) Dmitrijs Bindemanis/S, (cl) Library of Congress/digital version by Science Faction, (bl) Bettmann/Corbis, (br) Dominik Michálek/S 33(tl) Jacqueline Abromeit, (tr) RF, (cl) Bettmann/Corbis, (bl) Graeme Dawes/S, (bc) NASA-MSFC, (br) Reuters/Corbis 34–5(m) Russell Kightley/SPL 34 NASA/ESA/STSCI/J.Kenney & E. Yale, Yale University/SPL 35 Chandra X-ray Observatory/NASA/SPL 36–7(bg) David Parker/SPL, (clockwise starting bl) Christophe Vander Eecken/Reporters/SPL, Adam Hart-Davis/SPL, Tim Wright/ Corbis, optimarc/S, Sylverarts/S, Emilio Naranjo/epa/Corbis 38–9(border) gorica/S 38(tl) INSAGO/S, (cl) R-studio/S, (bl) GI 39(tl) Christophe Boisvieux/Corbis, (bl) Time & Life Pictures/GI, (r) Omikron/SPL 40–1 Jose Antonio Peñas/SPL (c) T Carrafa/ Newspix/RF, (r) Anan Kaewkhammul/S

BODY SCIENCE 42–3 Segalen/Phanie/RF; 44–5 aliisik/S, Sarunyu_ foto/S, aopsan/S; 44(tr) Willdidthis/S, (tr) R-studio/S; 45 Cordelia Molloy/SPL, (b) Viacheslav A. Zotov/S, (bl) vvoe/S, (br) Andrea Danti/S, (tl) Twelve/S, (tl) SeDmi/S; 46 Steve Gschmeissner/SPL, (br) SPL/GI; 47 Dr. Kessel & Dr. Kardon/Tissues & Organs/GI, (bl) Alexey Khromushin/F, (br) J.C. Revy, ISM/SPL, (t) Aaron Amat/S; 48–9 Science Picture Co/GI, Palsur/S; 48(bl) GRei/S, (bl) Linali/S; 50–1 R-studio/S, (tc) TebNad/S; 50(bl) Michal Kowalski/S, (bl) R. Bick, B. Poindexter, Ut Medical School/SPL, (br) Litvinenko Anastasia/S, (br) Olivier Le Queinec/S, (br) B Calkins/S, (cl) kedrov/S, (cr) Nixx Photography/S, (cr) Anusorn P nachol/S, (cr) Prof. P. Motta/Dept. of Anatomy/University "La Sapienza", Rome/SPL, (tl) Oleksii Natykach/S, (tl) ZoneFatal/S, (tl) wmedien/S, (tl) ojka/S, (tr) Yevgen Kotyukh/S; 51(bl) happykanppy/S, (br) Anthony DiChello/S, (cl) Scimat/SPL, (cr) nikkytok/S, (tl) Yaraz/S, (tl) Steve Gschmeissner/SPL, (tr) Volker Steger/SPL; 52–3 Sergey Panteleev/IS; 52(bl) St Bartholomew's Hospital/SPL, (br) Paul Gunning/SPL, (cr) Fedor Kondratenko/S; 53(br) SPL, (t) Dr. Richard Kessel & Dr. Randy Kardon/Tissues & Organs/Visuals Unlimited/CO; 54 Leigh Prather/S, (br) Diego Cervo/S, (cr) Mikhail/S, (cr) Bill Longcore/SPL, (l) Scientifica/GI, (tr) Ozerina Anna/S; 55 Gunnar Pippel/S, (r) Colleen Petch/ Newspix/RF, (bc) Alex Staroseltsev/S, (bl) AFP/GI, (bl) Alex Varlakov/IS, (br) Martin Dohrn/SPL, (cr) Alex073/S, (tl) Eric Gevaert/S; 56–7 Neliyana Kostadinova/S, Ramon Andrade 3Dciencia/SPL; 56(br) 3d4medical.com/SPL, (l) Sebastian Kaulitzki/S, (l) Zephyr/SPL; 57(tr) Sovereign, ISM/SPL; 58–9 Medical Images, Universal Images Group/SPL; 58(bl) Sergey Furtaev/S, (cr) Steve Gschmeissner/SPL; 59(bl) Gunnar Pippel/S, (br) Kannanimages/S, (tl) Similar Images Preview/GI;

PHIL VICKERY'S
Ultimate
DIABETES
COOKBOOK

PHIL VICKERY'S
Ultimate
DIABETES
COOKBOOK

**Delicious recipes to help
you achieve a healthy,
balanced diet**

**WITH
BEA HARLING BSc**

photography by Sean Calitz

KYLE BOOKS

First published in Great Britain in 2017 by
Kyle Books, an imprint of Kyle Cathie Ltd
192–198 Vauxhall Bridge Road
London SW1V 1DX
general.enquiries@kylebooks.com
www.kylebooks.co.uk

10 9 8 7 6 5 4 3 2 1

ISBN 978 0 85783 407 2

Editor Judith Hannam
Editorial Assistant Hannah Coughlin
Copy Editor Anne Sheasby
Design Ketchup
Photographer Sean Calitz
Food Stylist Annie Rigg
Prop Stylist Tonia Shuttleworth
Production Nic Jones and Gemma John

A Cataloguing in Publication record for this title is available from the
British Library.

Colour reproduction by f1 Colour
Printed and bound in China by C&C Offset Printing Co., Ltd.

Contents

Foreword by Diabetes UK

Hello,

We all know how important eating well is, whether you've got diabetes or not. But if you do have diabetes then you have to think about food every meal time. Yet that doesn't mean you can't eat delicious food. And this book will give you plenty of great ideas to help you get busy in the kitchen.

Making sure people are confident about their diet is just one of the things Diabetes UK does to help the 4.5 million people in the UK living with diabetes. With someone diagnosed with diabetes every 2 minutes our work has never been more important. When people don't get the right care and support diabetes can cause complications like strokes, heart attacks, blindness and amputations.

We make sure people do get the care and support they need, whether that's through our Helpline, online information, events or local support groups. We also campaign to make sure everyone gets the care they need from the NHS. And we fund research which develops new treatments and will, ultimately, find a cure.

To find out more about how we help people with diabetes and how we might be able to help you or someone you know, check out our website diabetes.org.uk.

We're fighting for a world where diabetes can do no harm. By buying this book you've become part of that fight.

Thank you,

Chris Askew
Chief Executive of Diabetes UK

Introduction

For anyone living with diabetes it is essential to eat well, to ensure you have a balance of foods, that your overall diet is low in sugar, saturated fat and salt, and high in fruit, vegetables, fibre, wholegrains, beans and pulses. There isn't a special diet for people with diabetes, so our recipes celebrate the fact that a healthy, balanced diet is good for everyone and doesn't need to be restrictive.

The trend for so-called 'healthy eating' is not always what it seems. All too often the accompanying books turn out to be ill conceived and full of spurious claims. All the recipes in this book, however, have been tested several times to ensure not only that they work but that they are nutritionally sound and are in line with healthy eating principles.

Our aim with this book was to avoid the 'you poor thing' approach and instead create friendly, rounded, easy-to-cook recipes that just happen to be perfect for those living with diabetes.

Please note, when managing diabetes, it is essential to talk to your doctor or to consult a registered dietitian with a referral from a doctor, to assess your individual dietary needs. One size does not fit all for diabetes management. Nutritional information is provided for each recipe that can help you make choices and plan your meals. This information can also be helpful if you're trying to lose weight or need to know how much medication (like insulin) to give yourself.

Phil Vickery and Bea Harling

So the key messages are:
- This is a recipe book about eating well that also contains modern cooking ideas for people living with diabetes. There isn't a special diet for people with diabetes
- It also has wider appeal for people interested in eating healthily for the longer term.

And the recipes are designed to help those who:
- Are interested in eating healthily in general.

- Want to lose weight, but in a less drastic fashion, and also eat tasty, interesting food.

- Want to maintain their weight, with a well-balanced but delicious diet.

- Want to really look at their lifestyle and make some positive tweaks.

What is diabetes?

Diabetes is a condition that occurs when the amount of glucose (sugar) in the blood is too high, either because the body is not producing any or enough insulin, or because the insulin it is producing is not effective. If left untreated, it can cause serious health complications.

A hormone produced by the pancreas, insulin is sometimes described as a key that opens the doors to the body's cells. Normally, once foods containing carbohydrates have been digested and broken down into glucose, insulin helps move this glucose into our cells, where it is used as fuel for energy. In those with undiagnosed/untreated diabetes, the body can't use glucose to provide energy and that's why some people may feel tired or lose weight.

There are two main types of diabetes – Type 1 and Type 2:
Type 1 is an autoimmune condition where the body attacks and destroys insulin-producing cells, meaning no insulin is produced. It can develop at any age, but usually appears before the age of 40, and especially in childhood. It is not caused by diet or lifestyle – a common misconception is that it is caused by eating too much sugar. Nobody knows the exact cause, so it can't be prevented. The least common of the two types, occurring in about 10 per cent of people with diabetes, there is currently no cure. It is treated by daily insulin doses, taken either by injection or via an insulin pump as well eating healthily and being regularly active.

Type 2 develops when the body doesn't make enough insulin, or the insulin it makes doesn't work properly (known as insulin resistance). It is caused by a combination of genetic and environmental factors. It usually appears in people over the age of 40, though in people of South Asian descent, who are at greater risk, it often appears from the age of 25. Other factors that increase risk of developing Type 2 diabetes include coming from an African–Caribbean or Black African background and having a close family member (sibling or parent) with diabetes. But being overweight is one of the main reasons people develop Type 2 diabetes. It is also increasingly common in children, adolescents and young people of all ethnicities. Type 2 is treated with a healthy diet and being regularly physically active. Quite often medication (including insulin) will be needed.

Achieving a healthy lifestyle

Following a healthy diet lifestyle, by eating healthily, being regularly active and managing your weight is a big part of managing your diabetes. There is more on healthy eating later, but regular physical activity means spending less time sitting down and more time on your feet. Government guidance also recommends doing 150 minutes of moderate intensity activity per week. This is any kind of activity where breathing is increased but you can talk comfortably. This could be walking quickly, cycling on flat ground or a leisurely swim. It's also recommended to do exercises that improve muscle strength such as heavy gardening, carrying groceries or yoga on at least two days a week. If you don't do much activity, it's best to start slowly and gradually build up. Walking is a great activity to start with.

What does a healthy, balanced diet look like?

In a nutshell, it means having a diet high in fruit and vegetables, fibre, wholegrains, beans, pulses and oily fish and eating less red meat and processed meat, salt, sugar and saturated fat. Importantly, it also means keeping to healthy portion sizes, see www.diabetes.org.uk/portion-sizes. The good news is: a healthy, balanced diet is good for everyone and your family and friends can continue to enjoy interesting food and the lifestyle with you. You will find more explanation about main food groups, ingredients, kitchen and cooking tips throughout the book.

Getting the essentials right

Eating is a confusing business with so much information around. Keep your goals in mind and become more aware of what you are eating. Focus on the quality and composition of your food: your aim is to make healthier choices and develop good eating habits. For starters, here's a 3-step plan:

1. Start by looking at what you eat – it might be helpful to keep a food diary for a week.
2. Follow with shaping some idea of the healthier foods you aim to eat more of and the foods you want to eat less of, then make a plan about how you are going to do this – it might be helpful to make a meal plan for a week and you could use some recipes from the book. Speak to a dietitian for more individual, tailored advice. Start off with small changes and build on them.
3. Then give some thought to including a wide variety of foods from the main food groups, in the recommended proportions, every day.

For further information, look at at the Enjoy Food section of the Diabetes UK website: www.diabetes.org. uk/Guide-to-diabetes/Enjoy-food/

Eating smart

Knowing more about the benefits of different foods and nutrient groups can help you improve your diet.

Carbs All carbohydrates – found in foods such as bread, rice, pasta, potatoes and yams – affect blood sugar levels, so you need to keep an eye on the amount you eat. They are a source of energy: the body converts carbohydrates into glucose to fuel cells. The three main types of carbohydrates are starch, sugar and fibre. Some carbs are more filling than others. Wholegrain versions naturally have higher fibre and help keep you feeling full longer and can help you manage your diabetes better.

You need to include some carbohydrate in your diet every day. How much depends on how old you are, how active you are and the targets you are trying to achieve. Speak to a dietitian about how much you need and what types are healthier.

Sugars can be natural, such as those found in dairy foods (lactose) and in vegetables and fruit (fructose). Then there's the 'free sugars' that you add yourself or are added by the manufacturer in foods such as sweets, chocolate and sugary drinks. Free sugars also include the natural sugars in honey and syrups like maple and agave, and juices and smoothies – all of these foods need to be limited in your diet. We all eat too much sugar and could do with reducing the amount we eat. Sugary foods and drinks are high in calories and eating too much can lead to weight gain and can affect your blood sugar levels.

Cooking from scratch also puts you in control of the amount in foods. The best thing to do is to reduce sugar and your taste for sweet things and instead get natural sweetness from fruit and vegetables – but sometimes you may want to use an artificial sweetener. For more information see: https://www.diabetes.org.uk/Guide-to-diabetes/Enjoy-food/Carbohydrates-and-diabetes/Sugar-sweeteners-and-diabetes/. If you do use an artificial sweetener, powdered sweeteners work best in baking. Granulated sweeteners work well in softer sweet things, such as Soft Chinese five-spice meringues on page 159. If you're adding sweetener to general cooking, any sweetener will work.

Fibre Insoluble fibre, such as is found in wholegrain bread, cereals and pasta, brown, wild and basmati rice, nuts and seeds helps to keep your gut healthy. Soluble fibre as found in fruit and vegetables, linseed, soya, oats and barley, beans and pulses, helps to keep your blood glucose and cholesterol under control.

Make sure you eat more foods containing fibre regularly. Good sources include fruits and vegetables, nuts and seeds, oats, wholegrain breads and pulses like beans and lentils.

Fat is fat and – however it is packaged – it is high in calories. Your mantra should be 'cut the fat: cut the calories', especially if you are trying to lose weight. Eat less saturated fat (found mainly in animal products like butter and ghee) and substitute with unsaturated plant fats like avocado and olive oil, rapeseed and vegetable oil. Eating healthier types of fat is better for your cholesterol levels and heart. Do include some low fat dairy foods every day, like yogurt and milk. Dairy options are good sources of protein, some vitamins and calcium.

Protein Foods like beans, pulses, fish, eggs and meat are high in protein, which helps with building and replacing muscles. They also contain vitamins and minerals. Oily fish, such as mackerel, salmon and sardines also provide omega-3, which can help protect the heart. Aim to have some food from this group every day, with 2 portions of oily fish a week. Choose lean cuts of meat and try to add beans and pulses to dishes.

Using a good quality non-stick pan will mean you can use less oil to cook with. Keep a pump bottle or spray oil next to the cooker.

Fluids It's important to drink enough fluid. Aim for 8–10 cups or glasses a day. Water is a good option. We have some suggestions for making water more interesting later (see page 161). All drinks count, including tea, coffee and milk (skimmed or semi skimmed) or go for low or no calorie and sugar free drinks. Fruit juice and smoothies, sugary fizzy drinks and alcohol? Try to limit these for calories sake and they can also affect your blood sugar levels: the health guidelines for alcohol apply to everyone, including those with diabetes.

Smarter choices

Plan your meals and shopping list first – and do so with the intention of eating wholesome, homemade food. Aim for a balanced diet: and make sure you also eat a variety of different foods from all the food groups.

Include some starchy foods every day. Keep an eye on portion sizes and vary the type. For example, swap potatoes for sweet potato, or choose carrots, beetroot or squash instead. Swap white starchy bread, pasta and rice for wholegrain versions as they contain more fibre. Remember, though, that wholegrains will need more cooking time. If you are aiming to lose weight, check your portion sizes of all foods, not just carbs.

Resolve to eat real food and cook from scratch as much as is practical. Fish and eggs can be the simplest fast food, quick to cook and they contain protein, which keeps you feeling full for longer. Having some basic ingredients in the cupboard and freezer, will help with faster home cooking. Make double quantities when you can, eat some and freeze the rest in portions for the microwave. Watch out for the amount of extras you add, like salad dressings and oil that you cook with. We've added more tips throughout the book, to help keep your healthy diet on track.

Creating good habits

Making small changes to your usual habits, slowly over time, really will make a difference. You can still enjoy favourite foods without cutting out everything and feeling deprived. Some of these tips may seem very obvious, but it is worth trying out healthier habits.

- Out of sight out of mind! Reorganise your kitchen and put healthy food in vision first, both in the fridge and in your cupboards. Have a clear out of things you know will be a problem, like family sized 'share' packets of sweets and crisps, or chocolate biscuits.
- When shopping, put a visual prompt in the basket to load vegetables and fruit.
- Portion food out and don't leave the serving dish on the table for seconds.
- Bump up the veg. In recipes, try reducing the meat portion and stretch it out with extra vegetables, beans or pulses instead. Meals like Bolognese sauce, chilli or stews will go further and it will save you money too.
- Try using smaller serving plates as well, to make the portions appear fuller.
- Invest in a heavy, non-stick pan and use less or no oil. A griddle pan is great for this too.
- Leave the pepper pot on the table and put the salt back in the cupboard. Ingredients with strong flavours like dried mushrooms, chilli, spices and herbs are all great replacements for salt.
- Mature and strong cheeses like Parmesan are so powerful in flavour you can use less and so lower the calories contributed by fat.

If you are trying to lose weight, it might help to remember a single fact about losing weight: how much you eat overall is the important point. If you eat more calories than you burn then you will put on weight. To maintain a healthy weight, keep a keen eye on portion sizes. Speak to a dietitian for more advice.

Portion sizes

Keeping to healthy portion sizes is an important part of eating healthier too and can also help to manage your weight. Think about the size of the slice, for example, and how often you have it, especially with treats and snacks. It may also be helpful to weigh things out and not guess at portion sizes.

It's difficult to guess at a portion and to get it right: using familiar objects to visualise portion sizes is an easy way to go with this. Tablespoons, golf balls and a computer mouse size will all help. Remember, everybody's needs are different so the number of portion sizes you need is individual – and your weight, gender, body composition and activity levels all make a difference. Your dietitian will be able to advise you on the portion sizes that are right for you. See www.diabetes.org.uk/portion-sizes for a visual guide to portion sizes.

Store cupboard staples

Stock up on a few dried, canned and frozen stores so that you have ingredients on hand for making fresh, quick meals.

• Grains, seeds and pulses offer a world beyond white rice and pasta: upgrade to wholegrain versions of carbohydrates and mix in grains, seeds, beans and pulses. Many are high in fibre and more filling, which helps to sustain energy levels right through the day.
• Wholegrains are the seeds of cereal plants and the benefits of adding more of these ingredients to your meals are many as they provide protein, vitamins and minerals.
• Beans also contain these nutrients and add fibre. So stir in some beans next time you are cooking rice, or a main meal.
• Dried pasta shapes made from bean or lentil flour are really worth a try instead of the usual refined wheat pasta; the flavour is good and the change will boost a whole range of nutrients in one meal.
• Cooking pasta al dente so that it is slower to digest is the best cooking method and chilling cooked pasta, even if you reheat it after, helps to reduce the rise in blood sugar levels after eating and also adds more fibre.

Follow food safety guidelines when cooling, storing and reheating foods in order to minimise the risk of potential food poisoning. See the NHS website for more information on this.

It is best to check the pack instructions for preparing grains and pulses because the same ingredient can be processed differently: some need soaking and some are 'quick cook' for convenience. If the long cooking time puts you off, go for the canned versions of chick peas, lentils, etc. I love the inspired combinations of wholegrains, seeds and pulses to be found in ready-to-heat pouches, they make wonderful shortcuts.

Here is a general method of preparing most dried wholegrains and pulses before using in recipes, to make them digestible. Place them in a glass bowl with double the volume of cold water. Cover and leave overnight. Drain and rinse; ready to cook. Keep in the fridge for up to 3 days. Some alternate grains are:

Buckwheat is a versatile fruit seed, related to rhubarb and sorrel, not wheat at all. It is a heart-healthy option, because it contains rutin, a compound that protects against the effects of high cholesterol. It's rich in magnesium, (for healthy bones and muscle function) and zinc (good for your skin health) plus iron. The whole grains are a great base to use instead of all rice, for risottos and salads. Try swapping in some buckwheat flour in baking and breakfast pancakes. The flavour can taste bitter to some people; always rinse and try sparingly first.

A recommended portion size for buckwheat is around 4 tablespoons (about 75g) cooked.

Preparation time: 5 minutes
Cooking time: 10 minutes

70g whole buckwheat grains, rinsed
160ml cold water

Eating your 5-a-day

Research shows that eating fruit and vegetables has substantial health benefits and can help protect our health from a range of conditions. The advice is to aim for at least 5 portions a day for this to work. A portion is about 80g, or roughly a handful. Fresh, frozen, dried and canned all count towards your total. Don't forget to include the vegetables you add when cooking, like onions, or tomatoes in a pasta sauce, or in a vegetable soup, for example. Potatoes don't count because they mainly contribute starch, so fall into the starchy carbohydrate food group. A variety of fruit and vegetables everyday will supply you with plenty of vitamins, minerals and fibre. Including fruit and vegetables in your diet can help with losing and maintaining weight.

Don't bother peeling vegetables such as sweet potatoes, to leave more fibre and antioxidants.

Place the buckwheat in a pan with the water and bring to the boil. Reduce the heat, simmer gently for 8–10 minutes and then remove from the heat. Leave the pan to stand until all the water is absorbed into the grains.

A recipe may call for a reduced salt stock cube to add to flavour the buckwheat; use ½ cube to 160 ml.

Lentils are great – they include all the beneficial nutrients like fibre, protein, minerals and vitamins and are low in calories. They are perfect to eat in warming casseroles in winter, in the summer added to salads, or puréed in spreads, for crudité and crackers. An easy way to add the useful nutrients from lentils is to purée them after cooking and use to thicken soups and sauces. Puy lentils are fantastic whole, in soups, or mixed with finely diced carrots, celery and onions as a side for lamb or meat. See the recipe on page 71.

Amaranth A small seed like grain, rich in iron and a source of protein. Swap some into porridge for a great breakfast alternative.

Bulgar is a form of whole wheat that has been parboiled and dried, making it a quicker to cook. You can find packs of quick cook whole wheat bulgar mixed with other grains such millet and red rice: lovely in warm salads. Contains fibre as well as supplying energising B vitamins. See the recipe on page 65.

Quinoa This grain-like seed contains higher protein content than most other grains. To cook from dry: rinse the quinoa (to remove a slightly bitter coating on the seeds) place it in a pan with half a reduced salt stock cube if you like, and cover it with the water. Bring to the boil and cook for 12–15 minutes, (you will see the little 'tails' appear) and then leave to cool and drain well. Spread it over a shallow dish to dry and fluff up.

Oats also contain a soluble fibre, beta-glucan, and eating them regularly can offer the benefit of helping to lower blood cholesterol levels. You can also find packets of oat bran (a by-product of making flour from whole oats) and adding a spoonful of this in with the oats you are cooking is a good tip to boost the beta-glucan even more.

You will see many types available; processed in different ways from jumbo to fine and the size of the grain really does count. Jumbo rolled oats are better than quick-cook and instant oats as they are slower to digest than the more processed variety and cause less of a rise in blood sugar levels after eating.

Look at the label

You've read all the advice and written your shopping list, so don't allow panic to set in once you start looking at the labels on food packaging. 'Back of pack' labelling – found by law on both food and drink products – gives essential information about the ingredients, nutritional composition (calories, fats, sugars, salt, etc.) and known allergens. The ingredients are listed in order, starting with the highest-quantity ingredient first and ending the lowest-quantity ingredient last. If sugar appears in the first three, that food is likely to be high in sugar.

Colour-coded labelling

Colour-coded labelling – known as traffic light labelling – is not yet compulsory. It's an easy way to check at a glance how healthy a food or drink is, based on how much fat, saturated fat, sugars and salt it contains. The amounts are colour-coded green to red to show whether a particular nutrient is low (green), medium (amber) or high (red). Always try to choose foods with more greens and few ambers and avoid, where possible, foods with reds. If you do eat them, try to only to have occasionally and in small quantities.

There are two versions of how these traffic light labels appear:

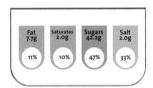 

The nutritional analysis in this book includes everything listed under ingredients, including optional extras.

Nutritional claims

Many products found in our supermarkets make claims such as fat free or low fat, which can be confusing. Here's the difference:

- Fat free: has to have no fat, but check the ingredients list for free (added) sugar, which is often used to replace the fat.
- Sugar free: the product doesn't contain sugar. Check the ingredients list to see what the sugar has been replaced with.
- No added sugar: although no sugar is added there may be naturally occurring sugar in the food.
- Low fat: the product has 3g or less of fat per 100g.
- Low sugar: has less than 5g of sugar per 100g.

Reduced fat or sugar: contains 30 per cent less fat or sugar than the standard version of the product. This doesn't necessarily mean it's healthy and in some cases the reduced-fat version can have the same amount of calories and fat as the standard version made by another brand.

Adapting your own recipes

Being diagnosed with diabetes doesn't mean that you have to learn a whole new way of cooking or banish all your favourite recipes. With a little modification most recipes can be made healthier and more suited to someone with diabetes, and you won't need to cook separate dishes for the rest of the family either. You can modify your usual recipes by:

- Reducing the amount of fat and type of fat you use.
- Cutting down on the salt.
- Cutting down on the amount of sugar – try replacing some sugar with dried fruit in baking.
- Increasing the amount of fibre by using more pulses, fruits and vegetables and wholegrain and wholemeal ingredients.

BREAKFAST

Buckwheat pancakes

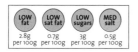

ENERGY *234kcals*, **PROTEIN** *9.3g*, **FAT** *4g*, **SATURATED FAT** *1g*, **CARBOHYDRATE** *43g*, **TOTAL SUGARS** *4.4g*, **SALT** *0.8g*

Buckwheat is the fruit seed of a plant in the dock family. It is gluten-free and a rich source of magnesium, zinc and iron. This recipe uses wholemeal buckwheat flour to make thick pancakes. If you cook smaller drops of batter, then you will have blinis to serve for another occasion (in which case, it might be nice to add in a teaspoon of mixed seeds before cooking). If you prefer, you can swirl the blueberries into the batter before cooking. You could also top with smoked salmon and pepper for something savoury.

175g wholemeal buckwheat flour

1½ level teaspoons baking powder

2 eggs

200ml skimmed milk

1 teaspoon olive oil

2 teaspoons vegetable oil, for cooking

80g prepared seasonal fresh fruit (such as blueberries), per person

MAKES 8–10 / SERVES 4 / PREP TIME *10 minutes* / **COOKING TIME** *20 minutes*

1. For the pancakes, mix the flour and baking powder together in a mixing bowl. Whisk the eggs, milk and olive oil together in a jug, then gradually whisk this into the flour mixture, to make a smooth batter. It should be thick and a bit gloopy, but will still drop from a tablespoon, so add a touch of water if it's too thick as the flour can vary a bit.

2. Heat 1 teaspoon of the vegetable oil in a 23cm non-stick frying pan over a medium heat. Cook two or three pancakes at a time – spoon in separate tablespoons of batter and spread each one out to about 8cm in diameter.

3. Cook for 2–3 minutes until bubbles and little holes appear on the surface and the underside is golden, then turn and cook the other side for a further 2–3 minutes until light brown. Remove the cooked pancakes to a warm plate, cover with foil and keep warm, whilst you cook the remaining pancakes in the same way, adding the remaining oil, as needed. (You will make 8–10 pancakes in total.)

4. Serve the pancakes warm, topped with some fresh fruit scattered over.

Lacy pancakes with zesty lemon yogurt

ENERGY *205kcals*, **PROTEIN** *14g*, **FAT** *5.1g*, **SATURATED FAT** *1.2g*, **CARBOHYDRATE** *20g*, **TOTAL SUGARS** *4g*, **SALT** *0.5g*

This is a nice easy recipe, which looks quite impressive, too. You could also add more fruit, if you like, and possibly serve them for dessert rather than breakfast.

2 eggs
2 teaspoons sweetener
100g plain wholemeal flour
150–200ml skimmed milk
1 tablespoon olive oil
1 tablespoon vegetable oil

FOR THE ZESTY LEMON YOGURT
200g low-fat natural yogurt
finely grated zest and juice of 1 lemon
2 tablespoons sweetener

MAKES 8 / SERVES 4 / PREP TIME *10 minutes* / **COOKING TIME** *15 minutes*

1. First make the pancakes. Break the eggs into a mixing bowl, then add the sweetener and flour and whisk together well. Gradually whisk in 150ml of the milk until you have a thick batter, then add more milk if needed; the batter should have the consistency of thick double cream. Finally, whisk in the olive oil.

2. Gently heat 1 tablespoon of the vegetable oil in a 23cm non-stick frying pan. Using a tablespoon, spoon some batter into the pan drizzling it in using a back and forth motion to make a lacy/web pattern over the base of the pan.

3. Cook over a high heat for a minute or so until nicely browned, then flip over and cook until browned on the other side. Carefully lift out of the pan and leave to cool on a piece of greaseproof paper.

4. Repeat the process, until all the batter is used up, adding the remaining oil as you need it (you'll make about eight pancakes in total), layering the cooked pancakes on top of each other with greaseproof paper in between.

5. Once they are all cooked, fold each pancake in half and half again.

6. Mix the yogurt, lemon zest and juice and sweetener together well.

7. To serve, for each portion, spoon a little lemon yogurt over a folded pancake, top with another folded pancake, and then top with a little more yogurt. Repeat to make your four servings (using two pancakes per serving), then serve straight away.

Vitality smoothie

MED fat	LOW sat fat	MED sugars	LOW salt
5.9g per 100g	1.2g per 100g	5.9g per 100g	0g per 100g

ENERGY *113kcals*, **PROTEIN** *1.7g*, **FAT** *7.9g*, **SATURATED FAT** *1.6g*, **CARBOHYDRATE** *9.4g*, **TOTAL SUGARS** *7.9g*, **SALT** *0g*

Fruit is best consumed whole rather than juiced as most of the fibre is in the skin, plus some smoothies can be high in calories and sugar. But, you can make homemade ones healthier. Choose a combination of fruits and add some green goodness too, for a nutritious liquid breakfast or snack on the go.

½ ripe avocado, peeled and stoned (you want about 80g flesh)

50g fresh strawberries or mixed fresh or frozen berries (see Cook's Tips)

juice of 1 large orange

a few fresh mint leaves, chopped

1 tablespoon fresh blueberries

SERVES 2 / **PREP TIME** *5 minutes* / **COOKING TIME** *none*

1. Put the avocado, strawberries and orange juice into a blender and purée until smooth.

2. Add about 100ml of water to thin it down (or add enough water to achieve the consistency you like) and blend briefly to mix. Pour the smoothie into two glasses.

3. Add the chopped mint and a few blueberries to the top of each smoothie and serve immediately to benefit from maximum vitamins.

COOK'S TIPS

It's a good idea to use frozen berries and blitz them straight from the freezer – this makes your smoothie nicely thick and chilled to drink.

Instead of avocado, use ½ peeled banana as this will add a lovely thick, smooth texture.

Some other combinations you might like to try for this smoothie include:
- *Papaya, lime juice and orange juice*
- *Mango, kiwi, avocado and lime juice*

Some nutrient-boosting ingredients you could add as extras, if you like, include one of the following:
- *a small handful of porridge oats*
- *a little peeled grated fresh ginger, along with some peeled carrot and cored (but not peeled) eating apple*
- *a small handful of baby spinach leaves or kale*
- *a teaspoon of powdered 'greens' (such as spirulina)*
- *1 teaspoon ground linseeds (flaxseeds), rice bran or wheatgerm*
- *1 teaspoon maca powder (maca is a small Peruvian root vegetable and it's a magnificent source of vitamin B2, iron, calcium, zinc and fibre)*

In general, use cold water to thin a fruit purée.
If you use fruit juice (red grape juice or pressed apple juice tastes great), watch out for the extra calories (and sugar) from the fruit sugar in the juice. Alternatively, try using cooled green tea instead of fruit juice to make a smoothie.

Blackberry, pear & pomegranate porridge

ENERGY *192kcals*, **PROTEIN** *9.7g*, **FAT** *2.9g*, **SATURATED FAT** *0.7g*, **CARBOHYDRATE** *33g*, **TOTAL SUGARS** *18g*, **SALT** *0.2g*

Porridge made with wholegrain oats provides slow release energy, which can help to manage blood sugar levels. Oats contain vitamins B and E, zinc, calcium, magnesium and iron and they are thought to be beneficial in helping to lower cholesterol and reduce the risk of heart disease. Try my other breakfast recipes containing oats, such as Swiss-style Bircher Muesli (see page 27).

50g jumbo porridge oats
350ml skimmed milk or water
1 ripe pear
2 tablespoons fresh blackberries

TO SERVE
2 tablespoons pomegranate seeds

SERVES 2 / **PREP TIME** *10 minutes* / **COOKING TIME** *10 minutes*

1. Put the oats into a small saucepan with the milk or water and bring gently to the boil, then simmer for 5 minutes, stirring occasionally. Remove from the heat.

2. Meanwhile, wash, quarter and core the pear, leaving the skin on, then cut into small chunks.

3. Add the pear and blackberries to the porridge and gently stir to combine, then divide between two bowls.

4. Serve each portion with a sprinkling of the pomegranate seeds.

COOK'S TIP
Whilst porridge is familiar when made with oats, for a change, try swapping a quarter of the oats for buckwheat flakes, and add any fruit in season.

Yogurt berry breakfast smoothie

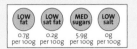

ENERGY *62kcals*, **PROTEIN** *2.6g*, **FAT** *0.9g*, **SATURATED FAT** *0.3g*, **CARBOHYDRATE** *11g*, **TOTAL SUGARS** *8g*, **SALT** *0.1g*

The combination of raspberry and pomegranate is just a suggestion for this recipe and it works very well, but why not try a delicious mix of ripe peaches or nectarines and raspberries when they're in season? Alternatively, make this smoothie with a colourful mixture of frozen fruit, as it's good value and the fruit is frozen when it's very fresh and in season.

100g low-fat natural yogurt
80g frozen and defrosted or
    fresh raspberries
1 tablespoon porridge oats
50ml fresh fruit juice
    diluted with 50ml water
    (pomegranate, pressed apple
    or cranberry
    juice all work well)
½ tablespoon pomegranate
    seeds, to serve

SERVES 3 / **PREP TIME** *5 minutes* / **COOKING TIME** *none*

1. Put all the ingredients, except the pomegranate seeds, into a blender and blitz together until smooth. Add a little more water to adjust the thickness, if needed.

2. Pour the smoothie into a glass, sprinkle the pomegranate seeds over the top and serve straight away.

Swiss-style bircher muesli

| MED fat 6.2g per 100g | LOW sat fat 1.1g per 100g | MED sugars 7g per 100g | LOW salt 0g per 100g |

ENERGY *279kcals*, **PROTEIN** *9.9g*, **FAT** *12g*, **SATURATED FAT** *2.2g*, **CARBOHYDRATE** *33g*, **TOTAL SUGARS** *16g*, **SALT** *0.1g*

Apples contain vitamin C, so can help with iron absorption. The kiwi fruit adds an antioxidant boost. This recipe is an easy way of combining good plant fats with protein and fibre from the nuts and nutrient packed seeds. Blackberries or red berries make a great alternative to kiwi.

50g jumbo porridge oats

2 tablespoons (20g) mixed seeds

1 tablespoon (10g) chopped mixed nuts

50ml pressed apple juice

100g low-fat natural yogurt

1 green-skinned eating apple, cored and grated or finely chopped

squeeze of lemon juice

1 kiwi fruit, peeled and sliced, to serve

SERVES 2 / **PREP TIME** *10 minutes, plus overnight standing* / **COOKING TIME** *none*

1. Put the oats, seeds, nuts and apple juice into a bowl with the yogurt and mix well. Stir in the grated apple and lemon juice.

2. Cover and chill in the fridge for at least 2 hours or overnight.

3. To serve, divide the bircher muesli between two bowls and top with the slices of kiwi fruit.

Baked rhubarb

ENERGY *18kcals*, **PROTEIN** *1.4g*, **FAT** *0.1g*, **SATURATED FAT** *0g*, **CARBOHYDRATE** *3.1g*, **TOTAL SUGARS** *3.1g*, **SALT** *0g*

Some foods naturally complement each other in flavour, but also when eaten in combination, can interact to make them more effective. A spoonful of yogurt with this rhubarb for breakfast is a delightfully nutritious way to start the day.

250g rhubarb, trimmed and sliced into 2cm pieces
juice of 1 orange (about 50ml)
1 tablespoon low-fat natural yogurt, per person

SERVES 2 / **PREP TIME** *10 minutes* / **COOKING TIME** *15 minutes*

1. Preheat the oven to 200°C/gas mark 6.

2. Tear off a sheet of thick foil, pile the rhubarb pieces in the centre and pull up the sides of the foil around the rhubarb to make an open parcel. Pour over the orange juice, then fold over the foil and close to make a loose parcel.

3. Place the foil parcel on a baking tray and bake for about 15 minutes until the rhubarb is soft.

4. Remove from the oven and cool slightly, then mash or blend the rhubarb to a purée, or leave it in chunks and serve with the juices, as you prefer.

5. Serve warm or cold with a spoonful of natural yogurt, or on top of a bowl of porridge (see page 25).

Fruity chia porridge

ENERGY *141kcals*, **PROTEIN** *5g*, **FAT** *5g*, **SATURATED FAT** *0.5g*, **CARBOHYDRATE** *19g*, **TOTAL SUGARS** *13g*, **SALT** *0.1g*

Chia seeds are a rich source of fibre, protein and omega-3 fatty acids. The tiny seeds are packed with vitamins, calcium and many antioxidant benefits. They thicken to form a gel when liquid is added. Drink plenty of water, and don't eat chia seeds dry. Here they are soaked and will expand before eating.

100g mixed berries, fresh or frozen (defrosted)
2 tablespoons chia seeds
100ml skimmed milk
¼ teaspoon ground cinnamon
1 teaspoon sweetener (optional)
2 teaspoons fresh blueberries or half a sliced banana and a few slivered whole almonds (skin on), to serve

SERVES 2 / PREP TIME *10 minutes, plus overnight chilling /* **COOKING TIME** *none*

1. Put the berries into a bowl and crush them lightly with a fork. Stir in all the remaining ingredients (except those for serving) and mix together until evenly combined.

2. Spoon the mixture into two serving bowls (ramekins are good), then cover and chill in the fridge for about 2 hours or overnight to thicken.

3. Serve with the blueberries or sliced banana and almonds scattered over.

Mushroom and parsley omelette

MED fat 8g per 100g | MED sat fat 1.9g per 100g | LOW sugars 0.1g per 100g | LOW salt 0.2g per 100g

ENERGY *236kcals*, **PROTEIN** *17g*, **FAT** *18g*, **SATURATED FAT** *4.4g*, **CARBOHYDRATE** *0.5g*, **TOTAL SUGARS** *0.3g*, **SALT** *0.4g*

Eggs are incredibly versatile and can be cooked so many ways. They contain a good amount of high quality protein and all nine essential amino acids.

1 teaspoon olive oil

100g mushrooms, sliced

2 eggs

1 tablespoon chopped fresh parsley

MAKES 1 OMELETTE / **PREP TIME** *10 minutes* / **COOKING TIME** *5 minutes*

1. Heat the olive oil in a non-stick omelette pan. Sauté the mushrooms for a few minutes until the water evaporates and the mushrooms are golden and dry.

2. Crack the eggs into a small bowl and beat lightly with a fork, then pour into the hot pan over the filling base. Stir and shake the pan to make an even layer of eggs and then cook gently for a few minutes until set.

3. Sprinkle over the parsley, then use a spatula to lift one edge of the omelette and fold over. Slide onto a warm plate and serve.

Tomato toast topper

LOW fat	LOW sat fat	LOW sugars	MED salt
0.6g per 100g	0.1g per 100g	2.9g per 100g	0.3g per 100g

ENERGY *117kcals*, **PROTEIN** *4.5g*, **FAT** *1.2g*, **SATURATED FAT** *0.3g*, **CARBOHYDRATE** *24g*, **TOTAL SUGARS** *6g*, **SALT** *0.6g*

An occasional swap to rye bread or toast for breakfast will help to keep you fuller for longer and avoid energy swings that lead to snacking. Some grains, such as rye, are higher in fibre and lower on the glycaemic index than wheat and so affect blood glucose levels more slowly compared to other foods like white bread.

spray of olive oil

4 ripe tomatoes, sliced

splash of balsamic vinegar

2 slices of rye bread

a few sprigs of fresh thyme
   or basil, leaves picked and
   chopped

freshly ground black pepper

SERVES 2 / PREP TIME *10 minutes* / **COOKING TIME** *5 minutes*

1. Spray a large frying pan with the oil, then add the tomato slices and cook over a high heat until the edges are browning, about 5 minutes. Remove the pan from the heat and sprinkle over the balsamic vinegar.

2. Toast the rye bread on both sides, then place a slice on each serving plate.

3. Tip the cooked tomato slices onto the rye toast, dividing evenly, then season with black pepper, sprinkle over the herbs and serve.

COOK'S TIP

Instead of using fresh tomatoes, tip a 227g can of chopped tomatoes into a small saucepan, add a dash or two of Worcestershire sauce to taste, then simmer, uncovered, over a low heat for 5–10 minutes until the liquid has reduced, stirring occasionally. Season to taste with black pepper, then serve as above and finish with the herbs.

Breakfast mini muffins

ENERGY *59kcals*, **PROTEIN** *3g*, **FAT** *3.5g*, **SATURATED FAT** *0.4g*,
CARBOHYDRATE *3.6g*, **TOTAL SUGARS** *0.7g*, **SALT** *0g*

These muffins are not too sweet for breakfast and the recipe makes mini-sized portions. You could make six bigger, blousy muffins instead, but remember to increase the cooking time a little.

Making your own muffins allows you to control what goes into them. Almond and oat flour, fresh fruit and mixed seeds are a healthy combination. Linseeds (flaxseeds) contain a mixture of soluble and insoluble fibre, and provide omega-3 oils and other beneficial nutrients. These tasty muffins are also gluten-free. They are best eaten on the day they are made.

50g almond flour (or finely ground almonds)

15g ground linseed (flaxseed)

25g oat flour

1 teaspoon gluten-free baking powder

¼ teaspoon ground cinnamon

15g (1 tablespoon) mixed seeds (such as linseeds/flaxseeds, sunflower and pumpkin seeds)

25g dark muscovado or soft dark brown sugar

1 tablespoon sunflower or rapeseed oil

60ml skimmed milk

1 egg, beaten

40g blueberries, apple chunks (cored , skin on) or other prepared fresh fruit

MAKES 12 MINI MUFFINS / PREP TIME *20 minutes, plus cooling /* **COOKING TIME** *20 minutes*

1. Preheat the oven to 180°C/gas mark 4. Line a 12-hole mini muffin tin with paper cases.

2. Mix the almond flour, linseeds, oat flour, baking powder, cinnamon, mixed seeds and sugar together in a bowl. Combine the oil, milk and egg in a measuring jug.

3. Make a well in the centre of the dry ingredients, add the egg mixture and mix just until you have a rough batter, being careful not to over mix. Add the blueberries or other fruit, mixing them lightly through the batter.

4. Spoon about 1 tablespoon of the mixture into each paper case, dividing the mixture evenly. Bake for 15–20 minutes until golden brown and firm to touch.

5. Remove from the oven and cool slightly in the tin before transferring to a wire rack. Serve warm, or cool completely, then freeze.

Spiced cherry tomato and ricotta omelette

ENERGY *268kcals*, **PROTEIN** *18g*, **FAT** *20g*, **SATURATED FAT** *5.4g*, **CARBOHYDRATE** *3.9g*, **TOTAL SUGARS** *3.1g*, **SALT** *0.5g*

Sometimes when you only have a few ingredients, it's a bit daunting knowing what to make. Here is an example of what can be made if paired together with a little thought. With only 6 ingredients you can produce a very tasty meal indeed – the combination of tomatoes, chilli and a seasoning of garam masala are terrific, with soft cooked eggs and a little acidic ricotta really hits the mark.

1 teaspoon olive oil

6 cherry tomatoes, quartered

1 fresh green chilli, deseeded
   and sliced (or ¼ teaspoon
   dried chilli flakes)

1 teaspoon curry powder or
   garam masala

2 eggs

15g ricotta cheese

MAKES 1 OMELETTE / **PREP TIME** *10 minutes* / **COOKING TIME** *5 minutes*

1. Heat the olive oil in a non-stick omelette pan. Sauté the tomatoes with the chilli and spice for 1–2 minutes.

2. Crack the eggs into a small bowl and beat lightly with a fork, then pour into the hot pan over the filling base. Stir and shake the pan to make an even layer of eggs and then cook gently for a few minutes until set.

3. Crumble over the ricotta, then use a spatula to lift one edge of the omelette and fold over. Slide onto a warm plate and serve.

LIGHT BITES, SOUPS & LUNCH

Chicken kebabs with peanut dipping sauce

ENERGY *349kcals*, **PROTEIN** *29g*, **FAT** *19g*, **SATURATED FAT** *2.9g*, **CARBOHYDRATE** *4.7g*, **TOTAL SUGARS** *5.3g*, **SALT** *0.4g*

A good tip here, which applies to all Chinese cooking, is to pre-blanch the onions or any vegetable first. This softens them slightly and ensures they're not only quicker to cook, but also nicer to eat. If you are using wooden skewers, soak them in cold water for 20 minutes first, to prevent burning.

2 x 150g boneless chicken breasts, skin removed, cut into 20–30 small pieces

4 tablespoons low-fat natural yogurt

1 tablespoon finely chopped fresh coriander

2 large red onions, cut into chunky pieces

115g peanut butter (smooth or crunchy)

pinch of chilli powder

juice of 1 lemon

freshly ground black pepper

SERVES 4 / PREP TIME *15 minutes, plus 15 minutes standing, plus cooling and chilling /* **COOKING TIME** *25 minutes*

1. Put the chicken pieces in a bowl. Mix together the yogurt and coriander, season with black pepper, then spoon this mixture over the chicken and stir gently to coat the chicken. Cover and leave at room temperature for 15 minutes.

2. Meanwhile, put the red onions in a saucepan and cover with cold water. Bring to the boil, then immediately remove from the heat, drain well and cool.

3. Thread the chicken pieces onto skewers, alternating with the cooled onion pieces, then place on a plate, cover and chill in the fridge for several hours.

4. If you are cooking your kebabs over a barbecue, make sure you preheat it in advance. Otherwise, preheat your grill to medium. Alternatively, you can use a non-stick frying pan for cooking your kebabs, if you prefer. I often cook in a non-stick pan with no oil whatsoever, but you have to cook over a very low heat or the food will burn.

5. Place the kebabs on a rack over the barbecue or under the grill and cook gently for 8–10 minutes on each side, turning once, until the chicken is cooked through.

6. Meanwhile, put the peanut butter, chilli powder, lemon juice and 100ml of water into a small saucepan and heat gently, stirring occasionally, until you have a warm sauce for dipping. Remove from the heat and keep warm.

7. Serve the hot kebabs with the warm dipping sauce.

'Leftover' chicken chopped salad

ENERGY *316kcals,* **PROTEIN** *20g,* **FAT** *10g,* **SATURATED FAT** *1.8g,*
CARBOHYDRATE *34g,* **TOTAL SUGARS** *10g,* **SALT** *1g*

Any leftover meat will work in this salad, which is very simple to make.

½ large cucumber

6 spring onions

2 little gem lettuces

4 celery sticks

8 radishes

2 vine-ripened tomatoes

150g frozen peas, defrosted
    and drained

400g can borlotti beans,
    rinsed and drained

198g can sweetcorn
    kernels, drained

4 tablespoons chopped
    fresh mint

4 tablespoons chopped
    fresh coriander

150g cooked chicken (no
    skin or fat), chopped

FOR THE DRESSING

2 tablespoons extra virgin
    olive oil

2 tablespoons light
    mayonnaise

2 tablespoons sherry
    vinegar

1 tablespoon Dijon mustard

1 teaspoon sweetener

salt and freshly ground
    black pepper

SERVES 4 / **PREP TIME** *20 minutes* / **COOKING TIME** *none*

1. Finely chop the cucumber, spring onions, lettuce, celery, radishes and tomatoes, put into a bowl and mix well. Add the peas, borlotti beans, sweetcorn, mint, coriander and chicken and stir to mix well.

2. Meanwhile, make the dressing by placing all the dressing ingredients into a small bowl and whisking together until combined, adding a dash of water, if necessary.

3. Pour the dressing over the chilled salad and toss together to mix well, adjusting the seasoning to taste. Serve straight away with spoons.

Jalapeño rosemary yogurt dip

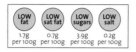

ENERGY *33kcals*, **PROTEIN** *1.9g*, **FAT** *1g*, **SATURATED FAT** *0.5g*, **CARBOHYDRATE** *3.5g*, **TOTAL SUGARS** *2.4g*, **SALT** *0.1g*

Sometimes when cooking, less is more, and here's a very simple recipe, absolutely delicious, using only three ingredients.

75g small green jalapeño chillies

150g low-fat natural yogurt

1 tablespoon finely chopped fresh rosemary

SERVES 4 / **PREP TIME** *10 minutes* / **COOKING TIME** *none*

This is very easy. Finely chop the jalapeños and then mix everything together in a small bowl and serve with your choice of fish.

Spiced red lentil & carrot dhal

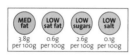

ENERGY *255kcals*, **PROTEIN** *11g*, **FAT** *10g*, **SATURATED FAT** *1.4g*, **CARBOHYDRATE** *32g*, **TOTAL SUGARS** *7.3g*, **SALT** *0.2g*

By combining a few spices with lentils, you can create a stunning dish packed full of flavours, and one that is extremely good for you.

½ teaspoon fennel seeds

½ teaspoon mustard seeds

½ teaspoon fenugreek seeds

½ tablespoon olive oil

2 carrots, peeled and diced

1 small onion, diced

1 garlic clove, crushed

75g dried red lentils

300ml reduced salt vegetable stock

squeeze of lime juice

2 heaped tablespoons chopped fresh coriander

SERVES 2 / **PREP TIME** *10 minutes* / **COOKING TIME** *30 minutes*

1. Crush the fennel, mustard and fenugreek seeds in a pestle and mortar.

2. Heat the olive oil in a saucepan, then add the carrots, onion and garlic and sauté for 5 minutes.

3. Stir in the lentils and stock, then bring to a gentle simmer and cook for about 20 minutes, stirring occasionally, until the lentils are soft and the mixture is thick. You can leave the cooked dhal with some texture or carefully blend the hot mixture until smooth (using a handheld stick blender in the pan) before serving, if you prefer.

4. Stir in the lime juice and chopped coriander and serve straight away.

Easy cauliflower, barley, spinach & parmesan sauté

ENERGY *134kcals*, **PROTEIN** *8.4*, **FAT** *6.6g*, **SATURATED FAT** *1.9g*, **CARBOHYDRATE** *13g*, **TOTAL SUGARS** *3.8g*, **SALT** *0.1g*

Cauliflower rice, or finely grated cauli, is very cool at the moment and, to be honest, it does make a nice change from boiled florets. I have added a little pearl barley, though not too much, to add a little bulk. The whole dish benefits from a little grated strong cheese such as Parmesan.

1 small cauliflower, thick stalks removed
1 tablespoon olive oil
1 large onion, finely chopped
2 garlic cloves, finely crushed
100g cooked pearl barley
about 75g baby spinach leaves
salt and freshly ground black pepper
25g finely grated Parmesan cheese, to serve

SERVES 4 / **PREP TIME** *20 minutes* / **COOKING TIME** *15–18 minutes*

1. Finely grate the cauliflower, or break off small florets of the cauliflower and gently process them in a food-processor, using the pulse function so you ensure the cauli pieces are not too fine.

2. Heat the olive oil in a wok or large frying pan. Add the onion, garlic and pearl barley and sauté over a medium heat for a few minutes, until the onion is softened.

3. Add the cauliflower and spinach and sauté quickly for about 10 minutes until the spinach has wilted and the cauli is cooked through but not overcooked. Remove from the heat and season well with salt and black pepper.

4. Spoon into serving bowls, then sprinkle over the Parmesan cheese and serve.

NUTRITION TIP

Cauliflower is surprisingly high in vitamin C and folic acid. We have become far more creative with the humble cauli, finding nutritious ways to sneak it into a mash, pizza bases and processing it into 'rice'. Barley is a close relative to oats; look for a whole grain product: it can contain even more of the heart-healthy beta-glucan, and fibre. Whole grains will take longer to cook, however.

Hummus with dukkah & dippers

ENERGY *169kcals,* **PROTEIN** *6.5g,* **FAT** *12g,* **SATURATED FAT** *1.5g,* **CARBOHYDRATE** *15g,* **TOTAL SUGARS** *0.4g,* **SALT** *0.3g*

I've always loved hummus after eating it in Jaffa, Israel, where I went to a restaurant that only served hummus. There were three versions: the queue was long but well worth the wait. Here is a very simple version, quick and easy.

FOR THE HUMMUS

2 x 400g can chickpeas, rinsed and drained
2 garlic cloves, peeled
½ teaspoon ground coriander
1 tablespoon olive oil
1 tablespoon tahini
1 tablespoon lemon juice
freshly ground black pepper

FOR THE DUKKAH

1 tablespoon sesame seeds, black or white
1 tablespoon coriander seeds
1 tablespoon cumin seeds
15g whole hazelnuts

TO SERVE

pinch of paprika, either sweet and mild or spicy and smoky
raw vegetable sticks

SERVES 6 / **PREP TIME** *10 minutes* / **COOKING TIME** *2 minutes*

1. For the hummus, reserve a few whole chickpeas, then put the remainder into a food-processor. Add the garlic, coriander, olive oil and tahini and blend together to form a thick paste. Add the lemon juice and pulse until the mixture is smooth and creamy. You may need to add a little water, if it is too thick. Taste the mixture and season with black pepper. Transfer to a serving bowl and sprinkle with paprika and reserved chickpeas. Set aside.

2. To make the dukkah, dry-fry the seeds and hazelnuts together in a frying pan over a medium heat for 1–2 minutes, shaking the pan regularly until lightly toasted. Remove from the heat, then crush them roughly into a coarse spice mixture using a pestle and mortar.

3. Serve the hummus and dukkah, separately, with a plate of raw vegetable sticks. First dip in hummus then gather some of the crushed spices on a second dip.

Sweetcorn & avocado salsa

ENERGY *110kcals*, **PROTEIN** *1.8g*, **FAT** *7.8g*, **SATURATED FAT** *1.6g*, **CARBOHYDRATE** *8.8g*, **TOTAL SUGARS** *4g*, **SALT** *0.2g*

A real favourite in the Vickery household, I have found, even kids will eat avocado prepared and served this way.

2 ripe tomatoes

1 spring onion, trimmed

100g drained canned
   sweetcorn kernels

1 ripe avocado

1–2 teaspoons lemon juice

SERVES 2 / **PREP TIME** *10 minutes* / **COOKING TIME** *none*

1. Finely chop the tomatoes and spring onion and mix together with the sweetcorn in a bowl.

2. Halve and stone the avocado, then scoop out and dice the flesh.

3. Add the avocado and lemon juice to the tomato mixture and mix together gently. Serve immediately.

NUTRITION TIP

Sweetcorn is a wholegrain vegetable and a medium ear of corn offers a helpful amount of dietary fibre. Cooking sweetcorn increases the beneficial effect from the antioxidants.

Vietnamese beef & noodle soup

ENERGY *221kcals*, **PROTEIN** *18g*, **FAT** *6.2g*, **SATURATED FAT** *2.5g*, **CARBOHYDRATE** *23g*, **TOTAL SUGARS** *1.2g*, **SALT** *0.5g*

Thin strips of rare beef steak are given the briefest heat in this fragrant spicy broth. To serve, some sliced and steamed mangetout, or purple sprouting broccoli, would complement nicely.

250g tender beef steak, very thinly sliced (see Cook's Tips)
2 teaspoons sesame oil
1 garlic clove, grated
1 tablespoon lime juice
100g dried rice noodles
2 spring onions, thinly sliced on the diagonal
freshly ground black pepper

FOR THE BROTH
1 small onion, thinly sliced
1 stick of lemongrass, slightly crushed
2cm piece of fresh ginger, peeled and sliced

2 star anise
¼ teaspoon ground allspice (or ground cinnamon)
1 cardamom pod, crushed
1 tablespoon Thai fish sauce (nam pla)

TO SERVE
1 fresh red chilli, deseeded and thinly sliced
small bunch of fresh coriander leaves, roughly chopped
small bunch of fresh mint or Thai basil leaves, roughly chopped
4 lime wedges

SERVES 4 / PREP TIME *10 minutes, plus marinating* / **COOKING TIME** *25 minutes*

1. Put the beef into a non-metallic dish with the sesame oil, garlic, lime juice and some black pepper and mix well, then cover and leave to marinate at room temperature for 30 minutes.

2. Meanwhile, put all the ingredients for the broth into a saucepan with 1 litre of water and bring to the boil. Reduce the heat, cover and simmer for 20 minutes. Remove from the heat and strain into a jug, discarding the flavourings and reserving the hot broth. Adjust the seasoning to taste and pour back into the pan.

3. Cook the rice noodles according to the packet instructions, then drain and add them to the beef broth. Bring back to barely simmering, then tip all of the marinated beef into the broth, along with the spring onions, and simmer for about 30 seconds – 1 minute only to briefly heat the beef.

4. To serve, ladle the beef broth and noodles into four warm serving bowls. Scatter the chilli slices and chopped herbs over the top, and serve with the lime.

COOK'S TIPS
The beef steak is easier to slice thinly if the meat is semi-frozen. Simply pop the fresh beef steak into the freezer for up to an hour beforehand, then slice it thinly, as required.

Don't be put off by the long list of ingredients here, it all creates a depth of flavour, but if you miss out one or two of the flavourings on the list, it will still be good.

COOK'S TIP

When you add the roasted chickpeas and cauliflower to the soup, stir in 200g chopped cooked skinless, boneless chicken or cooked (or raw) peeled prawns, then simmer as directed for a few minutes until the chicken or prawns are hot (or cooked, if using raw prawns).

Roasted cauliflower & chickpea laksa

ENERGY *266kcals*, **PROTEIN** *12g*, **FAT** *13g*, **SATURATED FAT** *5.1g*,
CARBOHYDRATE *27g*, **TOTAL SUGARS** *7.6g*, **SALT** *0.6g*

This soup is all about seasoning and adding layers of flavour, and yes, it takes a bit longer to prepare and cook, but it's well worth it. You can add a little shrimp paste to deepen the flavour, if you like, and 50g chopped cooked wholewheat noodles, which, although not authentic, work really well.

1 tablespoon vegetable oil

420g can chickpeas, rinsed and drained

1 small cauliflower, cut into small florets (about 2cm in size)

200ml light coconut milk

200ml skimmed milk

1–2 teaspoons sweetener

2 teaspoons Thai fish sauce (nam pla)

a small handful of beansprouts

4 spring onions, thinly sliced diagonally

juice of 2 large limes

freshly ground black pepper

FOR THE PASTE

2 small onions, very finely chopped

4 garlic cloves, peeled

2 tablespoons peeled and finely chopped fresh ginger

1 tablespoon finely chopped deseeded fresh red chilli

1 tablespoon lemongrass purée (jarred is great)

1 teaspoon ground cumin

1 teaspoon ground turmeric

50ml light coconut milk

1 reduced salt vegetable stock cube (10g)

TO SERVE

50g cooked wholewheat noodles

2–3 tablespoons roughly chopped fresh Thai basil

2–3 tablespoons roughly chopped fresh coriander

sliced fresh red chillies

lime wedges

SERVES 4 / **PREP TIME** *20 minutes* / **COOKING TIME** *55 minutes*

1. Preheat the oven to 220°C/gas mark 7.

2. Heat 1 tablespoon oil in an ovenproof frying pan, add the chickpeas and cook over a medium heat for about 10 minutes until lightly browned, stirring occasionally. Add the cauliflower florets and season with a little salt and black pepper, then cook for a further 10 minutes until lightly browned, stirring occasionally.

3. Transfer the pan to the oven and roast for 30 minutes to get a nice deeper colour without burning the mixture, but the more colour, the better the end flavour.

4. Meanwhile, blitz together all the ingredients for the paste in a blender (or using a small handheld stick blender in a bowl), until you have a paste.

5. Heat the remaining 1 tablespoon of oil in a wok, pour in the paste and cook for 2–3 minutes to cook through. Stir in the coconut milk, milk, the sweetener, fish sauce, beansprouts and spring onions and bring to a simmer. Add the roasted chickpeas and cauliflower and cook for a further 2–3 minutes, stirring occasionally. Stir in the lime juice and season well.

6. To serve, divide the cooked wholemeal noodles (if using) between four serving bowls, then ladle over the hot vegetable and chickpea broth. Sprinkle each portion with the herbs and chilli and serve with a lime wedge.

Warming Italian-style vegetable broth

ENERGY *234kcals*, **PROTEIN** *10g*, **FAT** *11g*, **SATURATED FAT** *2.8g*, **CARBOHYDRATE** *25g*, **TOTAL SUGARS** *12g*, **SALT** *1.3g*

The best thing about this soup is that there are no rules, or cutting sizes, it's entirely up to you! It can also be made in advance, plus it will freeze well for up to three months. To get even pieces of spaghetti in this soup, lay the spaghetti in a clean tea-towel and wrap it up tightly. Next, holding the tea-towel nice and tight, place one end over the side of a table, by about 5cm. Pull the end over the edge, pulling down at a ninety degree angle to the table, holding both ends. The pasta will crack into even pieces inside the tea-towel (you will hear it). Hold the tea-towel above the cooking pan and release the bottom end; the even lengths of pasta will fall into the pan – easy!

1 onion, chopped

2 carrots, peeled and chopped

2 garlic cloves, chopped

2 celery sticks, chopped

1 courgette, chopped

½ small Savoy cabbage (or any cabbage), finely sliced

400g can chopped tomatoes with herbs

1 reduced salt vegetable stock cube (10g)

75g raw wholewheat spaghetti, broken into even lengths (see intro)

2 tablespoons green pesto

2 tablespoons grated Parmesan cheese (optional)

freshly ground black pepper

1 tablespoon extra virgin olive oil, to finish

SERVES 4 / **PREP TIME** *20 minutes* / **COOKING TIME** *40 minutes*

1. Put all the prepared vegetables into a large saucepan (bear in mind they will cook down to about half their original volume, so don't panic that it looks too much!). Add the tomatoes, 500ml of water, crumble in the stock cube and stir well.

2. Bring to the boil, then reduce the heat to a simmer, add the spaghetti, pesto sauce and a little black pepper and stir well. Cover and simmer for 35–40 minutes, or until the spaghetti and vegetables are cooked and tender, stirring occasionally. By this stage, the broth should be thick and chunky.

3. Taste and adjust the seasoning, then stir in the cheese (if using).

4. Ladle into warm soup bowls and finish each serving with a drizzle of olive oil.

Chilli-spiced tuna & prawn broth

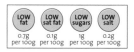

ENERGY *159kcals*, **PROTEIN** *28g*, **FAT** *2.8g*, **SATURATED FAT** *0.5g*,
CARBOHYDRATE *5.7g*, **TOTAL SUGARS** *4.3g*, **SALT** *0.8g*

I really like meat or fish broths, which are very satisfying and deliciously tasty. The secret is to pack in lots of lovely flavour by using vegetables and seasonings – I'm more than happy to use good-quality reduced salt stock cubes for a good background flavour. The new jelly bouillon (stock) that you can readily buy is also pretty good and has a lovely flavour profile, too.

600ml boiling water

2 reduced salt fish stock
  cubes (10g each)

½ teaspoon finely chopped,
  deseeded fresh red chilli

1 onion, finely chopped

2 garlic cloves, crushed

1 head of broccoli, cut into
  small florets, central
  stalk cut into 5mm cubes

75g baby spinach leaves

150g green or French beans,
  chopped

juice of 2 limes

4 tablespoons chopped
  fresh coriander

1 teaspoon sesame oil

250g can tuna in water,
  drained and flaked

150g raw freshwater
  prawns, peeled
  (prepared weight)

SERVES 4 / **PREP TIME** *10 minutes* / **COOKING TIME** *15 minutes, plus 5 minutes standing*

1. Put the boiling water, crumbled stock cubes, chilli, onion, garlic and broccoli stalks in a large saucepan, bring to the boil, then reduce the heat and simmer uncovered, for 10 minutes.

2. Stir in the broccoli florets, spinach and green beans and simmer for a further 3–4 minutes until the broccoli is tender.

3. Remove the pan from the heat, then stir in the lime juice, coriander, sesame oil, tuna and prawns. Cover the pan and leave the mixture off the heat for 4–5 minutes to warm the tuna and cook the prawns (the residual heat in the pan will cook the prawns and turn them pink).

4. Ladle the broth into warm bowls. I like to serve this on its own as a self-contained meal.

NUTRITION TIP

Fish is a great source of protein, providing the essential amino acids our bodies need constantly, yet can't make ourselves.

My version of Scotch broth

ENERGY *230kcals*, **PROTEIN** *19g*, **FAT** *7g*, **SATURATED FAT** *2.8g*, **CARBOHYDRATE** *25g*, **TOTAL SUGARS** *8.3g*, **SALT** *0.3g*

OK, so this is technically not a Scotch broth, but it's pretty close; all I have done is to remove the potatoes and turnips and add more leek, celery and sweet potato. I have also reduced the pearl barley content to just 25g. The end result is a light, fragrant and flavoursome vegetable-lamb stock. Slow and fairly long simmering not only softens the meat beautifully, but it also allows you to skim off all the fat during that time.

300g boneless lamb leg steaks (or mutton is better, if you can get it), cut into small cubes, all fat removed

25g pearl barley

1 large sweet potato (approx 200g), peeled and cut into small cubes

2 large leeks, washed and cut into small pieces

1 large onion, cut into small pieces

6 celery sticks, cut into small pieces

1 reduced salt vegetable stock cube (10g)

freshly ground black pepper

2 tablespoons chopped fresh parsley, to finish

SERVES 4 / **PREP TIME** *20 minutes* / **COOKING TIME** 1 hour, 50 minutes

1. Put the lamb and 2 litres of water in a saucepan and bring to the boil, then reduce the heat and simmer, uncovered, for 10 minutes, removing any scum or fat from the surface.

2. Stir in the pearl barley and all the prepared veg, crumble in the stock cube and season with some black pepper. Bring back to the boil, then reduce the heat and simmer for about 1½ hours, or until the lamb is tender, stirring occasionally and periodically removing any scum or fat from the surface.

3. Taste and adjust the seasoning, if necessary, then stir in the parsley to finish and serve.

NUTRITION TIP

This recipe is packed with nutritious vegetables. Sweet potatoes provide a rich source of vitamin A as well as powerful antioxidant carotenes that play a part in the growth of cells, healthy eyesight and good immune function. Sweet potatoes have significantly more potassium, calcium and vitamin K than normal spuds.
We tend to overlook onions, being so commonly used, but they contain inulin, a prebiotic that encourages healthy gut bacteria. They offer a range of antioxidant and anti-inflammatory compounds that are good for us, especially the brown and red type.

Easy black mushroom soup with mustard

ENERGY *195kcals*, **PROTEIN** *64g*, **FAT** *12g*, **SATURATED FAT** *1.9g*, **CARBOHYDRATE** *17g*, **TOTAL SUGARS** *5.7g*, **SALT** *0.2g*

The difference between this and many other mushroom soup recipes is that it uses fully open mushrooms. In fact, if you can leave them in your fruit bowl to open and turn nice and black, that's even better. You do end up with a wickedly black soup, but it's packed full of flavour.

500g open large mushrooms, the older the better

2 large onions, finely chopped

4 garlic cloves, finely chopped

20g pearl barley

1 small sweet potato, peeled and roughly chopped

1 reduced salt vegetable stock cube (10g)

1–3 tablespoons English mustard powder

freshly ground black pepper

1 tablespoon extra virgin olive oil, to finish (optional)

SERVES 4 / PREP TIME *15 minutes* / **COOKING TIME** *35–45 minutes*

1. Put the mushrooms, onions, garlic, pearl barley, sweet potato and crumbled stock cube into a deep saucepan. Pour in enough cold water to just cover the vegetables, bring to the boil, then reduce the heat to a simmer. Stir in the mustard powder to your taste and then simmer, uncovered, for 30–40 minutes, or until the barley is cooked, stirring occasionally.

2. Remove from the heat and cool briefly, then carefully blitz the soup to a fine purée either using a handheld stick blender in the pan or by transferring the mixture to a blender. Check the seasoning and adjust with a little black pepper, if needed.

3. Ladle the soup into deep bowls and swirl a little olive oil (if using) over each portion just before serving.

COOK'S TIP

I like English mustard so I add a lot, but anywhere from 1–3 tablespoons is lovely, as it really brings out the flavour of the mushrooms. I add pearl barley and sweet potato to bulk out the soup, but both can be omitted if you want just pure mushroom.

Pasta salad with roast tomatoes & basil

MED fat	MED sat fat	LOW sugars	LOW salt
4.9g per 100g	1.9g per 100g	2.9g per 100g	0.2g per 100g

ENERGY *279kcals*, **PROTEIN** *13g*, **FAT** *10g*, **SATURATED FAT** *3.7g*, **CARBOHYDRATE** *35g*, **TOTAL SUGARS** *6g*, **SALT** *0.5g*

Intensely flavoured tomatoes will make all the difference, so choose some ripe seasonal ones if you can. You might like to serve this pasta salad with some canned tuna and crumbled sushi nori (thin sheets of pressed seaweed, which are dried and toasted) that adds a wonderful umami taste to salads. Keep any leftovers in the fridge for a lunch box salad the next day.

500g cherry tomatoes on the vine or small, full-flavoured tomatoes on the vine
2 garlic cloves, thinly sliced
1 tablespoon olive oil
200g dried wholewheat pasta
small bunch of basil leaves, roughly chopped
freshly ground black pepper
4 tablespoons grated Parmesan cheese, to serve (optional)

SERVES 4 / PREP TIME *5 minutes* / **COOKING TIME** *20–30 minutes*

1. Preheat the oven to 200°C/gas mark 6. Line a roasting dish with foil.

2. Remove the stalks from the tomatoes and place the tomatoes in the lined roasting dish. Add the garlic slices to the tomatoes, drizzle over the olive oil and mix gently. Roast, uncovered, for about 20–30 minutes until the skins have split and begin to colour.

3. Meanwhile, cook the pasta according to the packet instructions, then drain well.

4. Remove the tomatoes from the oven and crush with a fork, then drop in the chopped basil and stir. Add the tomato mixture to the pasta, along with any juices, season with black pepper and toss together gently to mix. Serve, sprinkled with the grated Parmesan (if using).

Superbowl salad with quinoa

ENERGY *320kcals*, PROTEIN *10g*, FAT *11g*, SATURATED FAT *1.1g*,
CARBOHYDRATE *40g*, TOTAL SUGARS *10g*, SALT *0.1g*

Quinoa is a tiny little seed, rich in protein and other nutrients, including a good amount of calcium, iron and B vitamins. This salad makes a bold, colourful vegetarian main meal, high in antioxidants from the veggies, but it is also delicious served with grilled salmon or chicken (grilled with a smear of harissa paste mixed with a tablespoon of natural yogurt on top).

1 red onion, quartered
1 large courgette, diced
1 small butternut squash (about 500g), peeled, deseeded and diced (or you can use 350g sweet potatoes, peeled and diced)
1 red pepper, deseeded and diced
1 small yellow pepper, deseeded and diced
1 tablespoon rapeseed oil
200g quinoa (mixed red, black and white quinoa)
½ reduced salt vegetable stock cube (5g)
100g purple sprouting broccoli, trimmed
juice of 1 lemon or lime

1 garlic clove, finely chopped
2 tablespoons mixed toasted seeds
150g cherry tomatoes, halved
small bunch of mixed fresh basil and parsley, roughly chopped
freshly ground black pepper

TO SERVE
50g fresh pomegranate seeds

SERVES 4 / PREP TIME *15 minutes, plus cooling* / COOKING TIME *30–40 minutes*

1. Preheat the oven to 200°C/gas mark 6. Put the red onion, courgette, squash and peppers in a roasting tin. Drizzle over the rapeseed oil and season well with black pepper. Roast the veg for about 30–40 minutes until softened and beginning to colour at the edges.

2. Meanwhile, rinse the quinoa (to remove a slightly bitter coating on the seeds), put it in a saucepan with the crumbled stock cube and cover with 250ml of water. Bring to the boil, then reduce the heat, cover and cook for about 12–15 minutes until tender and the little 'tails' appear. Remove from the heat and leave to cool and absorb most of the water, then drain well. Spread it out over a shallow dish to dry and fluff up.

3. Snip the purple sprouting broccoli heads, stalks and leaves into bite-sized pieces. Boil or steam for a few minutes until just tender, then drain.

4. Put the quinoa in a large bowl. Add the lemon or lime juice, garlic, mixed seeds, cherry tomatoes, chopped herbs and the hot roasted vegetables and purple sprouting broccoli and stir to mix.

5. To serve, stir through the pomegranate seeds. Serve warm or cold.

Roasted butternut squash, feta & hazelnut salad with chickpeas

LOW fat 2.8g per 100g — LOW sat fat 0.4g per 100g — LOW sugars 3.1g per 100g — LOW salt 0.1g per 100g

ENERGY *268kcals*, **PROTEIN** *12g*, **FAT** *11g*, **SATURATED FAT** *1.5g*, **CARBOHYDRATE** *26g*, **TOTAL SUGARS** *13g*, **SALT** *0.3g*

A delicious, nutritious combination of flavours that work really well together.

350g butternut squash (prepared weight), or sweet potatoes, peeled, deseeded and diced

1 red onion, cut into 8 wedges

1 mild fresh red chilli, deseeded and sliced into thick strips

1 tablespoon olive oil

1 teaspoon garam masala

100g broccoli, cut into small florets

100g (4 tablespoons) canned (rinsed and drained) chickpeas

50g fresh (podded weight) soya (edamame) beans (or swap for all chickpeas)

FOR THE DRESSING

2 tablespoons olive oil

1 tablespoon lime juice

1 teaspoon cider vinegar

1 fat garlic clove, crushed

TO SERVE

75g mixed rocket, watercress and baby spinach leaves, washed and patted dry

80g feta cheese

4 tablespoons hazelnuts, in their skins, lightly crushed (or walnuts)

SERVES 2 / **PREP TIME** *15 minutes* / **COOKING TIME** *30 minutes*

1. Preheat the oven to 180°C/gas mark 4.

2. Put the diced squash and red onion wedges in a large roasting dish, along with the chilli, olive oil and garam masala and toss to coat. Roast for about 30 minutes until soft. Stir the mixture after about 20 minutes, adding in the broccoli florets for the remaining 10 minutes of the cooking time.

3. Put all the ingredients for the dressing in a large bowl and whisk together well. Toss the chickpeas and soya beans in the dressing and then mix in the hot roasted vegetables, coating well.

4. To serve, arrange a bed of the mixed salad leaves on a platter. Make a high pile of the roast vegetable mixture on top. Crumble the feta over the vegetables, then scatter over the crushed hazelnuts and serve.

TIP

Get used to baking or roasting vegetables like sweet potatoes, for retaining the most nutrients.

With greens and vegetables, keep cooking light and brief: steam, sauté or microwave for the best retention of vitamins.

Beetroot & broccoli salad with goat's cheese

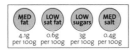

ENERGY *255kcals*, **PROTEIN** *11g*, **FAT** *9.6g*, **SATURATED FAT** *1.4g*, **CARBOHYDRATE** *32g*, **TOTAL SUGARS** *7g*, **SALT** *0.8g*

This is a great salad for a lunch box to go; simply keep it chilled until you are ready to eat. You can chop and change the main ingredients – for example, you could use ricotta rather than goats' cheese.

75g mixed red, black and white quinoa

1 teaspoon any mixed seeds (such as pumpkin, sunflower, hemp or seame)

1 teaspoon chopped almonds, skin on

80g small broccoli florets

a large handful of spinach leaves

50g cucumber, finely diced

100g cooked beetroot, peeled and sliced into strips

small bunch of mixed fresh herbs, finely chopped

2 tablespoons fat-free salad dressing

25g goats' cheese

SERVES 2 / PREP TIME *15 minutes* / **COOKING TIME** *15 minutes*

1. Cook the quinoa according to packet instructions (or see Superbowl Salad with Quinoa on page 61 for cooking instructions), then drain well and leave to cool.

2. Meanwhile, heat a small, dry frying pan over a medium heat and dry fry the seeds and almonds until toasted, about 1 minute (shake the pan and watch them, as they burn easily!). Set aside to cool. Cook the broccoli in a pan of boiling water for 3 minutes until just tender, then drain well and leave to cool.

3. When everything has cooled, put the cooked quinoa, toasted seeds and almonds and broccoli into a serving bowl. Add the spinach, cucumber, beetroot and herbs, then drizzle over the dressing and toss lightly to mix. Crumble the goats' cheese over the salad and serve.

NUTRITION TIP

This recipe is a super-charged combination of broccoli and beetroot. Beetroot is an excellent source of folate, fibre, manganese and potassium. The deep purple colour comes from betalains, plant chemicals similar to anthocyanins, which are thought to have antioxidant and anti-inflammatory properties. Beetroot contains an interesting amount of dietary nitrate, fuelling the potential for even more perceived health benefits. The green tops of beetroot are rich in calcium, iron and vitamins A and C; prepare and cook them as you would spinach.

Bulgar wheat with lemon & herbs

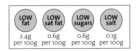

ENERGY *143kcals*, **PROTEIN** *4g*, **FAT** *5.3g*, **SATURATED FAT** *1.2g*, **CARBOHYDRATE** *21g*, **TOTAL SUGARS** *1.4g*, **SALT** *0.1g*

Bulgur wheat is parboiled, dried, then ground coarsely, so it needs less cooking and soaking to prepare. It is rich in protein and minerals and is also a good source of fibre. Substitute it for couscous for a change or, for a gluten-free version, use quinoa mixed with wholegrain buckwheat. Check the packet instructions for the bulgar wheat as the cooking time can vary a bit.

This dish goes nicely with grilled chicken or fish, and the flavours develop well if you make it a day in advance (keep it chilled in the fridge overnight).

100g bulgar wheat

½ reduced salt vegetable stock cube (5g) (optional)

finely grated zest and juice of 1 unwaxed lemon

1 garlic clove, crushed

1 tablespoon olive oil

2 tablespoons finely chopped fresh mint

2 tablespoons finely chopped fresh flat-leaf parsley

2 tablespoons chopped fresh coriander leaves

2 spring onions, sliced on the diagonal

1 large tomato, diced

freshly ground black pepper

SERVES 4 / **PREP TIME** *10 minutes, plus optional overnight chilling* / **COOKING TIME** *10 minutes, plus 10 minutes standing*

1. Cook the bulgar wheat according to the packet instructions. Or, rinse the bulgar wheat in a fine sieve and tip it into a saucepan. Add 600ml of water and the stock cube and bring to the boil. Cover and simmer for 10 minutes, then turn off the heat and leave to soak, with the lid on, for about 10 minutes until the grains are soft. Rinse under cold running water and then drain well.

2. Transfer the cooked bulgar wheat to a large bowl and fork through the grains to separate them.

3. In a small bowl, mix together the lemon zest and juice, garlic, olive oil, chopped herbs and some black pepper to taste, stirring well to combine. Add this to the bulgar wheat along with the spring onions and tomato and mix through roughly. Serve immediately or cover and chill in the fridge overnight and serve the next day.

Courgette linguine

ENERGY *87kcals*, **PROTEIN** *5g*, **FAT** *6.2g*, **SATURATED FAT** *1.9g*, **CARBOHYDRATE** *2.9g*, **TOTAL SUGARS** *2.7g*, **SALT** *0.1g*

The firm texture of courgettes makes them perfect for creating long twirls of vegetable noodles using a spiraliser. Alternatively, you can create vegetable ribbons using a food-processor, vegetable peeler or coarse grater. You can also mix in a variety of different vegetables, like sweet potatoes, squash, beetroot or carrots, for this alternative 'pasta' dish.

4 courgettes
15ml vegetable or olive oil
2 tablespoons lemon juice
freshly ground black pepper
25g parmesan, grated

SERVES 4 / **PREP TIME** *10 minutes* / **COOKING TIME** *5 minutes*

1. Depending on the type of spiraliser you have, there are different settings and blades. For the courgette pasta, spiralise the courgettes following the instructions for your spiraliser, or shave the courgettes into ribbons or strips using a vegetable peeler or coarse grater. (You can then repeat this with any other vegetables you would like to mix in, if you like – see recipe intro).

2. Heat the oil in a large frying pan, add the courgette noodles and stir-fry over a medium heat for 3–5 minutes until hot and just softened.

3. Stir in the lemon juice and season with a good grind of black pepper. Serve hot as a side dish sprinkled with cheese.

COOK'S TIP

Once you have spiralised your courgettes (and/or other veg), instead of serving them as above, there are several other ways to go. Try lightly cooked courgette noodles as a base for your own favourite pasta sauces – simply blanch the spiralised courgettes in a pan of boiling water for about 30 seconds and then drain well. Stir through some pesto or hot pasta sauce and heat through gently, before serving.

Alternatively, stir-fry the courgette noodles in vegetable oil and add a squeeze of lime juice, or you can use the spiralised courgettes in a stir-fry recipe.

To serve them raw, toss the spiralised raw courgettes in a little lemon juice and extra virgin olive oil, then cover and leave to marinate at room temperature for 30 minutes. This creates a great salad base (snip the long noodles into manageable pieces before marinating, if you prefer).

Lentil, carrot & celery stew

ENERGY *313kcals*, **PROTEIN** *12g*, **FAT** *6.9g*, **SATURATED FAT** *1.4g*, **CARBOHYDRATE** *52g*, **TOTAL SUGARS** *4.7g*, **SALT** *0.2g*

This recipe for braised lentils is richly flavoured and delicious when meaty mushrooms like shiitake are stirred through just before serving. It is also a perfect base for game, such as pheasant or venison, served with steamed green beans or kale.

1 tablespoon vegetable oil

125g carrots, peeled and finely diced

1 small onion, finely diced

150g celery, finely diced

1 garlic clove, crushed or finely chopped

1 reduced salt vegetable stock cube (10g)

1 tablespoon tomato purée

2 teaspoons balsamic vinegar

1 teaspoon freshly ground black pepper

100g dried green or Puy lentils, rinsed and drained

TO SERVE

1 teaspoon olive oil

200g fresh shiitake mushrooms, sliced

6 tablespoons fresh flat-leaf parsley, stalks removed

SERVES 4 / **PREP TIME** *10 minutes* / **COOKING TIME** *1 hour, 10 minutes*

1. Heat the vegetable oil in a saucepan, then add all the diced vegetables and cook over a fairly high heat for 5 minutes, stirring occasionally. Cover the pan, reduce the heat to medium and sweat the vegetables for a further 5 minutes, stirring now and again, and adding in the garlic for the last couple of minutes. Pour in 500ml of water, crumble in the stock cube, then add the tomato purée, balsamic vinegar, sugar and black pepper. Bring to the boil, then stir in the lentils.

2. Partially cover the pan, leaving a small gap and reduce the heat to low. Cook gently for about 50 minutes until the liquid is absorbed and the lentils are soft and richly flavoured, stirring occasionally. You may need to top up with a little more water if necessary, depending on the pan and heat you are using. The cooked stew should not be too watery.

3. Just before serving, heat the olive oil in a frying pan and add the shiitake mushrooms. Sauté over a fairly high heat for about 5–10 minutes until golden and the juices have evaporated. Stir the sautéed mushrooms into the stew, then divide between deep bowls and serve with parsley snipped over each portion.

TIP

You might not think so, but cooking rather than eating raw actually increases the nutrient content of some vegetables, like spinach, carrots and tomatoes.

Tapas tortilla

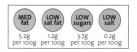

ENERGY *313kcals*, **PROTEIN** *16g*, **FAT** *16g*, **SATURATED FAT** *3.7g*, **CARBOHYDRATE** *30g*, **TOTAL SUGARS** *11g*, **SALT** *0.5g*

Eggs have impressive health credentials as they provide high-quality protein as well as several other key nutrients. They have a star role in this classic Spanish omelette, the tortilla, which can be served hot or cold and is perfectly portable for a lunch box. In Spain, they serve tortilla as tapas, cut into small cubes. I would definitely add a chopped fresh red chilli to this with the onion and garlic, but I leave that up to you.

450g (prepared weight) sweet
  potatoes, peeled and cut
  into thin slices
1 tablespoon rapeseed oil
1 red pepper, deseeded and
  chopped
1 onion, finely sliced
1 garlic clove, crushed
1 fresh red chilli, deseeded and
  chopped (optional)
6 large eggs
1 tablespoon chopped mixed
  fresh herbs (such as parsley,
  marjoram and basil)
freshly ground black pepper

SERVES 4 *as a main meal;* **SERVES 8** *as tapas/* **PREP TIME** *10 minutes /*
COOKING TIME *35 minutes*

1. Cook the sweet potato slices in a pan of boiling water for about 8 minutes until soft and cooked through, but still holding their shape. Drain well and leave until dry.

2. Meanwhile, heat the rapeseed oil in a 23cm non-stick frying pan, then add the red pepper, onion and garlic, and red chilli if using, and cook over a medium heat for about 10 minutes until soft and slightly coloured, stirring occasionally.

3. Beat the eggs together in a large jug, then add the herbs, sweet potato slices and the onion mixture and stir to coat in the eggs. Season well with black pepper. Pour this mixture back into the hot pan, spreading it evenly, and then cook until it is lightly set, about 8–10 minutes. Meanwhile, preheat the grill on high for 5 minutes.

4. Remove the pan from the hob and pop it under the hot grill (not too close to the heat) for a couple of minutes to finish cooking the top. Alternatively, if you are feeling brave, you could invert the tortilla onto a flat plate and turn it to cook the other side in the pan instead.

5. Slide the tortilla out onto a board, cut into squares and spear each square with a cocktail stick to eat as tapas. To serve as a main meal, cut into wedges and serve with a mixed salad and steamed broccoli, dressed with a squeeze of lemon and a pinch of mustard.

Tamarind-spiced lentils

 **ENERGY** *288kcals*, **PROTEIN** *16g*, **FAT** *5.9g*, **SATURATED FAT** *0.8g*, **CARBOHYDRATE** *43g*, **TOTAL SUGARS** *14g*, **SALT** *0.1g*

Lentils are an excellent source of protein, iron and fibre, and around 4 tablespoons of cooked pulses is one serving towards your 5-a-day. The earthy flavour of spinach combines well with the bold Indian spices in this version of dhal, as does kale or chard, if you prefer use these instead.

200g dried green or
  Puy lentils, rinsed and
  drained
1 tablespoon vegetable oil
1 onion, finely chopped
1 carrot, peeled and diced
2cm piece of fresh ginger,
  peeled and grated
1 garlic clove, finely crushed
1 fresh red chilli, deseeded
  and sliced (or use ¼
  teaspoon dried chilli
  flakes)
½ teaspoon ground
  turmeric
2 teaspoons tamarind

paste
400g can chopped
  tomatoes
20g dried dates, stoned
  and chopped
100ml boiling water
  (optional)
freshly ground black
  pepper

TO SERVE
200g chard, kale or
  spinach, washed and
  sliced
a little fresh coriander and
  a few fresh red chilli
  slices

SERVES 4 / PREP TIME *15 minutes* **/ COOKING TIME** *45 minutes*

1. Tip the lentils into a medium saucepan and cover with about three times their volume of cold water. Bring to the boil, reduce the heat to medium, partially cover the pan and cook for 25 minutes (you don't want to fully cook the lentils at this stage), topping up with more water during cooking, if necessary. Drain well.

2. Meanwhile, heat the vegetable oil in a separate saucepan, add the onion and carrot and cook over a medium heat for 5 minutes to soften, then stir in the ginger, garlic, chilli, ground turmeric and tamarind paste and season with some black pepper. Cook for a couple more minutes, then add the tomatoes and dates.

3. Add the lentils to the pan and return to a simmer. Partially cover the pan and cook gently for a further 15 minutes, stirring occasionally and adding the boiling water if the mixture begins to look dry.

4. If you are serving the dhal with chard, kale or spinach, add the leaves to the simmering pan for the last 5 minutes of the cooking time.

5. Spoon the dhal into shallow serving bowls, then snip a little fresh coriander on top and scatter over a few extra chilli slices if you like a bit of heat. Serve immediately.

COOK'S TIP

1 tablespoon curry paste (like makhani – a rich, tomatoey, Punjabi spice paste) can be used instead of mixing your own spices of ginger and turmeric.

You can freeze any leftovers, so you have your own ready meal available for an easy option midweek.

Papaya, green bean & chilli cabbage salad

MED fat 6.1g per 100g LOW sat fat 0.7g per 100g MED sugars 6g per 100g LOW salt 0g per 100g

ENERGY *105kcals*, **PROTEIN** *1.1g*, **FAT** *7.7g*, **SATURATED FAT** *0.9g*, **CARBOHYDRATE** *7.7g*, **TOTAL SUGARS** *0.9g*, **SALT** *0g*

A very tasty and simple summer salad that is best made up and left for half an hour before eating. Ideal as a starter on its own, or serve it for lunch with a few cooked peeled tiger prawns or some cold cooked skinless chicken for a snappy way to get the kids to eat raw vegetables. It's also great as an accompaniment to grilled chicken or pork chops.

1 red onion, very finely sliced

1 large ripe papaya, peeled, deseeded and thinly sliced

¼ small white cabbage, very finely sliced

8 stringless flat green or runner beans, cut into long thin slices

30g fresh ginger, peeled and cut into very thin strips

1 small fresh red chilli, deseeded and very finely chopped

FOR THE DRESSING

juice of 3 large limes

1 tablespoon sweetener

1 tablespoon sunflower or rapeseed oil

freshly ground black pepper

SERVES 4 / **PREP TIME** *10 minutes, plus 30 minutes standing* / **COOKING TIME** *none*

1. Put all salad ingredients in a serving bowl and mix together thoroughly.

2. In a separate small bowl, whisk together the dressing ingredients, seasoning with lots of black pepper.

3. Pour the dressing over the salad and toss to mix, then cover and set aside at room temperature for 30 minutes before serving, to allow the flavours to blend.

NUTRITION TIP

Chillies contain capsaicin, a substance that is showing an interesting effect on the body's ability to burn fat. Other health effects are also being investigated.

Flat mushroom 'buns'

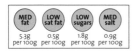

ENERGY *113kcals*, **PROTEIN** *6.3g*, **FAT** *8.3g*, **SATURATED FAT** *0.8g*, **CARBOHYDRATE** *3.6g*, **TOTAL SUGARS** *2.8g*, **SALT** *1.4g*

I modelled this idea on a burger bun; I once had a version of this in France and it was delicious. The secret is to get all the flat mushrooms the same size, and cut everything to fit in the mushroom 'bun' so when it's finally chilled it will look very impressive. Flat mushrooms are very good value for money, and when cooked in this way they take on a really meaty texture, plus they are a lot cheaper per kilo than button mushrooms and have much more flavour.

8 medium flat mushrooms

1 tablespoon extra virgin olive oil

4 wafer-thin slices of cooked ham, chicken or turkey

4 thin slices of Port Salut or tallegio cheese

1 beef tomatoes, sliced into 4 even slices

2 tablespoons smooth/ prepared English mustard

2 large pickled cucumbers, cut into long slices

8 fresh basil leaves

freshly ground black pepper

SERVES 4 / PREP TIME *25 minutes, plus cooling and overnight chilling /* **COOKING TIME** *10–12 minutes*

1. Preheat the grill to its hottest setting.

2. Cut the stalks out of the mushrooms and discard, then season the mushrooms well with salt and black pepper. Drizzle over the olive oil and then cook under the hot grill for 5–6 minutes on each side, turning once (be careful not to overcook them). Remove from the heat and leave to cool.

3. Meanwhile, take a plain cutter the same size as the flat mushrooms (or use a paper template if you don't have a suitable cutter), then cut the meat and cheese slices to the same size as the mushrooms. Slice the tomato into four roughly the same size as well.

4. Place four of the mushrooms on a chopping board, open sides up. Top each mushroom with a slice of meat and season with black pepper, then smear over some mustard. Add a cheese slice, some pickled cucumber slices and a tomato slice on top of each, seasoning each layer as you go, then add two basil leaves. Finally, top each with one of the remaining mushrooms, placing them open side down.

5. Lightly press down on each one, then wrap each 'bun' in clingfilm and chill in the fridge for at least 1 hour, but preferably overnight.

6. To serve, cut each mushroom 'bun' into quarters and skewer them with fancy cocktail sticks.

Nutty waffles with avocado, Thai basil & red onion

 **ENERGY** *273kcals*, **PROTEIN** *9.6g*, **FAT** *15g*, **SATURATED FAT** *3g*, **CARBOHYDRATE** *29g*, **TOTAL SUGARS** *4.3g*, **SALT** *0.2g*

This dish was a pure fluke, created one day when I was in my kitchen and just cooked what I had lying around. It's very simple, but filling and really tasty, and is ideal for a quick lunch or supper. I sometimes just use the topping and serve it on toasted pumpernickel or seeded wholewheat toast.

FOR THE WAFFLES
2 eggs, separated
115g rye or plain wholemeal flour
1 level teaspoon baking powder
15g pecan nuts, finely chopped
150–175ml cold skimmed milk
5ml olive oil
vegetable oil, for greasing

FOR THE TOPPING
1 ripe medium avocado, peeled, stoned and finely chopped, or mashed
½ small red onion, very finely chopped
1–2 tablespoons balsamic vinegar, to taste
2 tablespoons finely chopped fresh Thai basil
dash of extra virgin olive oil
freshly ground black pepper

SERVES 4 *(4 large or 8 small waffles)* / **PREP TIME** *15 minutes* / **COOKING TIME** *5–8 minutes*

1. First make the waffles. Put the egg yolks, flour, baking powder and pecans into a bowl and mix well, then whisk in 150ml of the milk until combined. Add a little more milk if the mixture is too thick, it should be the consistency of lightly whipped cream, then stir in the olive oil.

2. Whisk the egg whites in a separate clean bowl until they are soft and foamy, then gently fold them into the flour mixture until combined.

3. Lightly oil a 4-slice waffle iron/maker (see also Cook's Tip) and preheat it until hot. Ladle the waffle batter into the waffle iron/maker, close the lid and cook for 5–8 minutes until golden brown and crispy on the outside. Carefully remove the cooked waffles and keep warm.

4. Meanwhile, combine the topping ingredients in a small bowl, mixing well and seasoning to taste with black pepper.

5. Serve the hot waffles with the avocado topping spooned on top.

COOK'S TIP
If you don't have a waffle iron you can cook the batter in a large, griddle pan. Oil a griddle pan and preheat it until hot, then pour in all the batter (to make one large waffle) and cook over a medium heat for about 5 minutes until golden brown underneath and lightly set on top. Carefully turn over, then cook for a further 4 minutes until the underside is golden and the waffle is cooked. turn out and cut into four even portions, then spoon the avocado mixture on top to serve.

Apple & smoked mackerel salad

ENERGY *172kcals*, **PROTEIN** *7.5g*, **FAT** *14g*, **SATURATED FAT** *2.4g*, **CARBOHYDRATE** *5g*, **TOTAL SUGARS** *5g*, **SALT** *0.5g*

I really like this salad because it is simple, easy and straight to the point. I use no salt, preferring to use fish sauce and the acid from the lime to bring out the flavours. Any oily fish works well with this dressing, plus any type of nut will also work well.

1 medium Bramley or other cooking apple

100g smoked mackerel fillets, skin removed and flesh flaked

2 heads of Little Gem lettuce (or similar firm lettuce), sliced into long wedges

200g watercress (or rocket leaves)

8 walnut halves, roughly chopped

FOR THE DRESSING

1 tablespoon extra virgin olive oil

2 tablespoons vinegar (any type)

juice of 1 large lime

pinch or two of freshly ground black pepper

½ teaspoon sweetener

SERVES 4 / **PREP TIME** *15 minutes* / **COOKING TIME** *none*

1. First make the dressing. In a small bowl, mix together all the ingredients really well, then set aside.

2. For the salad, peel and core the apple, then finely grate or very finely slice the flesh into thin, matchstick-sized pieces. Add the apple to the dressing and mix well.

3. Put the mackerel, lettuce and watercress in a serving bowl and lightly mix. Add the dressing and apple mixture and toss together, then finally scatter in the walnuts.

4. Check and adjust the seasoning and serve straight away. I sometimes like to serve with a seeded cracker or a slice of toasted ciabatta to add a little crunch.

Salmon, quinoa, rice & salted cashew salad

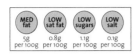

ENERGY *330kcals*, **PROTEIN** *17g*, **FAT** *13g*, **SATURATED FAT** *2.2g*, **CARBOHYDRATE** *35g*, **TOTAL SUGARS** *2.8g*, **SALT** *0.3g*

I love the nuttiness of quinoa, and once it's combined with a small amount of basmati rice, it makes a lovely bulky side dish or a tasty salad for supper or lunch. Here I'm using salmon, but any oily fish, such as mackerel, herring or sardines, will work really well. The only cooking the fish will need is the residual heat from the hot quinoa and hot rice, so long as you cover the mixture straight away with clingfilm.

250g quinoa

1 reduced salt vegetable stock cube (10g)

100g hot cooked basmati rice

300g skinless fresh salmon fillet (or other oily fish fillet), cut into 2cm pieces

90g rocket leaves

90g watercress

100g cashew nuts, chopped

freshly ground black pepper

FOR THE DRESSING

1 tablespoon olive oil

juice of 2 large limes

juice of 1 orange

1 garlic clove, crushed

1 large red onion, finely sliced

SERVES 6 / PREP TIME *10 minutes* / **COOKING TIME** *15 minutes, plus 10 minutes standing*

1. Put the quinoa in a saucepan and cover with plenty of cold water. Bring to the boil, crumble in the stock cube, then reduce the heat, cover and cook until the quinoa is nice and nutty, about 15 minutes should be fine (but don't overcook it).

2. Drain the quinoa well, add the hot rice and mix well, then transfer to a heatproof bowl, stir in the salmon pieces, quickly cover with clingfilm and set aside – the residual heat from the quinoa and rice will cook the salmon perfectly in about 10 minutes.

3. Meanwhile, for the dressing, put the olive oil and lime and orange juices in a separate bowl and whisk together, then add the garlic and red onion and mix well.

4. Once the fish is cooked, roughly chop the rocket and watercress, then add these to the quinoa and salmon mixture, along with the cashews. Add the onion dressing mixture and season well with black pepper, tossing everything together to mix well. Serve.

Sardines with chermoula

MED fat	MED sat fat	LOW sugars	LOW salt
8.g per 100g	2.2g per 100g	0.4g per 100g	0.2g per 100g

ENERGY *130kcals*, **PROTEIN** *14g*, **FAT** *7.1g*, **SATURATED FAT** *1.9g*, **CARBOHYDRATE** *2.2g*, **TOTAL SUGARS** *0.3g*, **SALT** *0.2g*

This North African recipe usually features fresh anchovies, but here I'm using fresh sardines instead. Fresh mackerel also work really well. Simplicity is the key to this delicious dish.

12 very fresh sardines, gutted, scaled, cleaned and heads removed (400g prepared)
plain wholemeal flour, for dusting
spray of olive oil
freshly ground black pepper

FOR THE CHERMOULA
3 large garlic cloves, crushed
2 pinches of ground cumin
pinch of freshly ground black pepper
4 heaped tablespoons chopped fresh flat-leaf parsley
5 tablespoons chopped fresh coriander
finely grated zest and juice of 2 large lemons

SERVES 6 / PREP TIME *15 minutes* / **COOKING TIME** *15 minutes*

1. First make the chermoula. Put all the ingredients for the chermoula in a food-processor and blend together well, then taste and adjust the seasoning if necessary. Scrape into a bowl, cover and set aside.

2. Season each sardine inside and out with black pepper, then dust each one all over with flour.

3. Spray a shallow griddle pan with olive oil and heat until hot. Put the sardines in the hot oil (you'll need to cook them in a couple or so batches, depending on the size of your pan), then cook over a fairly high heat for about 2 minutes on each side, or until the flesh is cooked and turns opaque, turning once.

4. Carefully transfer the cooked sardines from the pan to a ceramic dish and keep warm, whilst you cook the remaining sardines, adding a little extra olive oil to the pan, if necessary.

5. Drizzle or spoon the chermoula over the fish and serve straight away.

NUTRITION TIP

Sardines, an oily fish, are a rich source of essential omega-3 fatty acids and a key part of a balanced diet. Combined with fresh herbs and garlic, this recipe will provide an excellent range of nutrients.

Prawns on rye, Scandi-style

ENERGY *201kcals*, **PROTEIN** *19g*, **FAT** *4.6g*, **SATURATED FAT** *2g*,
CARBOHYDRATE *22g*, **TOTAL SUGARS** *2g*, **SALT** *2.2g*

Open style sandwiches mean you can reduce the amount of bread you eat by half and pack in more protein and fibre at the same time: rye, pumpernickel or sourdough.

1 tablespoon half-fat crème fraîche
a few caraway seeds
a few gratings of lime zest
1 teaspoon lime juice
60g cooked peeled prawns
1 tablespoon chopped fresh dill
½ small fennel bulb, finely sliced
5cm piece of cucumber
1 slice of rye bread
25g smoked salmon (trimmings are ideal)

SERVES 1 / PREP TIME *10 minutes* / **COOKING TIME** *none*

1. Put the crème fraîche, caraway seeds, lime zest and lime juice into a bowl and mix together to combine. Gently mix in the prawns, most of the dill and the fennel.

2. Thinly slice the cucumber lengthways into ribbons using a vegetable peeler. Toast the bread (it's nicer toasted on one side only).

3. Place the toast on your plate, lay the cucumber ribbons on top, followed by the smoked salmon, then spoon over the prawn mixture. Sprinkle with the remaining dill and serve immediately.

Turkey ginger patties

ENERGY *158kcals*, **PROTEIN** *24g*, **FAT** *3.5g*, **SATURATED FAT** *0.6g*, **CARBOHYDRATE** *7.5g*, **TOTAL SUGARS** *6.5g*, **SALT** *0.6g*

Quick and easy starter, snack or main course. I tend to find that you can remove most if not all salt from some cooking, but you need to add a big robust flavour or ingredients in its place. Here I've added ginger, garlic and Thai basil if you can get it. If not then normal basil will be just fine. The sweet potato adds a nice structure to the patties.

250g minced turkey breast free of skin

4 tablespoons chopped fresh Thai basil

2 tablespoons fresh ginger, very finely chopped

2 cloves garlic, very finely chopped

medium egg white, lightly beaten

1 teaspoon Thai fish sauce

ground white pepper

75-95g cooked sweet potato mash (from 1 medium roasted sweet potato)

1 teaspoon olive oil

250g small iceberg lettuce, finely chopped

75g watercress, roughly chopped

juice ½ lemon

pinch or two black pepper

SERVES 4 / PREP TIME *20 minutes* / **COOKING TIME** *10–12 minutes*

1. Place the turkey meat, basil, ginger, garlic, egg white, fish sauce, pepper and sweet potato together into a bowl. Then mix really well. Mould into small balls the size of a small walnut, then flatten to about 2cm thick.

2. Add 1 teaspoon olive oil to a non-stick large frying pan and cook half the patties for 3–4 minutes. Turn over and cook for a further 2–3 minutes to take a little colour.

3. Mix the lettuce and watercress together and add the lemon juice and pepper and mix well.

4. Serve the patties with the light salad.

Simple pea, mint & lettuce stew with crispy bacon

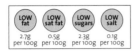

ENERGY *139kcals*, **PROTEIN** *8.9g*, **FAT** *4.7g*, **SATURATED FAT** *0.8g*, **CARBOHYDRATE** *16g*, **TOTAL SUGARS** *4g*, **SALT** *0.2g*

This is an easy, fresh and very flavoursome stew, and the addition of a little crispy bacon really lifts the whole dish.

1 rasher lean bacon

2 teaspoons olive oil

1 small onion, very finely chopped

250g frozen peas (ideally petits pois)

250ml reduced salt vegetable stock

15g plain flour

1 Little Gem lettuce (125g), very finely shredded

2 tablespoons chopped fresh mint

2 tablespoons chopped fresh coriander

freshly ground black pepper

SERVES 4 / PREP TIME *10 minutes* **/ COOKING TIME** *15 minutes*

1. Finely chop the bacon. It doesn't look like much, but you will be amazed at how much flavour comes from 1 lean rasher once cooked.

2. Heat 1 teaspoon of oil in a shallow saucepan, then add the bacon and onion, and cook until softened, about 3–4 minutes. Stir in the frozen peas and cook for 2 minutes. Pour in the vegetable stock, season well with salt and black pepper, then cover and cook for a further 2 minutes. Remove the lid and stir well.

3. Mix the remaining oil with the flour to make a paste, then divide the paste into small pieces and drop each one into the pea mixture, stirring until incorporated before adding the next one; keep the mixture boiling and it will gradually thicken as you add the paste. Once all the paste is incorporated, simmer for 5 minutes to cook out the flour.

4. Stir in the lettuce, mint and coriander, then check and adjust the seasoning, if necessary. If the mixture is a bit too thick, stir in a little hot water from the kettle; it should have a nice soupy consistency.

5. Ladle the stew into deep bowls to serve.

MAIN MEALS

Seven vegetable tagine

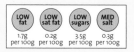

ENERGY *287kcals,* **PROTEIN** *10g,* **FAT** *0.7g,* **SATURATED FAT** *0.9g,*
CARBOHYDRATE *51g,* **TOTAL SUGARS** *5.6g,* **SALT** *1.6g*

Perfect for a slow cooker, this stew is fuss-free and undemanding and you can simply leave it to cook in one pot and return when it's fragrant and ready to eat (also, the recipe can easily be adapted to hob or oven cooking if you don't have a slow cooker). Feel free to play around and use different vegetables – Moroccans traditionally use seven because seven is a lucky number in Moroccan culture. Ras el hanout is a North African spice mix, which usually contains cloves, cardamom, cinnamon, rosebuds, turmeric and black pepper.

1 tablespoon rapeseed oil

1 large onion, chopped

1 large garlic clove, crushed

1 tablespoon ras el hanout spice mix

1 teaspoon ground turmeric

2cm piece of fresh ginger, peeled and grated

2 carrots (300g prepared weight), peeled and cut into small chunks (or use parsnips or swede)

300g (prepared weight) sweet potatoes, peeled and cut into small chunks

1 yellow or green pepper, deseeded and cut into large chunks

1 medium courgette (150g), cut into 5cm lengths

1 small fennel bulb, cut into 5cm lengths

400g can chickpeas or cannellini beans, rinsed and drained

400g can chopped tomatoes

50g ready-to-eat dried apricots (or stoned dates), chopped

1 small preserved lemon, chopped, or 1 tablespoon fresh lemon juice

350ml reduced salt vegetable stock

TO SERVE

400g cooked couscous (or buckwheat or quinoa, for a gluten-free accompaniment)

4 tablespoons chopped fresh parsley

4 teaspoons harissa paste

SERVES 6 / PREP TIME 25 minutes / COOKING TIME 4–6 hours in a slow cooker (on low) or 1–1½ hours in the oven

1. Preheat the slow cooker according to the manufacturer's instructions, or preheat the oven to 160°C/gas mark 3.

2. Heat the rapeseed oil in a large saucepan or flameproof casserole dish. Add the onion and cook over a medium heat for about 5–10 minutes until golden, stirring occasionally.

3. Stir in the garlic, ground spices and fresh ginger and cook for a further couple of minutes. Stir in all the remaining ingredients, then bring to the boil, stirring once or twice.

4. Transfer the mixture to the slow cooker, then cover and cook on low for 4–6 hours. Alternatively, cover the casserole dish, transfer it to the oven and cook for 1–1½ hours until the vegetables are tender and cooked down into the sauce. If you are oven cooking, stir the mixture halfway through.

5. Serve with cooked couscous, the parsley sprinkled over and a spoonful of harissa paste on the side.

Barley & mushroom 'risotto'

ENERGY *213kcals*, **PROTEIN** *3.3g*, **FAT** *8.2g*, **SATURATED FAT** *1.1g*, **CARBOHYDRATE** *34g*, **TOTAL SUGARS** *1.7g*, **SALT** *0g*

Not strictly a risotto, but quite similar in appearance and texture, this is quite a hearty meal so you will only need to cook 200g of barley for four servings (50g per person). By all means add or omit ingredients to your liking. The barley will soak up the gravy base, especially during the 5 minutes resting time, so adjust with a little more gravy base or add a little boiling water.

150g pearl barley

1 tablespoon olive oil

2 small onions, very finely chopped

2 garlic cloves, finely chopped or crushed

200g chestnut, portobello or brown mushrooms, sliced

approx. 400ml Bean and Barley Gravy Base (see page 187), depending on the consistency

freshly ground black pepper

50g grated Parmesan cheese, plus a little extra for serving

4 tablespoons roughly chopped fresh parsley

SERVES 4 / **PREP TIME** *20 minutes* / **COOKING TIME** *40–50 minutes*

1. Put the pearl barley in a saucepan and cover with plenty of cold water. Bring to the boil, then reduce the heat, cover and simmer for 35–45 minutes, or until the barley is soft but not stodgy. Drain well.

2. Meanwhile, heat the olive oil in a separate saucepan, add the onions and garlic and cook gently for 10 minutes until softened, stirring occasionally. Stir in the mushrooms, mixing well, then cook for a further 10 minutes until softened.

3. Add the gravy base and simmer gently for about 10 minutes until the sauce coats the barley in a similar way to a risotto consistency, stirring occasionally. Season with black pepper, then stir in the Parmesan and parsley.

4. Remove from the heat, cover and leave to rest for 5 minutes. Re-stir and then serve with a little extra Parmesan sprinkled over.

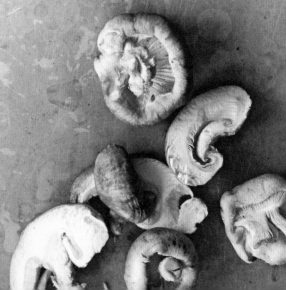

Vegetable curry

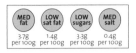

ENERGY *245kcals*, **PROTEIN** *6.1g*, **FAT** *10g*, **SATURATED FAT** *3.8g*, **CARBOHYDRATE** *32g*, **TOTAL SUGARS** *9.3g*, **SALT** *1.3g*

An easy curry, packed with vegetables and cooked in creamy coconut milk. I use a Thai curry paste to save time and keep it simple. The amount and variety of vegetables is flexible and you can leave some out and add others. If you find you have some left over, then freeze for up to three months; simply defrost overnight in the fridge and reheat gently until hot, before serving. This dish is perfect for cooking either in a slow cooker (if you have one) or in the oven.

1 tablespoon rapeseed oil

1 onion, chopped

1 large garlic clove, crushed

2 tablespoons Thai red curry paste

250ml light (reduced fat) coconut milk

300ml reduced salt vegetable stock

2 teaspoons Thai fish sauce (nam pla) (omit if vegetarian)

250g carrots, peeled and cut into small chunks

500g (prepared weight) peeled sweet potatoes or butternut squash (peeled and deseeded) and cut into small chunks

1 red pepper, deseeded and cut into large chunks

100g green or French beans, trimmed and halved

400g can chickpeas, rinsed and drained

50g cashew nuts

TO SERVE

2 heaped tablespoons cooked basmati rice (per person)

4 tablespoons chopped fresh coriander

1 small lime, cut into 4 wedges

SERVES 6 / PREP TIME *20 minutes* / COOKING TIME *4–6 hours in a slow cooker (on low) or 1½ hours in the oven*

1. Preheat the slow cooker according to the manufacturer's instructions, or preheat the oven to 160°C/gas mark 3.

2. Heat the rapeseed oil in a saucepan or flameproof casserole. Add the onion and cook over a medium heat for about 5 minutes until golden, stirring occasionally.

3. Stir in the garlic and Thai curry paste and cook for 1 minute, then stir in the coconut milk, stock and fish sauce (if using) and bring gently to the boil.

4. If using a slow cooker, put the carrots, sweet potatoes or squash, red pepper, green beans, chickpeas and cashew nuts into the slow cooker, then pour over the coconut sauce and stir well, making sure the veg are pressed down into the liquid. Cover and cook on low for 4–6 hours.

5. Alternatively, add all the veg, the chickpeas and cashew nuts to the coconut sauce in the casserole dish and stir well, then cover with the lid, transfer it to the oven and cook for about 1½ hours until the vegetables are tender and cooked down into the sauce, stirring the mixture halfway through.

Braised aubergines with cucumber yogurt, chilli & peanuts

ENERGY *225kcals*, **PROTEIN** *9g*, **FAT** *18g*, **SATURATED FAT** *3.4g*, **CARBOHYDRATE** *8.4g*, **TOTAL SUGARS** *6.4g*, **SALT** *0.4g*

I love braised aubergines because they readily absorb so many flavours. I once had a version of this dish in Israel and the soft succulence of the aubergines coupled with the crunchy peanuts was so delicious, I knew it had to go in a book. The cucumber yogurt cuts through the richness perfectly.

2 medium aubergines, cut in half lengthways, stalks left on
1 tablespoon olive oil
1 teaspoon finely chopped fresh red chilli
4 garlic cloves, crushed
50–100ml boiling water
½ reduced salt vegetable stock cube (5g)
freshly ground black pepper

FOR THE PEANUT TOPPING
60g crunchy peanut butter
2 tablespoons chopped unsalted peanuts
1 garlic clove, crushed
2 tablespoons warm water

FOR THE CUCUMBER YOGURT
½ small cucumber, coarsely grated
150g low-fat natural yogurt
2 tablespoons light mayonnaise

SERVES 4 / **PREP TIME** *25 minutes* / **COOKING TIME** *45–55 minutes*

1. Preheat the oven to 200°C/gas mark 6.

2. Place the aubergines, side by side, in a roasting tray so they are nice and snug. Mix the olive oil, chilli and garlic together, then spoon this evenly over the aubergines. Season well with salt and black pepper, then pour the boiling water around and crumble in the stock cube. Cover with foil, then if you can, place the tray on the hob and heat over a medium heat until you can hear bubbling. (If you can't or don't want to do this, then add 30 minutes or so to the oven cooking time.)

3. Place the tray in the oven and cook for 30–40 minutes or so, once or twice spooning any liquid or juices over the aubergines to make them even more succulent. Check to see if the aubergines are cooked – they should be very soft, but not falling apart. Once cooked, remove the foil and spoon any cooking juices over the aubergines.

4. For the peanut topping, combine the ingredients in a bowl, then dot this mixture over the aubergines. Re-spoon any cooking juices over the top and then pop the tray back into the oven for 10 minutes to warm the topping through.

5. Meanwhile, for the cucumber yogurt, gently squeeze any excess water from the grated cucumber (do this by placing it in a sieve and pressing down gently), then mix the cucumber with the yogurt and mayonnaise and season.

6. Remove the tray of aubergines from the oven and carefully lift them onto warm serving plates, then top with the cucumber yogurt and serve.

Rich tomato, chickpea & sweet potato braise with paprika

ENERGY *180kcals,* **PROTEIN** *6g,* **FAT** *5.5g,* **SATURATED FAT** *1.1g,* **CARBOHYDRATE** *28g,* **TOTAL SUGARS** *16g,* **SALT** *1g*

This is a great vegetable braise, full of flavour, colour and texture.

1 tablespoon olive oil

2 red onions, thinly sliced

4 garlic cloves, crushed

2 teaspoons cumin seeds

400g can chopped
   tomatoes

400g can chickpeas in
   water, rinsed and drained

2 teaspoons sweetener

2 tablespoons vinegar (any
   type)

1 reduced salt vegetable
   stock cube (10g)

2 medium sweet potatoes
   (about 300g), peel on,
   scrubbed and cut into
   2cm cubes

1 small butternut squash
   (about 600g) peeled,
   deseeded and cut into
   4cm pieces

1 heaped teaspoon smoked
   paprika

freshly ground black
   pepper

TO FINISH

200g low-fat natural
   yogurt

2 teaspoons smoked
   paprika

6 tablespoons roughly
   chopped fresh parsley

SERVES 4 / **PREP TIME** *20 minutes* / **COOKING TIME** *35 minutes*

1. Heat the oil in a large saucepan, then add the onions, garlic and cumin seeds and cook over a medium heat for 3–4 minutes until they take on a little colour and soften slightly.

2. Add the tomatoes, chickpeas, sweetener, vinegar, crumbled stock cube, sweet potatoes, squash and smoked paprika and stir well. Pour in enough water to just cover the vegetable mix, then season.

3. Bring to the boil, then reduce the heat and simmer for 15–20 minutes until the sweet potatoes and squash are cooked, stirring occasionally.

4. Spoon the braise into warm serving bowls, then top each portion with a dollop of yogurt and finish with a sprinkling of smoked paprika and some chopped parsley. Serve straight away.

Tasty veg chilli

ENERGY *423kcals*, **PROTEIN** *18g*, **FAT** *16g*, **SATURATED FAT** *3.9g*, **CARBOHYDRATE** *56g*, **TOTAL SUGARS** *18g*, **SALT** *1.2g*

A good alternative to a meat-based chilli, this one is packed full of tasty vegetables. In fact, I sometimes prefer this version to the meat-based one. If you simmer the chilli until most of the liquid has been absorbed or evaporated and the sweet potato has broken down, the chilli will thicken nicely.

The cream cheese is an optional extra, and sometimes I also add 300g diced plain tofu, added right at the end and warmed through, to bulk it out further. I do like adding the coriander to finish, but I'm well aware that some people dislike it, so just leave it out if you are not so keen.

1 tablespoon rapeseed or olive oil

2 onions, finely chopped

2 small carrots, peeled and finely chopped

1 red pepper, deseeded and finely chopped

4 garlic cloves, finely crushed

1 small sweet potato, (about 175g) cut into small cubes

1 teaspoon ground cumin

½ teaspoon ground cinnamon

½ teaspoon dried chilli flakes

400g can kidney beans in water, rinsed and drained

400g can pinto beans in water, rinsed and drained

400g can chopped tomatoes

1 reduced salt vegetable stock cube (10g)

freshly ground black pepper

TO FINISH

4 tablespoons chopped fresh coriander (optional)

4 tablespoons low fat cream cheese (optional)

1 small avocado, peeled, stoned and roughly chopped

1 small lime, cut into 4 wedges

SERVES 4 / PREP TIME *20 minutes* / **COOKING TIME** *35–40 minutes*

1. Heat the oil in a large saucepan, then add the onions, carrots and red pepper and cook over a medium heat for 5 minutes to soften.

2. Stir in the garlic and sweet potato, then add the spices, beans and tomatoes, crumble in the stock cube and mix well. Stir in about 600ml water and bring to the boil, then reduce the heat and simmer gently uncovered for 25–30 minutes, or until the veg are all cooked, stirring occasionally. Season to taste with black pepper.

3. Meanwhile, to finish, mix the coriander, cream cheese and avocado together in a small bowl and season well with black pepper.

4. Serve the veg chilli topped with the avocado mixture and a wedge of lime.

Braised butter beans with white wine, ginger & shallots

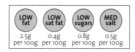

ENERGY *114kcals,* **PROTEIN** *5.2g,* **FAT** *4.7g,* **SATURATED FAT** *0.8g,* **CARBOHYDRATE** *11g,* **TOTAL SUGARS** *1.5g,* **SALT** *0.9g*

This simple dish is good with any meat or fish, or just served on its own. Any canned or dried (soaked and cooked) beans instead of butter beans will work equally well.

1 tablespoon vegetable oil
2 small shallots, finely chopped
2 garlic cloves, finely chopped
1 tablespoon peeled and finely chopped fresh ginger
50ml white wine
1 reduced salt vegetable stock cube (10g)
400g can butter beans in water, rinsed and drained
pinch of freshly ground black pepper

SERVES 4 / **PREP TIME** *15 minutes* / **COOKING TIME** *25 minutes*

1. Heat the oil in a saucepan, then add the shallots, garlic and ginger and cook gently for a few minutes until softened.

2. Add the white wine, 300ml of water and the crumbled stock cube. Bring to the boil, then reduce the heat and simmer, uncovered, about 20 minutes until the sauce is reduced and syrupy.

3. Stir in the butter beans and warm through but do not overcook or they will fall apart.

4. Finally, season with black pepper and serve.

Braised cauliflower wedges with sweet potato, toasted seeds & ricotta

ENERGY *317kcals*, **PROTEIN** *12g*, **FAT** *18g*, **SATURATED FAT** *4g*, **CARBOHYDRATE** *28g*, **TOTAL SUGARS** *8.2g*, **SALT** *0.2g*

This is a simple, easy recipe. I add no extra salt and use only what is provided by the stock cube, but I do add black pepper and vinegar to balance out the whole dish. This is further enhanced with fresh coriander and gently toasted seeds and fragrant spices. This dish can be made a day or so beforehand and gently heated in a microwave or moderate oven to serve.

1 large cauliflower, trimmed and cut into 8 wedges

1 reduced salt vegetable stock cube (10g)

200ml boiling water

3 tablespoons pumpkin seeds

3 tablespoons sunflower seeds

2 tablespoons sesame seeds

½ teaspoon cumin seeds

½ teaspoon ground turmeric

4 medium sweet potatoes, microwaved or oven-baked whole until very soft

1 tablespoon vinegar (any type)

4 tablespoons chopped fresh coriander (optional)

100g ricotta cheese

freshly ground black pepper

SERVES 4 / **PREP TIME** 20 minutes / **COOKING TIME** 30 minutes

1. Preheat the oven to 230°C/gas mark 8.

2. Lay the cauliflower wedges in a roasting tray, overlapping slightly. Season well with black pepper. Dissolve the stock cube in the boiling water, then pour this over the cauli, cover with foil and pop into the oven for 15 minutes until almost cooked. Remove the foil and return to the oven for a further 10 minutes so that the cauliflower takes on a little colour. It must be cooked but not too soft or falling apart.

3. Meanwhile, gently toast the seeds and spices together in a dry pan over a medium heat for a couple of minutes until fragrant (but don't let them burn), shaking the pan regularly. Set aside to cool.

4. Peel the warm sweet potatoes and gently mash the flesh with a fork. Season well with the vinegar and some black pepper.

5. Once the cauli wedges are cooked, lift them out of the tray, place in four warm bowls (two wedges per serving) and keep warm. Pour any cooking juices from the tray into a small saucepan and gently bubble down until you have a very reduced stock, about 3–4 minutes. Add this to the mashed sweet potatoes and mix well.

6. Just before serving, stir the seeds and spices into the sweet potato mix (this ensures they stay crunchy), along with the coriander (if using). Spoon over the warm cauli wedges, dot the top with ricotta cheese and grind over a little extra black pepper.

Cauliflower, broccoli & carrot salad

ENERGY *81kcals*, **PROTEIN** *5.7g*, **FAT** *2.6g*, **SATURATED FAT** *0.4g*, **CARBOHYDRATE** *8.9g*, **TOTAL SUGARS** *8g*, **SALT** *0.4g*

For this recipe, a food-processor is a real advantage for blitzing the vegetables. However, you can still make it using a sharp knife, a bit of elbow grease and patience. I leave the salad to marinate for at least 30 minutes to allow the seasonings to soften the raw vegetables. A little fruit like fresh pomegranate seeds can be added for extra flavour and texture, if you like.

I serve this as an accompaniment, side dish or topped with a poached, fried or soft-boiled egg for a tasty snack or quick supper.

1 small head of cauliflower, trimmed and cut into florets (stalks left on)
1 small head of broccoli, trimmed and cut into florets (stalks left on)
1 small carrot, peeled
100g green or French beans, finely sliced
1 small lemon, very finely sliced, pips removed, but skin left on
4 tablespoons chopped fresh parsley
4 tablespoons chopped fresh basil

FOR THE DRESSING
juice of 1 large lime
1 tablespoon tamarind paste
1 teaspoon Thai fish sauce (nam pla)
1 large garlic clove, finely chopped
1 heaped teaspoon finely chopped deseeded fresh red chilli
1 tablespoon reduced salt soy sauce
1 teaspoon sweetener
1 tablespoon olive oil

SERVES 4 / **PREP TIME** *20 minutes, plus 30 minutes marinating* / **COOKING TIME** *none*

1. The first job is to set up your food-processor, if you have one. (If not, get your sharp knife and chopping board at the ready, and some extra time and patience.)

2. Add the cauliflower florets to the food-processor and pulse until you have a fine breadcrumb texture, then tip into a bowl. Repeat with the broccoli florets and carrot. (Alternatively, very finely chop the vegetables by hand.) Add the green beans and lemon slices to the bowl and mix well.

3. Combine all the dressing ingredients in a small bowl, then add this to the raw vegetables and mix together really well. Cover and leave to marinate at room temperature for 30 minutes.

4. Stir again, then sprinkle over the herbs, toss to mix and check the seasoning. Serve in deep bowls.

NUTRITION TIP
'At risk' groups such as infants, children, pregnant women, the elderly and those who are unwell should avoid soft/lightly cooked and raw eggs, unless they can guarantee that they are produced under the Lion code quality assurance scheme.

Tomato, roasted squash & rice salad

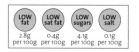

ENERGY *301kcals*, **PROTEIN** *5.4g*, **FAT** *12g*, **SATURATED FAT** *1.9g*, **CARBOHYDRATE** *39g*, **TOTAL SUGARS** *13g*, **SALT** *0.4g*

This is another more filling salad that can double up as a main course quite easily. I sometimes grill lean pork chops to serve with it, or you could serve it with grilled bass or a few grilled sardines or mackerel fillets. You can also swap the iceberg for any lettuce (like raddichio) for a slightly different taste or texture.

1 medium butternut squash (about 750g) peeled, deseeded and cut into 8–10 long slices
½ tablespoon olive oil
120g green beans, cut into 4cm lengths
4 ripe tomatoes, cut into wedges
½ iceberg lettuce, finely sliced
4 spring onions, cut on the diagonal into long shards
250g packet microwaveable basmati rice
freshly ground black pepper

FOR THE DRESSING
4 tablespoons white wine vinegar
1 tablespoon sweetener
juice of 2 large limes
1 teaspoon freshly ground black pepper
½ tablespoon extra virgin olive oil
2 tablespoons roughly chopped fresh coriander

SERVES 4 / **PREP TIME** *20 minutes* / **COOKING TIME** *30 minutes*

1. Preheat the oven to 200°C/gas mark 6.

2. Put the squash slices in a roasting tray, drizzle over the olive oil, season with black pepper and toss to mix. Roast for 30 minutes until lightly browned and cooked through. Remove from the oven and leave to cool.

3. Meanwhile, cook the green beans in a small pan of boiling water until just tender, about 4–5 minutes. Drain well and leave to cool.

4. Put the tomatoes, cooked beans, lettuce and spring onions in a deep serving bowl and mix together carefully but well. Add the cooled roasted squash and mix gently.

5. Cook the rice in the microwave according to the packet instructions, then gently stir the hot rice into the squash mixture.

6. Whisk together the dressing ingredients in a small bowl, then spoon over the rice mixture while it's still warm and serve immediately.

Simple seafood stew

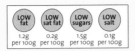

ENERGY *219kcals*, **PROTEIN** *28g*, **FAT** *5.8g*, **SATURATED FAT** *0.9g*,
CARBOHYDRATE *9.4g*, **TOTAL SUGARS** *7.2g*, **SALT** *0.5g*

This is a simple and delicious stew – a base of tomatoes is transformed into a taste of the Mediterranean with a few tasty extras. Just choose your fish depending on what's available and in season. Frozen seafood also works well in this recipe; simply defrost it first.

1 tablespoon olive oil

1 small onion, finely chopped

1 garlic clove, crushed

1 leek, washed and diced

1 small fennel bulb, sliced, then chopped

1 small red pepper, deseeded and diced into 2cm pieces

1 fresh green chilli, deseeded and finely chopped

150ml white wine

400g can chopped tomatoes

250ml reduced salt fish or vegetable stock

350g firm white fish fillets, cut into chunks

200g cleaned and prepared mixed fresh or frozen (defrosted) seafood (such as mussels, king prawns and squid)

a handful of mixed fresh herbs (such as marjoram and fennel tops – reserved from fennel bulb above), roughly chopped, to finish

SERVES 4 / **PREP TIME** *10 minutes* / **COOKING TIME** *40 minutes*

1. Heat the olive oil in a heavy-based saucepan until hot. Add the onion, garlic, leek, fennel, red pepper and chilli and cook gently for about 10 minutes until softened, stirring occasionally. Pour over the wine and bubble for 2 minutes to boil off the alcohol.

2. Stir in the tomatoes and stock, bring gently to the boil, then simmer, uncovered, for about 20 minutes, or until the liquid has reduced and thickened a little, stirring occasionally.

3. Place the fish and seafood on top of the tomato sauce, pressing it lightly into the liquid. Cover the pan, bring back to a simmer and cook gently for 5–10 minutes, or until the fish is just cooked through. You may need to gently turn the fish and seafood in the tomato sauce once. The fish and seafood are cooked when the flesh flakes, the prawns are pink and any mussels are open (discard any that are still closed before serving).

4. Spoon into serving bowls, then scatter over the chopped herbs to finish.

Squid, prawn & almond cakes with mint & coriander dipping sauce

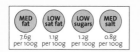

MED fat	LOW sat fat	LOW sugars	MED salt
7.6g per 100g	1.1g per 100g	1.2g per 100g	0.8g per 100g

ENERGY *256kcals*, **PROTEIN** *24g*, **FAT** *16g*, **SATURATED FAT** *2.2g*, **CARBOHYDRATE** *5.7g*, **TOTAL SUGARS** *98g*, **SALT** *1.7g*

The idea for this recipe came from chef, José Pizarro, and the texture and flavours of it are really unique. Almonds provide a good protein kick, whilst omitting the need for high carb flour to bind everything together. Freshwater prawns, puréed in a food-processor, help as a binder, too.

1 tablespoon plus a spray of olive oil

1 small onion, very finely chopped

2 garlic cloves, very finely chopped

300g prepared small squid, very finely chopped

200g peeled freshwater prawns, very finely chopped or puréed in a food-processor

1 egg

4 tablespoons chopped fresh coriander

2 tablespoons ground almonds

1 teaspoon Thai fish sauce (nam pla) (optional)

freshly ground black pepper

FOR THE DIPPING SAUCE

6 tablespoons light mayonnaise

1 tablespoon reduced fat hummus

2 tablespoons chopped fresh mint

2 tablespoons chopped fresh coriander

1 teaspoon sweetener

1 tablespoon vinegar (any type)

SERVES 4 / **PREP TIME** *25 minutes, plus chilling* / **COOKING TIME** *10 minutes*

1. Heat 1 tablespoon of the olive oil in a saucepan, add the onion and garlic and cook over a medium heat for 2–3 minutes to soften. Remove from the heat, spoon into a bowl and leave to cool.

2. Once the onion mixture is cool, add the squid, prawns, egg, coriander, ground almonds, fish sauce (if using) and some black pepper and mix together really well. Divide and shape the mixture into eight small balls, place them on a plate and press down lightly, then cover and chill well in the fridge for about an hour.

3. When you are ready to cook and serve, put all the ingredients for the dipping sauce in a bowl and mix together well. Set aside whilst you cook the patties.

4. Heat the remaining 1 tablespoon of oil in a non-stick frying pan until hot (or, if you are using a spray oil, spray the frying pan with the oil, then heat until hot).

5. Add the squid and prawn patties to the hot pan and cook gently for 2–3 minutes on each side, until lightly coloured and cooked through, but do not overcook.

6. Serve the cooked patties with the dipping sauce.

Crab, rocket & baby plum tomato omelette

ENERGY *257kcals*, **PROTEIN** *27g*, **FAT** *16g*, **SATURATED FAT** *4g*, **CARBOHYDRATE** *1.8g*, **TOTAL SUGARS** *1.8g*, **SALT** *1.3g*

This is another really simple but great recipe. I adore fresh crabmeat; in fact, I prefer it to lobster if push comes to shove. However, it's not always available, so when I tasted canned crabmeat a few years back in a dish my good pal Ken Hom was preparing, I rather liked it. Now the purists may sneer, but as a store cupboard ingredient it's spot on, so here I have partnered it with rocket leaves and juicy, ripe baby plum tomatoes. This is a flat omelette and creates a perfect light lunch or supper dish.

50g rocket leaves

100g ripe baby plum tomatoes, sliced in half lengthways

120g drained canned crab meat, not broken up too much

1 teaspoon sunflower oil

3 large eggs, lightly beaten

freshly ground black pepper

SERVES 2 / **PREP TIME** *10 minutes* / **COOKING TIME** *5–6 minutes, plus 5 minutes standing*

1. Roughly chop the rocket leaves and put in a bowl. Add the tomatoes and crabmeat and season well with black pepper.

2. Heat the oil in a 23cm non-stick frying pan over a medium heat.

3. Pour in the beaten eggs, then carefully stir with the back of a spatula, bringing in the egg from the outsides of the pan as the centre begins to thicken. Once the omelette is lightly set on top, remove the pan from the heat. Top the omelette with the rocket and crab mix, then leave aside for 5 minutes to set.

4. Cut the omelette in half and serve straight from the pan.

Steamed mussels with white wine, spicy sausage & parsley

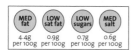

MED fat	LOW sat fat	LOW sugars	MED salt
4.4g per 100g	0.9g per 100g	0.7g per 100g	0.6g per 100g

ENERGY *216kcals*, **PROTEIN** *22g*, **FAT** *10g*, **SATURATED FAT** *2.1g*, **CARBOHYDRATE** *6.2g*, **TOTAL SUGARS** *1.5g*, **SALT** *1.3g*

Spicy sausage such as chorizo and merguez counts as processed meat. It tends to be high in saturated fat and salt and so it shouldn't be eaten regularly, but a little goes a long way in this recipe and overall it's healthy. I really like the simplicity of this dish and nothing else is really needed.

1 tablespoon vegetable oil

2 garlic cloves, crushed

1 small onion, very finely chopped

1 small spicy sausage, thinly sliced (40g in weight) – chorizo or merguez are perfect

75ml medium-dry white wine, or water

pinch of a crumbled reduced salt fish stock cube

1.5kg large fresh mussels, washed and scrubbed well (discard any open ones that don't close when sharply tapped)

4 tablespoons chopped fresh parsley

freshly ground black pepper

couple of squeezes of lemon juice, to finish

SERVES 3 / PREP TIME *15 minutes* / **COOKING TIME** *15 minutes*

1. Heat the vegetable oil in a large, deep saucepan until hot, then add the garlic and onion and cook for 1 minute. Add the sausage and sauté over a high heat for 3–4 minutes.

2. Pour in the white wine or water, add the stock cube, then bring to the boil and cook for 3 minutes.

3. Stir well, then add the cleaned mussels, cover with a tight-fitting lid and cook over a medium heat for about 4–5 minutes until all the mussels have opened, shaking the pan occasionally.

4. Remove the lid and enjoy the gorgeous aroma. Discard any mussels that remain closed. Stir in the parsley, taste a little of the juice to check the seasoning and adjust if necessary with some black pepper (you shouldn't need any salt).

5. Spoon the cooked mussels into two deep serving bowls, add a squeeze of lemon juice to each, then ladle over the delicious liquor.

Mediterranean tuna pasta salad

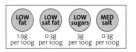

ENERGY *344kcals,* **PROTEIN** *29g,* **FAT** *6.6g,* **SATURATED FAT** *1.1g,* **CARBOHYDRATE** *42g,* **TOTAL SUGARS** *10g,* **SALT** *1.2g*

This is a different take on the usual tuna pasta that we made up on holiday in Minorca. It was the girls' turn to cook one night and they invented this version from ingredients they found in a Spanish supermarket. I am a fan of herb dressings like this salsa verde, as herbs are packed full of good stuff and this way you get to eat more of them.

200g wholewheat pasta

FOR THE GREEN HERB DRESSING (SALSA VERDE)
small bunch of fresh mint leaves
small bunch of fresh parsley
2 canned anchovy fillets, drained
juice of 1 small lemon
1 garlic clove, peeled
1 tablespoon olive oil
1 tablespoon balsamic vinegar
1 tablespoon 0%-fat Greek yogurt

FOR THE TUNA AND TOMATO SAUCE
4 ripe tomatoes, quartered
3 spring onions, finely sliced
1 tablespoon stoned black olives, drained and halved
1 red pepper, deseeded and cut into rough chunks
175g (½ a jar) passata
large handful of baby spinach leaves, washed and drained
2 x 160g cans tuna chunks in spring water, drained

SERVES 4 / **PREP TIME** *15 minutes* / **COOKING TIME** *15 minutes*

1. Cook the pasta according to the packet instructions, then drain well and return to the pan.

2. Meanwhile, make the green herb dressing. Put all the ingredients, except the yogurt, in a jug or small bowl and blend to a paste using a handheld stick blender. Stir in the yogurt to loosen the mixture a little, then cover and set aside.

3. Next, make the tuna and tomato sauce. Combine the tomatoes, spring onions, olives, red pepper and passata in a medium saucepan and bring gently to a simmer. Stir in the spinach and tuna chunks, then warm through for just a few minutes.

4. Add half of the green herb dressing to the hot pasta and toss to coat evenly. Keep the remainder of the dressing to serve at the table.

5. To serve, spoon the pasta mixture onto warm serving plates. Spoon the warm tuna and tomato sauce on top and then drizzle or spoon a few blobs of the remaining green herb dressing around the plates. Serve straight away.

Easy almond tuna fishcakes with avocado sauce

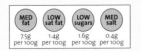

MED fat	LOW sat fat	LOW sugars	MED salt
7.5g per 100g	1.4g per 100g	1.6g per 100g	0.4g per 100g

ENERGY *318kcals*, **PROTEIN** *33g*, **FAT** *17g*, **SATURATED FAT** *3.1g*, **CARBOHYDRATE** *7.8g*, **TOTAL SUGARS** *4.3g*, **SALT** *1.1g*

Fishcakes are usually made with cooked mashed potatoes or rice to bind the ingredients together, but here I use tofu – the type you can buy easily in the supermarket. The mix is softer than the normal one, but it's still delicious. Lightly coated with ground or flaked almonds, then pan-fried, the end result is superb. I sometimes use sardines, pilchards or mackerel instead of tuna.

FOR THE FISHCAKES
2 teaspoons olive oil
1 onion, finely chopped
1 garlic clove, finely chopped
300g plain tofu, well drained and blitzed in a food-processor or finely mashed
2 x 130g cans tuna in spring water, well drained
1 egg, beaten separately
1 tablespoon plain wholemeal flour
30g toasted flaked almonds, finely chopped, or ground almonds
freshly ground black pepper
a spray of oil, for frying

FOR THE AVOCADO SAUCE
1 ripe avocado
150g low-fat natural yogurt
1 garlic clove, crushed
1 tablespoon vinegar (any type)
2 tablespoons roughly chopped fresh Thai basil (optional)

SERVES 4 / PREP TIME *25 minutes, plus chilling* / **COOKING TIME** *20 minutes*

1. Heat the olive oil in a pan, then add the onion and garlic and cook gently for 8–10 minutes until softened, stirring occasionally. Tip into a large bowl and leave to cool.

2. Add the tofu, tuna and 1 egg to the cooled onion and mix well. Season with black pepper, then add 2 tablespoons of the low-fat yogurt from the sauce ingredients to moisten the mix slightly. Stir in 1 heaped tablespoon wholemeal flour.

3. Divide the mixture into four or eight equal pieces (or you could make more, if you prefer smaller fishcakes) and shape each one into a round patty. Place on a plate, cover and chill well in the fridge for about 10 minutes before cooking.

4. For the avocado sauce, halve, stone and peel the avocado, then chop the flesh into 5mm pieces and put in a bowl. Crush the avocado pieces slightly with a fork, then mix in the yogurt, garlic and vinegar and season with a little salt and some black pepper. Add the Thai basil (if using) and mix together well. Cover and chill until ready to use.

5. When you are ready to cook, brush the fishcakes all over with the other egg, then lightly dust both sides with the almonds.

6. Heat a spray of vegetable oil in a non-stick frying pan until hot, then fry the fishcakes in batches over a medium heat for about 4–5 minutes on each side until they are nicely coloured and cooked through. Serve with the avocado sauce on the side, plus a small green salad.

Braised salmon & mackerel with spring vegetables & tarragon

3.6g per 100g   0.9g per 100g   3.4g per 100g   0.3g per 100g

ENERGY *342kcals*, **PROTEIN** *25g*, **FAT** *16g*, **SATURATED FAT** *4.2g*, **CARBOHYDRATE** *15g*, **TOTAL SUGARS** *7g*, **SALT** *1.5g*

I like this braise, it's delicious! You just need to ensure everything is cooked perfectly and all at the same time, hence the three stages of cooking. Any fish will do but the essential thing to remember is not to overcook it. No salt is needed, just a little black pepper to cut through the richness of the oily fish.

1 small carrot, peeled and roughly cut into 1cm cubes

2 large onions, finely chopped

1 medium sweet potato (225g), peeled and roughly cut into 1cm cubes

1 reduced salt fish stock cube (10g)

2 tablespoons reduced salt soy sauce

pinch of freshly ground black pepper

100g frozen peas

100g green beans, cut into 2cm lengths

200g fresh salmon, skinned, boned and cut into 2cm cubes

200g fresh mackerel fillets, skin on

4 tablespoons chopped fresh tarragon

TO SERVE

100g plain fromage frais

4 tablespoons snipped fresh chives

SERVES 4 / **PREP TIME** *20 minutes* / **COOKING TIME** *45 minutes, plus 10 minutes standing*

1. Put the carrot, onions, sweet potato, crumbled stock cube, soy sauce and black pepper in a saucepan, cover with cold water and place on the hob. Bring to the boil, then reduce the heat, cover and simmer for 30 minutes until the vegetables are tender, stirring occasionally.

2. Stir in the peas and green beans and cook for a further 5 minutes, then add the salmon, mackerel and tarragon and stir gently but well. Bring back to a simmer, then turn off the heat, cover with a lid and leave to stand for 10 minutes (the residual heat will cook the fish perfectly).

3. Mix together the fromage frais and the chives, then serve each portion with a small blob of the mixture.

Salmon & dill fishcakes

ENERGY *276kcals*, **PROTEIN** *26g*, **FAT** *15g*, **SATURATED FAT** *2.5g*, **CARBOHYDRATE** *9g*, **TOTAL SUGARS** *4.4g*, **SALT** *0.3g*

A classic way to enjoy more healthy oily fish; this works really well with a green salad and a yogurt, dill and mustard dip.

FOR THE FISHCAKES

400g skinless, boneless salmon fillet, finely chopped

1 large egg white

2 tablespoons plain wholemeal flour (such as sorghum or oat flour), plus extra for dusting

½ small bunch of fresh dill, finely chopped

2 teaspoons wholegrain mustard

2 teaspoons lemon juice

1 tablespoon vegetable or coconut oil

freshly ground black pepper

FOR THE YOGURT AND DILL DIP

100g 0%-fat Greek yogurt

½ small bunch of fresh dill, finely chopped

1 teaspoon wholegrain mustard

TO SERVE

4 bunches cherry tomatoes on the vine, roasted

4 lemon wedges

SERVES 4 / **PREP TIME** *15 minutes, plus chilling* / **COOKING TIME** *10 minutes*

1. For the fishcakes, put the salmon, egg white, flour, dill, mustard and lemon juice in a bowl, season with black pepper and mix well. Lightly squash the mixture together and then with clean, floured hands, divide it evenly and shape into four round patties. Place on a plate, then cover and chill in the fridge for about 10 minutes before cooking.

2. Meanwhile, combine all the ingredients for the dip (if making) in a small bowl, then cover and chill until you are ready to serve.

3. To cook the fishcakes, heat the oil in a shallow pan over a medium heat until hot. Place the fishcakes into the hot oil and cook for a few minutes to colour on the underside, then turn them over with a palette knife. Cook until lightly cooked on the inside and golden and crisp on the outside, about 8–10 minutes.

4. If you are making the dip simply stir the yogurt, dill and mustard together.

5. Serve each fishcake with a small bunch of roasted cherry tomatoes on the vine and a lemon wedge. Enjoy with a dollop of dip and some green salad.

COOK'S TIP

Alternatively, you can make eight smaller (mini) fishcakes and adjust the cooking time accordingly. Serve them hot or cold.

Steamed haddock with egg, caper & herb dressing

ENERGY *306kcals*, **PROTEIN** *43g*, **FAT** *14g*, **SATURATED FAT** *2.3g*, **CARBOHYDRATE** *2.3g*, **TOTAL SUGARS** *2.1g*, **SALT** *1.2g*

Serve this tasty dish on or with a selection of salad leaves, or with some baby spinach leaves mixed with soft herbs like basil, dill, chervil and/or tarragon. Lightly poaching fish or lean meat this way is not only easy but also very quick (just ensure you don't overcook it).

4 x 200g skinless haddock fillets

spray olive oil

½ reduced salt fish stock cube (5g)

FOR THE DRESSING

2 cold hard-boiled eggs, sieved or roughly chopped

1 tablespoon capers, drained and finely chopped

4 medium gherkins, drained and finely chopped

4 tablespoons roughly chopped fresh parsley

4 shallots, very finely chopped

1 tablespoon extra virgin olive oil

finely grated zest and juice of ½ lemon

freshly ground black pepper

TO SERVE

50g rocket leaves

50g watercress

SERVES 4 / **PREP TIME** *15 minutes, plus 20 minutes infusing* / **COOKING TIME** *5 minutes, plus resting*

1. First make the dressing. Put the sieved eggs, capers, gherkins, parsley and shallots in a bowl and mix together. Add the olive oil, lemon zest and juice and some black pepper and mix well, then cover and leave to infuse at room temperature for 20 minutes.

2. Meanwhile, season the haddock fillets all over with a little salt and black pepper. Dip a piece of kitchen paper into a little olive oil and wipe over the base of a non-stick sauté pan (or spray the pan with a little oil). Add the fish fillets to the pan, pour in 100ml of water, then crumble over the stock cube.

3. Place the pan over a low heat, cover with a piece of greaseproof paper or foil, then bring to a simmer and cook gently for 4–5 minutes, being careful not to overcook the fish. Remove the fish from the pan and place on a warm plate, cover with fresh foil and leave to rest in a warm place to finish cooking, about 10 minutes. The centre of the fish will be warm and slightly undercooked – just perfect.

4. To serve, arrange the rocket leaves and watercress in the centre of a large plate, top with the hot haddock fillets and then spoon over the dressing.

Fish parcels with herby greens

ENERGY *201kcals*, **PROTEIN** *30g*, **FAT** *7.8g*, **SATURATED FAT** *1.6g*, **CARBOHYDRATE** *1.7g*, **TOTAL SUGARS** *1.4g*, **SALT** *0.5g*

I really love Swiss chard, particularly with the rainbow stems, which makes a welcome change from spinach and kale. Packed full of good plant nutrition. This recipe uses the leafy greens, but the stems are also delicious served separately – sliced like celery and braise them in stock for 5 minutes to soften.

150g Swiss chard (or young spinach leaves)

small bunch of fresh dill, roughly chopped (or lemon thyme)

1 fresh red chilli, deseeded and cut into matchsticks

2 x 150g skinless, boneless white fish fillets (or salmon fillets)

2 teaspoons lemon juice

2 teaspoons olive oil

salt and freshly ground black pepper

1 tablespoon half-fat crème fraîche, to serve

SERVES 2 / **PREP TIME** *10 minutes* / **COOKING TIME** *10–15 minutes*

1. Preheat the oven to 180°C/gas mark 4. Cut 2 squares of baking parchment, each large enough to contain the fish and greens in a parcel with a fold over the top.

2. To prepare the chard, lay the leaves flat, then trim out the stalks. Pile the leaves together and roll them up (like a cigar), then slice and chop.

3. Pile the chard, dill and red chilli in the centre of each piece of baking parchment, dividing evenly, then place a fish fillet on top of each. Sprinkle with 2 teaspoons of water, the lemon juice and olive oil, dividing evenly between the two parcels. For each parcel, bring up the sides of the paper, make a fold over the top and seal the paper like a packet.

4. Place the parcels on a baking tray and bake for 15–20 minutes, or until the fish is just cooked. Carefully open up the parcels, season with salt and black pepper and then serve each with a small dollop of crème fraîche on top. Serve with Carrot, Chilli and Lime Mash (see page 167).

NUTRITION TIP

Chard tastes similar to spinach, only it's prettier: some have rainbow coloured stems and stalks. It reduces in size during cooking allowing you to eat more greens. It is a powerhouse of vitamins and minerals.

Vietnamese-style tuna

ENERGY *173kcals*, **PROTEIN** *24g*, **FAT** *8.5g*, **SATURATED FAT** *1.7g*, **CARBOHYDRATE** *0.4g*, **TOTAL SUGARS** *0.3g*, **SALT** *1.2g*

This simple recipe relies on a few ingredients only, but the end result is very pleasing. I serve it as a snack before a meal, but it also makes a great starter, or even a main course served with steamed vegetables or a light salad. The secret is to keep the tuna very undercooked (it is one of the few fish that is relatively safe to eat raw). No salt is needed either, as the fish sauce seasons it nicely.

400g fresh or frozen (defrosted) tuna steak, dried well on kitchen paper

finely grated zest and juice of 2 large limes

1 tablespoon Thai fish sauce (nam pla)

2 garlic cloves, finely crushed

½ teaspoon very finely chopped (almost a paste) deseeded fresh red chilli

½ teaspoon sesame oil

4 tablespoons very finely chopped fresh coriander, plus extra small sprigs to garnish

1 teaspoon sweetener

1 tablespoon sunflower or rapeseed oil

freshly ground black pepper

SERVES 4 / PREP TIME *15 minutes, plus cooling and 1 hour marinating /* **COOKING TIME** *10 minutes*

1. Cut the tuna into 2cm pieces and set aside.

2. To make the marinade, put the lime zest and juice and fish sauce in a mixing bowl, add some black pepper and whisk together. Add the garlic, chilli, sesame oil and chopped coriander and stir well. Taste and then add up to a teaspoon of sweetener and mix well. Set aside.

3. Heat 2 teaspoons of the oil in a non-stick wok over a high heat until smoking. Dust the tuna pieces with a little ground pepper and add a quarter of the pieces to the wok and stir-fry to seal the edges for 3–4 minutes maximum (the tuna will be raw inside, which is perfect as you don't want to overcook it).

4. Tip the stir-fried tuna onto a plate, then repeat the process a further three times, heating more oil, then stir-frying the remaining tuna in batches, as before.

5. Once all the tuna is cooked, set it aside to cool quickly, then add the cooled fish pieces to the marinade. Stir gently to mix, then cover and leave to marinate at room temperature or in the fridge for 1 hour before serving.

6. Spear two pieces of the marinated tuna onto a cocktail stick and repeat until all the fish is used up (discard the marinade), then top each stick with a small sprig of coriander and serve.

Carolina-style rubbed salmon

ENERGY *223kcals*, **PROTEIN** *24g*, **FAT** *15g*, **SATURATED FAT** *2.4g*,
CARBOHYDRATE *2.6g*, **TOTAL SUGARS** *0g*, **SALT** *0.1g*

This is a recipe I picked up many years ago whilst in North Carolina. It's a very simple recipe, but it's packed full of flavour. You can use the rub for other fish, shellfish and pork shoulder or chops. Serve with Celeriac and Carrot Slaw (see page 170).

4 x 120g pieces of fresh salmon fillet, skin on

FOR THE RUB

1 tablespoon sweet smoked paprika

2 teaspoons sweetener

½ teaspoon chilli powder

½ teaspoon celery salt

2 teaspoon dried garlic powder

1 teaspoon English mustard powder

1 teaspoon freshly ground black pepper

½ teaspoon ground cumin

SERVES 4 / **PREP TIME** *10 minutes* / **COOKING TIME** *8 minutes*

1. Preheat the grill to its hottest setting.

2. In a small bowl, mix together all the ingredients for the rub until well combined.

3. Put the salmon fillets into a non-stick, ovenproof frying or sauté pan, skin side down. Pile the rub mixture on top of the fish portions, dividing it evenly and spread to cover the flesh entirely.

4. Cook under the grill until the fish is half-cooked, about 3–4 minutes, depending on your grill. You will see the edges of the salmon turning lighter in colour. At this point, remove the pan from the heat and cover with foil, then leave to rest in a warm place for 10 minutes (the residual heat will finish cooking the fish perfectly).

5. Remove the foil. The fillets should now be firm enough to lift up with a spatula, being careful not to let them fall apart.

Sweet & sour chicken

ENERGY *345kcals*, **PROTEIN** *39g*, **FAT** *7.1g*, **SATURATED FAT** *1.1g*, **CARBOHYDRATE** *21g*, **TOTAL SUGARS** *17g*, **SALT** *1.5g*

This is a lighter version of a takeaway favourite, which is easy to make at home.

227g can pineapple pieces
  in natural juice
1 tablespoon rapeseed oil
4 small skinless, boneless
  chicken breasts (400g),
  each cut into 2.5cm cubes
1 red pepper, deseeded and
  cut into 2.5cm pieces
1 green pepper, deseeded
  and cut into 2.5cm pieces
1 fresh red chilli, deseeded
  and thinly sliced
2cm piece of fresh ginger,
  peeled and grated
1 large garlic clove, finely
  chopped
4 spring onions, cut into
  2.5cm lengths

FOR THE SAUCE
1 tablespoon cornflour
100ml pineapple juice
  (reserved from the can
  above)
2 teaspoons sweetener
1 tablespoon rice vinegar
  or red wine vinegar
2 tablespoons reduced salt
  soy sauce
200ml reduced salt chicken
  stock
2 tablespoons reduced
  sugar and salt tomato
  ketchup
¼ teaspoon Chinese five-
  spice powder

SERVES 4 / PREP TIME *10 minutes* / **COOKING TIME** *20 minutes*

1. Drain the pineapple, reserving the fruit and juice separately. Set aside.

2. Heat the rapeseed oil in a wok or large frying pan, then add the chicken pieces and stir-fry over a medium heat for 5 minutes. Add the peppers, chilli, ginger and garlic and stir-fry for a further 5 minutes. Stir in the spring onions and pineapple pieces and then remove the pan from the heat.

3. For the sauce, blend the cornflour with a little of the pineapple juice in a small bowl until smooth and combined, then stir in the remaining juice. Mix together all the remaining ingredients for the sauce in a separate bowl, then stir in the cornflour mixture.

4. Add the sauce mixture to the chicken and vegetables, then return the pan to the heat and bring to the boil, stirring. Reduce the heat, then simmer for about 5 minutes, or until the chicken is thoroughly cooked and the sauce is thickened slightly, stirring regularly. Serve straight away.

COOK'S TIP
It's handy to keep some fresh peeled ginger in the freezer and then grate it, straight from frozen, for recipes like this one.

Crunchy red cabbage & chicory salad with poached chicken

ENERGY *226kcals*, **PROTEIN** *25g*, **FAT** *10g*, **SATURATED FAT** *1.7g*, **CARBOHYDRATE** *3g*, **TOTAL SUGARS** *1.7g*, **SALT** *0.6g*

Red cabbage makes a great salad provided it is marinated first to soften the rawness. The salad is best marinated for at least a couple of hours or preferably overnight. In this recipe, I have cut the protein down quite a lot, as I find that 100g or a little over per serving is ample. Walnut oil was very trendy in the 1980s; I still rather like using it for its distinct flavour in salad dressings occasionally. Any poached meat or fish, such as chicken, turkey, salmon or even prawns will accompany this salad perfectly.

2 tablespoons Dijon mustard

2 garlic cloves, finely chopped or crushed

good pinch of sweetener (optional)

½ tablespoon extra virgin olive oil

½ tablespoon walnut oil (optional)

150g red cabbage, very finely sliced (using a mandolin, if possible)

1 head of red chicory, very finely sliced (using a mandolin, if possible)

1 head of yellow chicory, very finely sliced (using a mandolin, if possible)

4 small skinless boneless chicken breasts (about 100g each), any fat removed

freshly ground black pepper

SERVES 4 / PREP TIME *20 minutes, plus overnight marinating /* **COOKING TIME** *10 minutes*

1. Put the mustard, garlic, sweetener (if using) and some black pepper in a small bowl and mix well, then gradually whisk in the oil until combined.

2. Put the red cabbage and both types of chicory in a serving bowl, then pour over the dressing and mix well. Cover and leave to marinate in the fridge for at least 2 hours or ideally overnight.

3. When you are ready to serve, place the chicken breasts in a pan, cover with 350ml chicken stock and gently poach for 8–10 minutes, or until cooked through.

4. Slice the hot cooked chicken breasts and serve on a bed of the marinated cabbage salad, with a little of the dressing from the salad drizzled over the chicken.

Chicken fajitas with salsa

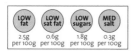

ENERGY *425kcals,* **PROTEIN** *44g,* **FAT** *8.2g,* **SATURATED FAT** *2g,* **CARBOHYDRATE** *33g,* **TOTAL SUGARS** *5.9g,* **SALT** *1g*

Everyone loves a fajita; here's a fast and easy version that's lighter on the calories and has wholegrain fibre in the wraps.

FOR THE FAJITAS

4 skinless, boneless chicken breasts (about 100g each), any fat removed and cut into thin strips

1 teaspoon smoked paprika

1 teaspoon Cajun spice mix

2 teaspoons rapeseed or olive oil

2 small red onions, halved and thinly sliced

1 large yellow or orange pepper, deseeded and cut into strips

4 small multi grain seeded tortilla wraps

FOR THE SALSA

2 ripe tomatoes

1 spring onion, trimmed

1 small fresh red chilli, deseeded

small bunch of fresh coriander, leaves only

1–2 teaspoons lemon juice

SERVES 4 / **PREP TIME** *15 minutes* / **COOKING TIME** *10 minutes*

1. For the fajitas, put the chicken into a small polythene food bag with the spices and shake to coat all over. Heat the oil in a frying pan, add the chicken strips and sauté over a medium heat for 5 minutes, stirring occasionally. Add the red onions and pepper and sauté for a further 5 minutes until the chicken is cooked through, stirring occasionally.

2. Meanwhile, to make the salsa, wash and finely chop the tomatoes, spring onion, red chilli and coriander leaves, then mix together with the lemon juice to taste in a small bowl.

3. Wrap the tortillas in clingfilm and warm in the microwave for about 1 minute until soft and piping hot.

4. Divide the warm chicken fajita mix between the wraps and then spoon over a little salsa. Roll up each tortilla and cut in half, then serve with any remaining salsa spooned alongside.

NUTRITION TIP

Without the skin on, chicken is a lean source of protein and the darker leg meat is rich in minerals such as iron, selenium and zinc.

Slow-cooked lemon chicken

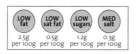

ENERGY *236kcals,* **PROTEIN** *30g,* **FAT** *6.5g,* **SATURATED FAT** *1.2g,* **CARBOHYDRATE** *4.4g,* **TOTAL SUGARS** *3.g,* **SALT** *0.5g*

I'm a big fan of slow cookers and this simple dish of chicken poached gently in lemon stock is really easy. Taking a Middle Eastern slant, I prefer to use preserved lemons for this recipe (they are available in many supermarkets or delis). The preserved lemons are brined, so if you are watching salt levels – which all of us should be – a small fresh lemon will be fine to use instead, just boil it in water for 5 minutes first, then drain. Ground sumac adds an intense, sharp and tart, fruity flavour to the dish, too.

1 tablespoon vegetable oil

4 skinless chicken portions, bone in (about 600g)

1 onion, chopped

1 large garlic clove, crushed

1 level teaspoon ground sumac

300ml chicken stock (made using ½ reduced salt stock cube – 5g)

1 preserved lemon (or 1 small lemon – see recipe intro), cut into quarters

SERVES 4 / **PREP TIME** *10 minutes* / **COOKING TIME** *3 hours in a slow cooker (on high)*

1. Preheat the slow cooker according to the manufacturer's instructions.

2. Heat the vegetable oil in a large frying pan, add the chicken portions and cook over a medium heat until browned on both sides. Remove from the pan and transfer to the slow cooker.

3. Add the onion to the pan and cook over a medium heat for about 5 minutes until softened, stirring in the garlic and sumac for the last minute. Add the stock, bring to a simmer and then pour this over the chicken in the slow cooker. Tuck the preserved lemon quarters in around the chicken.

4. Cover and cook on high for 3 hours. This lemon chicken is delicious served with wilted greens and couscous, along with some of the juices spooned over.

COOK'S TIP

If you don't have a slow cooker, you can of course make this in an ovenproof casserole dish. Simply follow the method above, using a casserole in place of the slow cooker, then cover and cook in a preheated low oven (at 180°C/gas mark 4) for about an hour, or until the chicken is cooked and tender (you may have to remove the lid for the last 20 minutes of the cooking time to reduce the liquid a little).

Steamed chicken with pickled peppers & black rice

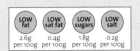

LOW fat	LOW sat fat	LOW sugars	LOW salt
2.6g per 100g	0.4g per 100g	1.8g per 100g	0.2g per 100g

ENERGY *450kcals,* **PROTEIN** *44g,* **FAT** *11g,* **SATURATED FAT** *2g,*
CARBOHYDRATE *8.2g,* **TOTAL SUGARS** *7.8g,* **SALT** *1g*

Black rice looks great with these pickled peppers and creates a lovely recipe with plenty of taste and colour – perfect for a light meal.

100g Nanjing black rice

200ml white wine vinegar

2 tablespoons black mustard seeds

¼ teaspoon freshly ground black pepper

1 red, 1 green and 1 yellow pepper, each deseeded and cut into long batons (about 2cm wide)

2 x 175g skinless, boneless chicken breasts, any fat removed and each cut into 4 pieces

about 250ml reduced salt chicken stock

1 tablespoon extra virgin olive oil

2 tablespoons chopped fresh basil

2 tablespoons chopped fresh parsley

squeeze of lemon juice

SERVES 4 / PREP TIME *20 minutes, plus overnight soaking, cooling and pickling /* **COOKING TIME** *25 minutes*

1. Put the black rice into a bowl, cover with cold water and leave to soak at room temperature overnight.

2. Next, make the pickled peppers, as these are also left overnight. Put 250ml of water, the vinegar, mustard seeds and black pepper in a saucepan, bring to the boil and simmer for 1 minute. Bring a separate pan of water to the boil, add the peppers and simmer for 2 minutes.

3. Pour the vinegar mixture into a non-plastic container and stir in the drained peppers. Cover, leave to cool then chill in the fridge overnight.

4. The following day, when you are ready to serve, place the chicken breasts in a single layer in a steamer set over a pan of simmering water and steam for about 15–20 minutes until cooked.

5. Meanwhile, rinse the soaked rice and drain well. Put the rice in a separate saucepan, cover with about double the amount of chicken stock, then bring to the boil, reduce the heat and simmer for 15 minutes until soft and tender. Drain well and keep warm.

6. Remove the chicken from the steamer and slice each breast. Drain the pickled peppers well. Put the olive oil and herbs into a small blender (or use a handheld stick blender in a bowl) and blend together until you have a beautiful green oil. Pour the herb oil into a serving bowl, then stir in the drained peppers.

7. To serve, add the lemon juice to the pepper mixture just before serving. Spoon the pickled pepper mixture into four serving bowls, dividing it evenly, then sprinkle over the warm black rice and top with the hot sliced chicken breasts.

Steamed chicken with jalapeño chillies, lime & basil

ENERGY *249kcals*, **PROTEIN** *31g*, **FAT** *7.6g*, **SATURATED FAT** *1.2g*, **CARBOHYDRATE** *5.1g*, **TOTAL SUGARS** *4.5g*, **SALT** *0.2g*

A really easy recipe with a bit of a spicy hit.

2 large courgettes, cut into thinnish (5mm) slices
1 red pepper, deseeded and roughly chopped
1 small red onion, very finely sliced
2 garlic cloves, finely chopped
4 small pickled jalapeño chillies, finely chopped
2 tablespoons chopped fresh coriander leaves
4 x 120g skinless, boneless chicken breasts, any fat removed
juice of 2 limes
4 tablespoons roughly chopped fresh basil
freshly ground black pepper

TO SERVE
4 teaspoons olive oil
4 lime wedges

SERVES 4 / **PREP TIME** *20 minutes* / **COOKING TIME** *15–20 minutes*

1. Preheat the oven to 220°C/gas mark 7.

2. Tear off four large pieces of foil, then place them on a chopping board, keeping them separate.

3. Arrange a quarter of the courgette slices (half a courgette in total) in the centre of each piece of foil, overlapping the slices.

4. Sprinkle the red pepper, red onion, garlic and jalapeños over the top, dividing evenly, then scatter over the coriander. Place a chicken breast on top of each portion of vegetables. Squeeze over the lime juice and sprinkle with black pepper, then add a tablespoon of basil to each.

5. For each foil packet, lift up both sides of the foil and scrunch together tightly over the top, then seal one of the ends well. Carefully pour 2–3 tablespoons of boiling water from the kettle into the packet through the open end, then close and seal this end tightly, too (you want the juices to stay inside the foil packet). Repeat to make four sealed foil packets.

6. Place the foil packets in a deep roasting tray and pour a little extra boiling water into the bottom of the tray to prevent the packets from catching. Bake for 15–20 minutes, or until the chicken is cooked through and tender.

7. Remove from the oven and open each packet, being careful as the steam will be very hot. To serve, pour the contents of each packet into a warm serving bowl, drizzle over a little olive oil, then garnish with a lime wedge and serve.

Simmered chicken with green vegetables & garlic mayo

ENERGY *318kcals*, **PROTEIN** *40g*, **FAT** *11g*, **SATURATED FAT** *2.6g*, **CARBOHYDRATE** *16g*, **TOTAL SUGARS** *8.5g*, **SALT** *0.9g*

Now, I know what you're thinking… yes this is so easy to prepare, can it really be that good? Well, sometimes the simple things are the best, and this recipe really does go to show that great food can be very, very simple. Remember, you just want to gently simmer the chicken, otherwise it will become dry and stringy.

8 large skinless chicken thighs, bone in (about 750g)

2 onions, roughly chopped

1 reduced salt chicken stock cube (10g)

4 garlic cloves, roughly chopped

1 small head of broccoli, broken into small florets

150g frozen peas

150g mangetout

75g fine green beans, cut into 2cm pieces

100g fresh baby spinach

FOR THE GARLIC MAYONNAISE

4 tablespoons light mayonnaise

2 garlic cloves, finely crushed

4 tablespoons chopped fresh coriander or parsley or a mixture of both

pinch of freshly ground black pepper

pinch of mild paprika

SERVES 4 / **PREP TIME** *15 minutes* / **COOKING TIME** *45–50 minutes*

1. Put the chicken thighs, onions, crumbled stock cube and garlic in a deep saucepan. Pour in enough water to just cover and then bring to the boil. Reduce the heat, partially cover with the lid and simmer for 35–40 minutes, turning occasionally. At this stage, check and ensure there is about 2cm of liquid above the top of the meat.

2. Meanwhile, towards the end of the cooking time, cook the broccoli florets in a separate pan of boiling water for 3–4 minutes until just tender (alternatively, you can cook the broccoli in the microwave). Drain well and keep warm.

3. Stir the peas, mangetout and green beans into the chicken stew and simmer for a further couple of minutes or so until tender. Add the cooked broccoli and the spinach to the stew and stir in gently but well (the spinach will quickly wilt down). Remove from the heat.

4. For the garlic mayonnaise, in a small bowl, mix together the mayo, garlic, herbs, black pepper and paprika until combined.

5. Serve the chicken and green vegetable stew in deep bowls with the garlic mayo served separately.

Tray roast chicken & vegetables

ENERGY *230kcals,* **PROTEIN** *27g,* **FAT** *4.5g,* **SATURATED FAT** *1.5g,* **CARBOHYDRATE** *18g,* **TOTAL SUGARS** *11g,* **SALT** *0.4g*

This involves putting everything into one dish and letting the oven do all the work, so it's ideal for a midweek meal. Use any seasoning mix you like for the chicken, just note though that if you use smoked paprika instead of sweet paprika, it can be very spicy hot, so use sparingly.

4 chicken legs, trimmed of fat with the skin left on

1 teaspoon mild sweet paprika (or smoked paprika, to taste)

2 sprigs of fresh thyme, leaves picked, or pinch of dried thyme

500g squash (any type will do), deseeded and thickly sliced, peel left on (prepared weight)

1 red pepper, deseeded and sliced

1 courgette, cut into batons

1 onion, cut into wedges

1 garlic clove, left whole and unpeeled

500ml reduced salt chicken stock

100ml white wine

olive oil spray

SERVES 4 / **PREP TIME** *15 minutes* / **COOKING TIME** *1 hour*

1. Preheat the oven to 200°C/gas mark 6.

2. Put the chicken legs in a polythene food bag with the paprika and thyme, then shake to coat the legs in the spice and herbs.

3. Scatter the prepared vegetables into a large roasting tray, then tuck the chicken legs in amongst the veg and add the garlic.

4. Pour the stock and wine around the base of the vegetables and chicken, then spray the chicken and veg with the spray oil.

5. Roast for about 1 hour or until the chicken is thoroughly cooked and the vegetables are tender and nicely coloured. Stir once or twice during cooking.

6. Remove from the oven, then carefully (as it will be hot) squeeze the roasted garlic from its skin and mix the pulp with the vegetables. Spoon the chicken and vegetables onto serving plates and spoon over any juices. Serve with a mixed leaf salad.

Crabcakes with Asian Coleslaw

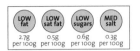

ENERGY *387kcals*, **PROTEIN** *33g*, **FAT** *10.2g*, **SATURATED FAT** *2.1g*, **CARBOHYDRATE** *43.4g*, **TOTAL SUGARS** *2.3g*, **SALT** *1.3g*

There's something very satisfying about crabcakes. This one, like many dishes from the US West Coast, owes much to Asian influences. As fresh crabmeat can be expensive you can swap it for drained canned crabmeat if you prefer.

2 spring onions, finely
  chopped
1 fresh red chilli, deseeded
  and finely chopped
1 tablespoon chopped fresh
  coriander
1 tablespoon snipped fresh
  chives
½ tablespoon chopped
  fresh mint
1½ tablespoons low-fat
  mayonnaise
½ teaspoon English
  mustard powder
½ teaspoon wasabi powder
  (optional)
1 egg yolk
450g fresh crabmeat
50g seeded breadcrumbs
  (see Tip)
spray sunflower oil

FOR THE COATING
115g plain flour
2 eggs, beaten
115g seeded breadcrumbs

FOR THE COLESLAW
2 tablespoons basil
1 fresh hot chillies
225g bok choi, shredded
125g carrots, julienned
4 shallots, sliced
½ tablespoon grated fresh
  ginger
2 tablespoons coriander
1 tablespoon mint leaves
1 clove garlic, chopped
grated zest of 1 orange
juice of 1 orange
juice of 2 limes
1 tablespoon Asian fish
  sauce
4 tablespoons peanut oil
freshly ground black
  pepper, to taste

SERVES 4 / **PREP TIME** *25 minutes, plus chilling* / **COOKING TIME** *8–10 minutes*

1. To make the Asian Coleslaw, shred the basil leaves, and finely chop the chillies, removing the seeds. Mix in a bowl with the bok choi, carrots, shallots, ginger, coriander, mint, garlic and orange zest. In a small bowl, whisk together the orange juice, lime juice, Asian fish sauce and sugar. Slowly whisk in the oil until emulsified. Add the dressing to the cabbage and toss well. Season with pepper. Chill, covered for 2–6 hours.

2. In a bowl combine the spring onion, chilli and herbs. In another bowl whisk together the mayonnaise, mustard, wasabi (if using) and egg yolk, then add the herb mixture to the mayo. Fold this mixture into the crabmeat, then add enough breadcrumbs to bind efficiently. Shape into 4 patties, then chill to firm up on an oiled plate, uncovered, for an hour but ideally overnight.

3. Preheat the grill to high. Lay out 3 plates to prepare the coating: one for the flour, one for the beaten egg and one for the breadcrumbs. Dip the crab cakes into the flour, then the egg (making sure all floury bits are covered) and then the breadcrumbs.

4. Spray the surface of each crabcake with sunflower oil, pop under the grill and cook for 3–4 minutes each side, ensuring they do not burn. Serve with Asian Coleslaw.

COOK'S TIP

To make seeded breadcrumbs, dry some seeded bread slices in a low oven (no higher than 130°C/gas mark 1) until brittle enough to snap. Break them up into pieces, pop in a food processor and blitz into crumbs. Do not pass the bread through a sieve as you want to retain a little texture.

Roast butterflied chicken with pomegranate, lemon, garlic & mint

ENERGY *189kcals,* **PROTEIN** *25g,* **FAT** *3.8g,* **SATURATED FAT** *0.8g,*
CARBOHYDRATE *12.5g,* **TOTAL SUGARS** *2.2g,* **SALT** *0.3g*

A colourful, tasty and satisfying recipe. Frying the garlic until crispy adds a different dimension, and butterflying the chicken cuts the cooking time, too.

800g oven-ready chicken

finely grated zest and juice of 2 lemons

½ tablespoon olive oil

4 garlic cloves, finely crushed

approx 150ml boiling water

5 tablespoons vinegar (any)

1 tablespoon sweetener

1 teaspoon cornflour

freshly ground black pepper

FOR THE SALAD

½ tablespoon extra virgin olive oil

6 garlic cloves, thinly sliced

200g cold cooked egg noodles, roughly chopped

finely grated zest and juice of 2 large lemons

1 tablespoon sweetener

1 small red onion, very finely chopped

4 tablespoons finely chopped fresh mint

1 small pomegranate, cut in half and seeds removed

SERVES 8 / **PREP TIME** *25 minutes* / **COOKING TIME** *1 hour, plus 30 minutes resting*

1. Preheat the oven to 200°C/gas mark 6.

2. To butterfly the chicken, slide a heavy, sharp knife into the cavity and to one side of the backbone. Press down sharply and cut through. Repeat on the other side and remove the backbone completely. (Or ask your butcher to do this.) Open the chicken up, press it flat, remove the skin, and place in a roasting tray.

3. Mix the lemon juice, olive oil, garlic and some salt and black pepper in a bowl. Rub the mix all over the chicken. Pour the boiling water around the chicken, then cover the roasting tray with foil and roast for 40 minutes.

4. Meanwhile, for the glaze, in a separate bowl, mix the lemon zest, vinegar and cornflour together until combined. Set aside.

5. Heat the olive oil for the salad in a non-stick frying pan, add the sliced garlic and sauté over a medium heat until golden brown and crisp, about 5 minutes. Remove from the heat, tip out onto a plate and leave to cool.

6. Check the chicken is cooked and, if it is, increase the oven temperature to 230°C/gas mark 8. (If it isn't, roast it for a further 5–10 minutes before increasing the oven temperature.)

7. Paint the lemon glaze all over the chicken, then return it to the oven, uncovered, for 15–20 minutes until well browned. Remove from the oven, cover with foil and rest in a warm place for 30 minutes before serving.

8. Meanwhile, finish the salad. Put the noodles in a deep serving bowl, add all the remaining ingredients, except the crispy garlic and pomegranate seeds, and mix well. Season with black pepper.

9. Break or cut the cooked chicken into big chunks and serve it with the salad. Scatter the pomegranate seeds and crispy garlic over the top to finish.

Slow-cooked lamb with apricots

ENERGY *284kcals*, **PROTEIN** *27g*, **FAT** *12g*, **SATURATED FAT** *4.9g*, **CARBOHYDRATE** *12g*, **TOTAL SUGARS** *4.7g*, **SALT** *0.3g*

Slow-cooking gives the flavours time to work their way into the meat and reduce the liquid to a rich sauce. Some mashed chickpeas, served hot and mingled with juices from the gravy, are a perfect accompaniment. If this makes more than you need, it's worth freezing the rest for a fast ready meal next time (it can be frozen for up to three months; simply defrost in the fridge overnight and reheat gently until hot before serving).

1 teaspoon vegetable oil

1kg stewing lamb steaks, including bone, visible fat trimmed off

1 large onion, thinly sliced

1 tablespoon coriander seeds, roughly crushed

2 tablespoons cornflour

150ml dry sherry (or dry cider or white wine)

600ml reduced salt chicken stock

40g ready-to-eat dried apricots, sliced

4 bay leaves

freshly ground black pepper

TO GARNISH

sprig of fresh rosemary

finely grated zest of ½ lemon

SERVES 6 / **PREP TIME** *20 minutes* / **COOKING TIME** *2 hours, 20 minutes*

1. Preheat the oven to 160°C/gas mark 3.

2. Heat the vegetable oil in a large saucepan over a medium-high heat. Add the lamb steaks in a couple of batches and brown on all sides (about 5–10 minutes per batch), then remove to an ovenproof casserole dish.

3. Reduce the heat, add the onion to the pan and cook for about 5 minutes until lightly browned, stirring occasionally. Add the crushed coriander seeds and cook for 1 minute, then stir in the cornflour. Gradually stir in the sherry and stock to initially make a paste and then a smooth liquid. Stir in all the remaining ingredients, seasoning with some black pepper, bring to the boil, stirring, and then pour over the lamb in the casserole dish.

4. Cover with the lid, then transfer the casserole to the oven and cook for 2 hours until the meat is very tender and falls off the bone. Periodically check that the meat is still tucked under the sauce during cooking and add a little water, if needed.

5. To serve, transfer the lamb steaks to a serving dish, discarding any visible bones and the bay leaves. Spoon the onion and apricot sauce over the lamb, then garnish with the rosemary and lemon zest.

Roast leg of lamb with easy ratatouille

ENERGY *245kcals*, **PROTEIN** *21g*, **FAT** *15g*, **SATURATED FAT** *5.7g*, **CARBOHYDRATE** *7.7g*, **TOTAL SUGARS** *6.7g*, **SALT** *0.2g*

Covering and resting the roast leg of lamb will give you a perfect rosy red leg of lamb. If you want the leg well done, roast it for 2 hours, then rest the same way for 30 minutes. When adding the tomatoes, basil and peppers, just warm them through, so the tomatoes just start to soften and release their juices.

1 medium-sized leg of British lamb (about 2kg or slightly more)

2 tablespoons extra virgin olive oil

2 onions, roughly chopped

4 garlic cloves, finely chopped or crushed

1 small aubergine, diced (skin and all)

1 large courgette, diced

2 red peppers, deseeded and roughly chopped

2 green peppers, deseeded and roughly chopped

250g cherry tomatoes, halved

2 small bunches of fresh basil, roughly chopped

freshly ground black pepper

SERVES 8 / **PREP TIME** *30 minutes* / **COOKING TIME** *1½ hours, plus 30 minutes resting*

1. Preheat the oven to 200°C/gas mark 6. Place the lamb in a roasting tray and season with pepper. Roast uncovered for 1½ hours.

2. Meanwhile, heat the olive oil in a deep saucepan, add the onions and garlic and cook over a medium heat for 10 minutes, stirring occasionally.

3. While the onions are cooking, bring a separate saucepan of lightly salted water to the boil. Add the aubergine, courgette and red and green peppers, bring back to the boil, then simmer for 3–4 minutes. Drain well. Add these veg to the onion and cook for a few minutes, so they all mix together well. Stir in the cherry tomatoes and basil and warm through for 2–3 minutes. Remove from the heat, season, then set aside.

4. Once the lamb is cooked to your liking, remove it from the oven and cover tightly with foil. Leave to rest in a warm place for 30 minutes.

5. Slice the leg of lamb, warm through any reserved juices and to spoon over the meat, and serve with the ratatouille alongside (either served at room temperature or gently warmed through in a microwave oven on medium for a few minutes before serving, if you prefer).

Juicy pork cutlets with lemon apple sauce

ENERGY *277kcals*, **PROTEIN** *45g*, **FAT** *8.3g*, **SATURATED FAT** *2.1g*,
CARBOHYDRATE *5.3g*, **TOTAL SUGARS** *4.4g*, **SALT** *0.3g*

You will be surprised how only a few basic ingredients can transform an ordinary pork chop into a juicy piece of meat. Resting the meat for the same length of time as you cook it makes all the difference. Delicious served with some roasted cauliflower and a few steamed greens.

FOR THE MARINADE

4 x 2cm thick boned pork cutlets or chops, fat removed
6 teaspoons sweetener
pinch freshly ground black pepper
1 tablespoon olive oil

FOR THE SAUCE

1 large Bramley or other cooking apple, peeled cored and roughly chopped
juice and finely grated zest of 1 lemon
2 teaspoons sweetener

SERVES 4 / **PREP TIME** *30 minutes* / **COOKING TIME** *10–15 minutes*

1. Put the cutlets in a glass or ceramic dish. Mix together the sweetener, pepper, then sprinkle evenly over both sides of the cutlets and leave to marinate at room temperature for 30 minutes.

2. Meanwhile, make the sauce. Put the apple, lemon zest and juice and sweetener in a saucepan, with 100ml water. Bring to the boil, then reduce the heat and simmer gently until you have pulpy, not too smooth sauce. Remove from the heat and leave to cool.

3. Heat the olive oil in a non-stick frying pan. Pat the pork steaks dry with kitchen paper, pop into the heated frying pan, and gently cook for 5 minutes, then flip over and cook for a further 3–5 minutes until thoroughly cooked through. Leave the pork to rest in the frying pan off the heat, loosely covered with foil for 5 minutes.

4. Transfer to warm plates and serve with the apple sauce.

NUTRITION TIP

Lean cuts of pork are high in protein, low in fat and have more B-vitamins (thiamine, niacin, B6 and B12) than many other types of meat. These vitamins play a role in a variety of body functions, including carbohydrate digestion, a healthy nervous system and heart function.

Braised pork with barley, sage & onion

ENERGY *245kcals*, **PROTEIN** *26g*, **FAT** *8g*, **SATURATED FAT** *2.2g*, **CARBOHYDRATE** *17g*, **TOTAL SUGARS** *5.5g*, **SALT** *0.3g*

This is another one pot meal for an easy supper. The only addition might be some steamed green beans or broccoli for the table. Instead of pork, venison or chicken are delicious alternatives.

20g dried wild mushrooms

300ml boiling water

1 tablespoon vegetable oil

1 onion, finely chopped

1 carrot, peeled and sliced

2 small celery sticks, chopped

4 x 100g lean pork fillet, trimmed of fat

1 parsnip, peeled and cut into 1–2cm cubes

30g pearl barley

1 teaspoon ground allspice

1 tablespoon dried sage

800ml reduced salt vegetable stock

1 bay leaf

freshly ground black pepper

SERVES 4 / **PREP TIME** *20 minutes, plus soaking* / **COOKING TIME** *1 hour, 5 minutes*

1. Put the dried mushrooms into a heatproof bowl, pour over the boiling water and set aside to soak while you cook the vegetables and the base.

2. Heat the oil in a large, heavy-based saucepan, then add the onion, carrot and celery and cook gently for 10 minutes to colour lightly, stirring occasionally.

3. Add the pork steaks, stir well and cook for a further couple of minutes, then stir in the parsnip, barley, allspice, sage, stock and the mushrooms with their soaking liquid. Season well with black pepper, pop the bay leaf in and cover the pan. Bring gently to a simmer and then cook over a low heat for about 45 minutes until the liquid is reduced and the pork is tender, stirring occasionally.

4. Serve with a bowl of wilted steamed spinach. And carrot or sweet potato mash to mop up the delicious juices.

TIP

The freezer is a great help to eating healthily: Allocate a regular slot in the week or month to do batch cooking, or make extra portions of some of your meals and freeze them to give you more flexibility to find something in a hurry.

Including some lighter dairy in the mix is fine but if using milk in sauces, try mixing it half and half with low salt stock.

Asian-style seared beef salad

ENERGY *239kcals*, **PROTEIN** *27g*, **FAT** *11g*, **SATURATED FAT** *2.9g*, **CARBOHYDRATE** *8.4g*, **TOTAL SUGARS** *5.6g*, **SALT** *0.6g*

Whole cuts of meat, such as steaks, are only ever contaminated by bacteria on the outside of the meat, which are destroyed during cooking even if the middle of the meat is pink, or rare. Sushi nori (pressed seaweed which is dried and toasted) is a good replacement for salt to crumble over this type of salad.

1 teaspoon vegetable oil

¼ teaspoon Chinese five-spice powder

2 x 100g sirloin beef steaks

FOR THE DRESSING

juice of 1 small lime

1 teaspoon rice wine vinegar

½ tablespoon reduced salt light soy sauce

1 teaspoon Thai fish sauce (nam pla)

5mm piece of fresh ginger, peeled and grated

1 garlic clove, grated

½ lemongrass stalk, very finely chopped (optional)

FOR THE SALAD

100g carrots, peeled and cut into thin ribbons using a vegetable peeler

½ cucumber, cut into thin ribbons using a vegetable peeler

½ fennel bulb, very finely sliced into thin strips

2 spring onions, sliced on the diagonal

75g beansprouts

TO SERVE

a handful of fresh coriander leaves, roughly chopped

a handful of fresh mint leaves, roughly chopped

1 fresh red chilli, deseeded and sliced

1 tablespoon toasted sesame seeds

SERVES 2 / PREP TIME *20 minutes* / **COOKING TIME** *5–10 minutes, depending on the thickness of the steaks*

1. Mix the vegetable oil with the five-spice powder, then brush this mixture all over the steaks. Set the steaks aside on a plate, whilst you prepare the dressing and salad vegetables.

2. Put all the ingredients for the dressing into a large bowl and mix until combined. Taste and adjust the flavour to your liking.

3. Add all the salad vegetables to the dressing in the bowl and tumble everything together to mix and coat. Pile the salad onto two serving plates and set aside.

4. Heat a heavy-based, non-stick frying pan or griddle pan over a high heat until very hot. Add the steaks to the pan and sear on both sides for a couple of minutes or so until cooked to rare, or cook for slightly longer, if you prefer.

5. Remove the steaks to a warm plate, cover with foil and leave to rest briefly, a couple of minutes, before thinly slicing into strips. Arrange the slices of beef on top of the salad.

6. To serve, scatter the beef salad with the chopped herbs, chilli slices and sesame seeds and serve immediately.

COOK'S TIP

You could use roughly chopped watercress instead of beansprouts, if you prefer, and some crushed, unsalted peanuts rather than sesame seeds, to finish.

Venison casserole with sour cherries & red wine sauce

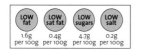

ENERGY *262kcals*, **PROTEIN** *25g*, **FAT** *6g*, **SATURATED FAT** *1.4g*, **CARBOHYDRATE** *19g*, **TOTAL SUGARS** *18g*, **SALT** *0.9g*

Venison is low in fat, high in protein and a source of useful vitamins and iron. Slow-cooked, as in this recipe, it becomes real comfort food; trust me on the cocoa, a small amount works well with the rich flavour. The nutritional analysis doesn't include the sweet potato mash or steamed leeks.

1 tablespoon rapeseed oil

400g venison braising steak, cut into 2cm chunks

250g carrots, very finely diced

300g shallots, left whole if small, or halved if large

1 garlic clove, crushed

FOR THE SAUCE

200ml red wine

300ml reduced salt beef stock

2 teaspoons tomato purée

2 sprigs of fresh thyme

½ tablespoon redcurrant jelly

½ teaspoon balsamic vinegar

4 dried juniper berries, crushed

small pinch of ground cinnamon

50g dried sour cherries (or use 100g stoned fresh cherries, halved

½ teaspoon unsweetened cocoa powder

coarsely ground black pepper

TO SERVE

sweet potato mash or cooked wholegrain buckwheat

steamed leeks

SERVES 4 / **PREP TIME** *20 minutes* / **COOKING TIME** *1½ – 2 hours*

1. Preheat the oven to 160°C/gas mark 3.

2. Heat the rapeseed oil in a large frying pan until hot, then add the cubed meat, carrots and shallots in three small batches, and cook over a medium-high heat for about 10 minutes (per batch) until browned, stirring occasionally. Add the garlic to cook with the last batch. Remove each batch of browned meat and vegetables to an ovenproof casserole dish and keep warm, whilst you cook the remainder.

3. To make the sauce, pour the red wine into the hot frying pan, scraping up all the tasty bits left in the pan, and let it bubble for a couple of minutes to cook off the alcohol. Stir in all the remaining ingredients for the sauce, seasoning with some black pepper, then bring gently to the boil and simmer for 5 minutes. Pour the sauce over the venison mixture in the casserole dish, stir to mix and then cover with a lid.

4. Transfer the casserole dish to the oven and cook for about 1½–2 hours until the venison is tender and the sauce is reduced and thickened slightly, stirring halfway through. Fish out the thyme stalks before serving.

5. Spoon the casserole onto warm serving plates and serve with sweet potato mash or buckwheat and steamed leeks.

SWEET THINGS
& DRINKS

Fruity yogurt ice cream

ENERGY *89kcals,* **PROTEIN** *4.2g,* **FAT** *3.3g,* **SATURATED FAT** *2g,*
CARBOHYDRATE *11g,* **TOTAL SUGARS** *11g,* **SALT** *0.2g*

Traditionally, ice cream is made with eggs and cream or custard. Using yogurt is a healthy alternative and makes a treat you can still enjoy. It's best to use full-fat yogurt; it is lower in fat than cream or custard and low-fat yogurt forms large ice crystals, which gives an icy texture. If you have an ice-cream maker, then all the better to achieve a silky texture, but it's not a problem if you don't. Any variety of soft fruit will work just as well as the strawberries or mango.

400g prepared fresh ripe mango flesh, chopped (or use canned mango and drain it well) or 400g strawberries, hulled and chopped
juice of 1 lime
300g full-fat natural yogurt
1 tablespoon sweetener

SERVES 4 / **PREP TIME** *20 minutes, plus freezing* / **COOKING TIME** *none*

1. Put the strawberries or mango and lime juice into a blender and blitz together to make a smooth purée. Put the yogurt and icing sugar in a mixing bowl and whisk together for a minute or so until light and combined. Pour in the fruit purée and stir to combine well.

2. Pour the yogurt mixture into a shallow, lidded freezerproof container and freeze until slushy, about 2 hours. Remove from the freezer and stir well with a fork to break down the ice crystals, then cover and freeze again until firm. Repeat a couple of times more for a smoother texture. Alternatively, pour the yogurt mixture into your ice-cream maker and churn according to the manufacturer's instructions.

3. When you are nearly ready to serve, remove the ice cream from the freezer 15 minutes or so beforehand, to allow it to soften slightly.

4. Serve the ice cream in scoops on its own or with some fresh mixed berries alongside.

Cherry compote

ENERGY *48kcals*, **PROTEIN** *1g*, **FAT** *0g*, **SATURATED FAT** *0g*, **CARBOHYDRATE** *12g*, **TOTAL SUGARS** *12g*, **SALT** *0g*

Deep-red juicy cherries are one of the joys of summer to eat fresh during their all-too-short season, but if there is ever an abundance, then do make this compote for dessert and enjoy a spoonful or two on natural yogurt or quark.

200g ripe, deep-red fresh cherries
3 fresh lemonbalm leaves (optional)

SERVES 2 / **PREP TIME** *10 minutes* / **COOKING TIME** *15 minutes*

1. Preheat the oven to 190°C/gas mark 5.

2. Halve the cherries and remove the stones. Pile the cherries on a large piece of foil, add the lemonbalm leaves (if you have some), then gather up the foil around the cherries and seal to make a parcel.

3. Put the foil parcel onto a baking tray and roast for about 15 minutes until the cherries are juicy but still holding their shape.

4. Remove from the oven, open the parcel and tip the hot cherries and all their lovely juices into a serving bowl. Serve the cherry compote hot, or leave it to cool, then cover and chill in the fridge until you would like it. The compote will keep in an airtight container in the fridge for up to two days.

NUTRITION TIP

The deep red colour of cherries comes from a beneficial plant pigment called anthocyanin, a powerful antioxidant thought to help prevent oxygen reacting with other substances in our body and creating damage. All cherries contain high concentrations, but sour cherries contain even more of the good stuff than the sweet ones: great for cooking with. More phytonutrients in cherries are under scientific investigation for many beneficial effects on our bodies.

Blush Poached Pears

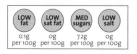

ENERGY *77kcals*, **PROTEIN** *0.4g*, **FAT** *0.2g*, **SATURATED FAT** *0g*, **CARBOHYDRATE** *19g*, **TOTAL SUGARS** *19g*, **SALT** *0g*

Pears are sublime at the peak of their season and readily available any time of year. This light dessert satisfies one of your 5-a-day servings, as well as providing a source of fibre and potassium. Simply poached in cranberry and grape juices the pears take on a subtle flush of colour.

2 ripe pears
300ml cranberry and grape
  juice (pre-mixed carton)
1 small sprig rosemary

SERVES 2 / **PREP TIME** *5 minutes* / **COOKING TIME** *30 minutes*

1. Peel the pears, retaining the stalks, and slice lengthways into halves or leave whole if you prefer.

2. Put the juice in a medium sized pan, slot in the pears and heat to a simmer. Poach uncovered for about 30 minutes until the pears are tender and the liquid has reduced by about half. Spoon the juice over frequently, so that the pears take on a pretty blush colour. About 5 minutes before the end, pop the sprig of rosemary in to flavour.

3. Serve warm or cold, with the juice.

NUTRITIONAL TIP
Check the nutrition label on the juice carton carefully to ensure it doesn't have any added sugar.

Banana chocolate drop scones

ENERGY *227kcals*, **PROTEIN** *8.4g*, **FAT** *1.2g*, **SATURATED FAT** *0.4g*,
CARBOHYDRATE *49g*, **TOTAL SUGARS** *11g*, **SALT** *0.6g*

These are also good for breakfast, as they can be made the day before and placed on a plate and wrapped in cling film. I warm them briefly in the microwave and serve with a few berries.

150g self raising flour

1 teaspoon baking powder

1 level tablespoon cocoa
powder

1 medium egg white

100ml skimmed milk

1 medium ripe banana, mashed

1 teaspoon sunflower oil

MAKES 10 SMALL SCONES / **PREP TIME** *5 minutes* / **COOKING TIME** *3–4 minutes*

1. Mix the flour, baking powder and cocoa powder in a bowl.

2. Add the egg white, milk and about 100ml water (enough to make a thick batter), then add the mashed banana and mix well.

3. Heat the oil in a non-stick frying pan then drop in spoonfuls of the mixture and cook until the top starts to bubble and is just set. Flip over carefully and cook for further 1 minute. Repeat until all the mixture is used up.

Berry, lime and grape sorbet

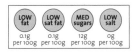

ENERGY *62kcals*, **PROTEIN** *3g*, **FAT** *0.1g*, **SATURATED FAT** *0g*, **CARBOHYDRATE** *13g*, **TOTAL SUGARS** *13g*, **SALT** *0g*

A deliciously simple sorbet to have if you feel like something refreshing or palate cleansing after a meal. It takes advantage of the high level of natural sugar found in grapes and doesn't need any further sweetener.

300g black grapes, frozen

50g blackberries, frozen (or blueberries)

50g 0%-fat Greek yogurt

juice and zest of ½ lime

fresh mint leaves to serve

SERVES 4 WITH 2 SMALL SCOOPS EACH / **PREP TIME** *5 minutes, plus chilling and freezing* / **COOKING TIME** *none*

1. Pureé the frozen grapes and blackberries or blueberries, yogurt and lime juice in a blender or food processor.

2. Transfer the slushy mixture to a plastic tub or container with a lid, and freeze until nearly solid.

3. Scoop into small serving bowls, with a few mint leaves.

COOK'S TIP

If you prefer, you can make a 'fruit bowl' variation: instead of yogurt, blitz 1 peeled and frozen banana with the grapes and lime juice until you have a pureé.

Thai basil & lime jelly

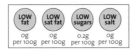

ENERGY *15kcals*, **PROTEIN** *3.2g*, **FAT** *0g*, **SATURATED FAT** *0g*, **CARBOHYDRATE** *0.2g*, **TOTAL SUGARS** *0.2g*, **SALT** *0g*

A very simple dessert but very refreshing. By boiling the water to dissolve the gelatine and then adding the lemonade you keep the freshness of the lime juice, zest and basil. Other herbs such as lemon verbena and rosemary work equally well.

3 small sheets leaf gelatine (10g) soaked in cold water until soft

500ml boiling water

500ml sugar free lemonade

juice and finely grated zest of 4 limes

4 tablespoons finely chopped fresh Thai basil

1 level teaspoon sweetener

a little low-fat fromage or quark, to serve

SERVES 4 / **PREP TIME** *15 minutes* / **COOKING TIME** *10 minutes*

1. Place the soaked gelatine in a bowl, pour over the boiling water and stir until dissolved.

2. Once dissolved, add the lemonade, lime juice, zest, basil and sweetener. Pour into tumblers and chill well.

3. I sometimes top with a little fromage frais or quark.

Vanilla mousse with blueberry crush

ENERGY *130kcals*, **PROTEIN** *8g*, **FAT** *1g*, **SATURATED FAT** *0.2g*, **CARBOHYDRATE** *21g*, **TOTAL SUGARS** *14g*, **SALT** *0.1g*

A lovely, simple dessert, very similar to a panna cotta, which is light but still packs a good flavour punch. Any milk will do. In fact, I have used just water and achieved the same texture, though it does lack a little depth of flavour.

I have used sugar-free jam to boost the blueberry flavour, but sweetener also works well, if you prefer. Removing the fromage frais from the fridge a good hour beforehand stops the mousse setting too quickly when whisking in the hot gelatine and milk mixture.

4 small leaves of gelatine (7g)
300ml unsweetened rice, soya or almond milk
500g fat-free Quark
2 teaspoons vanilla extract or vanilla bean paste
4 teaspoons sweetener

FOR THE BLUEBERRY CRUSH
200g fresh blueberries
2 teaspoons reduced sugar blackcurrant or blackberry jam
finely grated zest and juice of 1 large lemon
2 tablespoons chopped fresh mint or basil leaves

SERVES 6 / PREP TIME *20 minutes, plus 2 hours setting and chilling /* **COOKING TIME** *5 minutes*

1. Put the gelatine leaves in a bowl, cover with cold water and leave to soak for about 5 minutes until very soft and floppy.

2. Gently heat the milk in a saucepan until just boiling, then remove from the heat. Squeeze the excess water from the gelatine leaves, then add them to the hot milk and stir until dissolved. Cool slightly.

3. Put the Quark and vanilla extract in a separate bowl and gently beat together for a minute or two using a hand whisk (it will lighten slightly), then whisk in the sweetener. Quickly whisk in the dissolved gelatine mixture until combined, then spoon the mixture into four large tumblers or individual glass dishes. Cover and chill in the fridge for at least 2 hours before serving.

4. Meanwhile, for the blueberry crush, put the blueberries into a bowl and add the jam and lemon zest and juice. Using a fork, gently crush the berries to create a chunky sauce. Stir in the mint or basil and mix well, then cover and chill well before serving.

5. To serve, spoon some of the blueberry crush on top of each mousse and serve immediately.

English strawberries marinated with balsamic vinegar & fresh mint

ENERGY *73kcals*, **PROTEIN** *2.3g*, **FAT** *2.1g*, **SATURATED FAT** *1.4g*, **CARBOHYDRATE** *15g*, **TOTAL SUGARS** *7g*, **SALT** *0g*

Unfortunately, many strawberries available in the supermarkets are pretty tasteless, but English (and French) strawberries are some of the best in the world and always will be, and if you can pick your own they're even better. One good tip is to always wash strawberries before you remove the stalks, so they don't become waterlogged and go soggy in minutes.

400g small ripe English
    strawberries

2 heaped tablespoons
    sweetener

2 teaspoons balsamic vinegar

juice of 1 large lime

finely grated zest of 1 large
    orange

a few sprigs of fresh mint,
    leaves only

100g plain fromage frais,
    lightly whipped

SERVES 4 / **PREP TIME** *15 minutes, plus 1 hour marinating* / **COOKING TIME** *none*

1. Gently wash the strawberries, then remove the stalks. Cut them in half lengthways and put in a shallow dish. Sprinkle over the sweetener, balsamic vinegar, lime juice and orange zest.

2. Finely shred the mint leaves and reserve a little for decoration, then sprinkle the remainder over the strawberries.

3. Set aside and leave to marinate at room temperature for 1 hour, stirring occasionally.

4. To serve, pile the strawberry mixture into sundae glasses and top each portion with a spoonful of the lightly whipped fromage frais. Sprinkle with the reserved chopped mint to finish.

Soft Chinese five-spice meringues

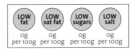

ENERGY *4kcals*, **PROTEIN** *1g*, **FAT** *0g*, **SATURATED FAT** *0g*,
CARBOHYDRATE *0g*, **TOTAL SUGARS** *0g*, **SALT** *0g*

This recipe is very similar in texture and taste to the classic French dessert 'Floating Islands'. The only difference is that you bake these meringues and rather than poach them in a thin egg custard (or crème anglaise). The end result is a delicious, sugar-free dessert.

3 egg whites (80g), at room
    temperature
pinch of cream of tartar
75g sweetener
1 tablespoon Chinese five-spice
    powder (optional)

MAKES 8–12 MERINGUES (SERVES 4) / **PREP TIME** *15 minutes, plus 10 minutes cooling* / **COOKING TIME** *1 hour*

1. Preheat the oven to 150°C/gas mark 2. Line a large baking tray with baking parchment.

2. Put the egg whites into a clean, grease-free mixing bowl and add the cream of tartar. By hand, just lightly whisk them together until combined, then using an electric whisk, whisk the mixture on a high speed until thick and foamy, about 2–3 minutes. Reduce the speed of the whisk, sprinkle over the sweetener, then increase the speed again and whisk for a further 4–5 minutes until you have a thick and glossy meringue mixture.

3. Using a dessertspoon, place blobs of the meringue onto the lined baking tray to make 8–12 meringues, leaving a little space between each one, then evenly sprinkle a little of the five-spice powder, if using, over each one. Bake for 1 hour, until soft but not sticky to the touch.

4. Remove from the oven and leave to cool for 10 minutes, then carefully transfer the meringues to serving plates (serve two or so meringues per serving). Serve with Exotic Fruit Salsa (see page 178).

Pink lemonade

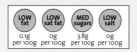

LOW fat	LOW sat fat	MED sugars	LOW salt
0.1g per 100g	0g per 100g	3.8g per 100g	0g per 100g

ENERGY *65kcals*, **PROTEIN** *0.4g*, **FAT** *0.1g*, **SATURATED FAT** *0g*, **CARBOHYDRATE** *16g*, **TOTAL SUGARS** *16g*, **SALT** *0g*

If you happen to have a juicer – it's fine to use it now and again to make homemade freshly squeezed juices (with no added sugar). Remember only up to 150ml/day counts as a portion of fruit and whenever you can try to eat the actual fruit itself. The eating apples in this drink are naturally sweet and balance the sharp citrus flavour of the lemon and lime, without the need to add any sugar. If you use pink- or red-skinned varieties, the juice will be pink, but you may like to add a few raspberries or even the odd blackberry or two, for a deeper colour.

250g sweet eating apples (with pink or red skins)
2 unwaxed lemons, washed (or 1 lemon and 1 lime)
3 fresh raspberries (to add colour)
600ml sparkling water

TO SERVE
crushed ice
a few fresh mint leaves, chopped

MAKES ABOUT 300ML; SERVES 2 / PREP TIME *10 minutes* **/ COOKING TIME** *none*

1. Every juicer is different, so follow the manufacturer's instructions for your model and juice all the fruit. It's usually a good idea to alternate the combination of fruits, as the firmer lemons will help push through the softer apples and raspberries. Mix the fruit juice with the sparkling water.

2. To serve, pour the mixture over crushed ice in two glasses. Add a little chopped mint, then serve.

COOK'S TIP
A spritzer made up of half freshly squeezed juice (from above) and half sparkling mineral water is also really refreshing.

Water, fruit & herb infusions

Most of us do need to keep an eye on staying hydrated throughout each day, and sipping water is the healthiest option, but how can you make water more interesting? It's simple enough to do when you add a few slices of fruit or veg to your glass of water, and you may find you can trick your mind into enjoying drinking more water than you usually do (and that's a good thing).

Anything goes really and you don't need very much of it. Here are a few suggestions of ingredients to add to sparkling or still water, to get you going...

- Slice or two of **cucumber** and a **sliced grape**, or a slice or two of cucumber and a slice of lime.

- Slice of **lime** or **lemon** has a way of refreshing any drink, and both are more fragrant with some fresh **mint leaves** added.

- Slice of **lemon** and a sliver of **fresh ginger**.

- Slice of **orange** and a few **fresh berries** (such as raspberries, strawberries or blackberries).

- **Fresh herbs** can star on their own... start with mint – try mint leaves (or basil) and a slice of cucumber. If you have some lemonbalm, or any favourite herb, a few leaves in a glass of water will infuse subtle flavour and make a more interesting drink.

- **Cinnamon stick** and a slice of **pear**.

TIP

It may sound obvious, but if the usual treats and sweets are not around, then you can't eat them! Think variety and try something different, like a small portion of almonds with the skin on, or walnuts mixed with seeds and dried berries.

Peach melba spritzer

og per 100g   og per 100g   3.8g per 100g   og per 100g

ENERGY *65kcals*, **PROTEIN** *0.4g*, **FAT** *0.1g*, **SATURATED FAT** *og*, **CARBOHYDRATE** *16g*, **TOTAL SUGARS** *16g*, **SALT** *og*

Peach melba is a summery sparkler, but any fruit and juice combination will be good to try in this simple drink. I also love pomegranate juice instead of apple juice with the raspberries. Diluting the juice with sparkling water is helpful to keep the calories and sugar lower, too.

160g fresh raspberries
1 ripe fresh peach, stoned and puréed or mashed
ice cubes
60ml pressed apple juice
60ml sparkling mineral water

TO SERVE
sprigs of fresh mint
slices of eating apple

SERVES 2 / PREP TIME *10 minutes* / COOKING TIME *none*

1. Rinse the raspberries, then drop them into the bottom of two large glasses. Add the peach purée to the raspberries, then half-fill the glasses with ice.

2. Mix the apple juice with the sparkling water in a small jug and then pour this over the ice and fruit. Serve straight away garnished with the mint and apple.

COOK'S TIP
You can get creative with the flavours in a non-alcoholic spritzer...
how about making a delicious and cooling mint tea? Simply mix
100ml of sparkling mineral water with a squeeze of fresh lime juice,
50ml of cold (brewed) green tea and a few fresh mint leaves. Pour over
ice and serve.

SIDES & DRESSINGS

Rainbow chard with olives & parsley

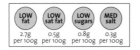 **ENERGY** *114kcals*, **PROTEIN** *5g*, **FAT** *8g*, **SATURATED FAT** *1.6g*,
CARBOHYDRATE *5g*, **TOTAL SUGARS** *2.5g*, **SALT** *0.8g*

Rainbow chard has showy, multi-coloured stalks with beautiful dark-green leafy tops that can be used in a similar way to spinach. Don't discard the stalks – simmer in a little stock, or cut into batons and lightly sauté, and serve with venison or fish. Replacing the stock with water will reduce the salt.

300g rainbow chard, washed and drained
300ml reduced salt vegetable stock
8 stoned black or green olives, drained and chopped
2 teaspoons lemon juice
2 teaspoons olive oil
a small handful of flat-leaf parsley, roughly chopped

SERVES **2** / **PREP TIME** *10 minutes* / **COOKING TIME** *15 minutes*

1. To prepare the chard, lay the leaves flat on a chopping board, cut out the central white stalks and slice the stalks into short lengths. Pile the leaves together, then roll them up like a cigar and slice thinly.

2. There are two stages to cooking the chard – the stalks need a bit longer, so put these in a saucepan with the boiling stock, then cover and braise them over a low heat for about 10 minutes, topping up the stock with a little more water, if needed.

3. Add the leaves to the pan, then cover and simmer for a further 5 minutes, until tender. Drain off any excess liquid, then toss the cooked chard with the olives, lemon juice, olive oil and parsley. Serve straight away.

4. Stir in the basil, season with black pepper and then serve hot or cold.

NUTRITION TIP
To reduce the salt content, replace the vegetable stock with water.

Carrot, chilli & lime mash

LOW fat 0.3g per 100g — LOW sat fat 0.1g per 100g — MED sugars 7.3g per 100g — LOW salt 0.1g per 100g

ENERGY *44kcals*, **PROTEIN** *1g*, **FAT** *0.4g*, **SATURATED FAT** *0.1g*, **CARBOHYDRATE** *10g*, **TOTAL SUGARS** *10g*, **SALT** *0g*

A great alternative to mashed potatoes. If you prefer, combine a mixture of carrot and sweet potato, or my favourite, carrot and swede. Just chop the vegetables into similar-sized pieces, boil them together until soft, then drain and mash until smooth. You can leave out the spice, but the lime really lifts the flavour of this mash. Overall, carrots have less carbs than white potatoes and contain more vitamin A.

500g carrots, peeled and sliced
juice of ½ lime
1 teaspoon freshly ground
**   black pepper**
½ teaspoon ground coriander
**   (or sweet paprika)**
½ teaspoon dried chilli flakes

SERVES 4 / PREP TIME *10 minutes* / **COOKING TIME** *20 minutes*

1. Cook the carrots in a pan of boiling water for about 15–20 minutes until tender.

2. Drain well (make sure they are dry), return the cooked carrots to the pan, then add all the remaining ingredients and mash together until smooth.

3. This delicious mash would work perfectly with the Venison Casserole with Sour Cherries on page 142, the Slow-cooked Lamb with Apricots, page 135, or the Braised Aubergines, page 90.

Garlicky greens with mushrooms

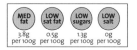

ENERGY *66kcals*, **PROTEIN** *3g*, **FAT** *4g*, **SATURATED FAT** *0.6g*,
CARBOHYDRATE *2g*, **TOTAL SUGARS** *2g*, **SALT** *0g*

Shiitake mushrooms are a good source of B vitamins, protein and iron. We all know that greens are good for us, and this is a tasty way of getting the vitamin and mineral boost they provide.

250g kale, washed, tough
    stalks removed
    and leaves chopped
1 tablespoon olive oil
1 red onion, finely chopped
200g fresh shiitake
    mushrooms
    (or brown cap button
    mushrooms), sliced
1 garlic clove, thinly sliced
1 teaspoon dried chilli flakes
    (or use 1 fresh
    red chilli, deseeded and
    finely sliced)

SERVES 4 / **PREP TIME** *10 minutes* / **COOKING TIME** *15 minutes*

1. Steam the kale leaves over a pan of boiling water for about 5 minutes until tender. Drain well, set aside and keep hot.

2. Meanwhile, heat the olive oil in a frying or sauté pan, add the red onion and mushrooms and sauté over a medium heat for about 10 minutes until the water has evaporated and the mushroom slices are golden brown, stirring occasionally and adding the garlic and chilli flakes for the last couple of minutes.

3. Add the kale to the mushroom mixture in the pan and heat through for a couple of minutes or so. Serve straight away with grilled fish.

Celeriac & carrot slaw

ENERGY *57kcals*, **PROTEIN** *1.5g*, **FAT** *3.2g*, **SATURATED FAT** *1g*, **CARBOHYDRATE** *5.5g*, **TOTAL SUGARS** *4.6g*, **SALT** *0.3g*

Creamy, crunchy coleslaw, dressed with apple cider vinegar and a touch of mustard. Travelling in Europe, and especially Switzerland, I found that slaw tended to be very simple, made with just celeriac and carrot. I loved it, so here is my version, but going a bit lighter on the dressing. You can use red or white cabbage for this slaw, the choice is yours.

FOR THE SLAW
¼ small red or white cabbage
½ small celeriac root, peeled
1 large carrot (about 150g), peeled
1 fresh jalapeño chilli, deseeded and finely chopped

FOR THE DRESSING
2 tablespoons light mayonnaise
2 tablespoons half-fat crème fraîche or quark
1 tablespoon apple cider vinegar
1 teaspoon wholegrain mustard
freshly ground black pepper

SERVES 4 / PREP TIME *15 minutes, plus 2 hours chilling /* **COOKING TIME** *none*

1. Put all the dressing ingredients into a clean screw-top jar and shake them together until well mixed. Set aside.

2. For the slaw, finely shred the cabbage and celeriac – you can do this by hand, but it's easiest and quicker if you use the grater attachment on a food-processor. Coarsely grate the carrot, either by hand or using a food-processor.

3. Put all the prepared vegetables into a large bowl and stir in the jalapeño chilli. Give the dressing a quick shake, then pour it over the vegetables and mix well. Check the seasoning and add a little more black pepper, if needed.

4. Cover and refrigerate for at least 2 hours before serving, so that the flavours mingle and develop and the vegetables soften.

COOK'S TIP
Instead of using mustard in the dressing, add a generous squeeze of fresh lime juice and snip in 2 tablespoons fresh coriander leaves to complement the jalapeño chilli.

If you prefer a more traditional coleslaw, use white cabbage, carrot and perhaps a small chopped onion instead of the celeriac and jalapeño.

Green beans with tomato dressing

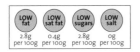

ENERGY *141kcals*, **PROTEIN** *3g*, **FAT** *8.4g*, **SATURATED FAT** *1.3g*, **CARBOHYDRATE** *10g*, **TOTAL SUGARS** *8.5g*, **SALT** *0g*

I came across this dish in Italy, served just as it is, a simple starter, but it also makes a great side salad.

½ tablespoon olive oil
1 small onion, finely chopped
1 garlic clove, crushed
½ teaspoon fennel seeds
4 ripe tomatoes, chopped
1 fresh red or green chilli, deseeded and finely chopped
50ml white wine (optional)
175g fine green beans, trimmed, left whole
freshly ground black pepper

SERVES 2 / **PREP TIME** *10 minutes* / **COOKING TIME** *20 minutes*

1. Heat the olive oil in a saucepan, then add onion, garlic and fennel seeds and cook over a low heat for about 5 minutes until softened.

2. Stir in the tomatoes, chilli and wine and then simmer gently for 10 minutes until reduced and thickened, stirring now and again. The cooking time will depend on how juicy the tomatoes are – the sauce should be quite thick but retaining enough liquid to cook the beans in.

3. Add the green beans to the tomato sauce, then cover and simmer gently for a further 5 minutes or so until the beans are cooked. Season with black pepper and serve.

NUTRITION TIP

Tomatoes contain lycopene; the red-tinged antioxidant linked to a protective effect in the body. Cooking tomatoes makes the lycopene more absorbable. Tomatoes are also abundant in vitamins, potassium and antioxidants such as a and ß-carotenes, xanthins and lutein. Altogether, these pigment compounds have multi benefits when eaten.

Peperonata

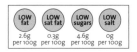

ENERGY *149kcals*, **PROTEIN** *3g*, **FAT** *8g*, **SATURATED FAT** *1g*, **CARBOHYDRATE** *17g*, **TOTAL SUGARS** *15g*, **SALT** *0g*

Peperonata is a Sicilian dish, somewhere between a stew and a relish. It's wonderful served alongside grilled or roasted meat or fish, spooned over steamed vegetables like broccoli, or stirred into hot pasta. The flavour intensifies after a day in the fridge, too. Eat it on its own hot or cold, as a snack on bruschetta (as shown here), or serve it with the Tapas Tortilla (see page 70).

½ tablespoon olive oil
1 red onion, finely diced
2 red peppers, deseeded and finely diced
1 garlic clove, crushed
½ teaspoon balsamic or red wine vinegar
2 tomatoes, chopped
small bunch of fresh basil, chopped
freshly ground black pepper

SERVES 2 / **PREP TIME** *10 minutes* / **COOKING TIME** *35 minutes*

1. Heat the olive oil in a saucepan, add the red onion and cook over a medium heat for 10 minutes until soft and translucent but not browned, stirring occasionally.

2. Stir in the red peppers, garlic and vinegar, then reduce the heat, cover and simmer for about 15 minutes until the peppers soften, stirring occasionally.

3. Stir in the tomatoes and continue to cook, uncovered, for a further 10 minutes or so, or until you have a thick not sloppy stew.

4. Stir in the basil, season with black pepper and then serve hot or cold.

NUTRITION TIP
Peppers rank very high in antioxidant power, plus they contain fibre, of course. All colours are a rich source of vitamin C and a great serving of vitamin A, though red peppers contain the highest amount of polyphenols and carotenes. A little bit of oil cooked with the peppers will enhance the absorption of the nutrients.

Guacamole

ENERGY *77kcals*, **PROTEIN** *1g*, **FAT** *7.4g*, **SATURATED FAT** *1.6g*, **CARBOHYDRATE** *1.7g*, **TOTAL SUGARS** *1.2g*, **SALT** *0g*

There are so many versions of guacamole that I had to include one classic version here, because it's such a great snack as well as an accompaniment to many dishes. Smooth or chopped, you can make it just as you like, and feel free to add some finely chopped ripe tomatoes and red onion, to make it into a kind of salsa. This guacamole is rather nice served with the Chicken Fajitas with Salsa (see page 122).

1 large ripe avocado

1 fresh jalapeno chilli, deseeded and roughly chopped

juice of ½ lime

1 small garlic clove, finely crushed

1 large tomato, chopped

a small handful of fresh coriander leaves, chopped, to finish

SERVES 4 / **PREP TIME** *10 minutes* / **COOKING TIME** *none*

1. Halve the avocado lengthways and remove the stone, then scoop out the flesh into a bowl.

2. Add jalapeno chilli, lime juice and garlic then mash together well.

3. Stir in the tomato and coriander leaves to finish, then serve straight away.

NUTRITION TIP

Avocados are high in fat and therefore high in calories, so keep to a small portion: half an avocado counts as one of your 5 a day. However, they contain mostly **MONOUNSATURATED FAT**, *which is thought to be better for heart health than* **SATURATED FAT**. *The oleic acid and linoleum acid in avocado oil is helpful, as part of a balanced diet, in maintaining normal blood cholesterol levels. Avocados are also packed with nutrients, antioxidants, vitamin E and carotenes, plus soluble fibre.*

Sautéed padrón peppers with garlic & baby spinach

ENERGY *69kcals*, **PROTEIN** *2g*, **FAT** *4.1g*, **SATURATED FAT** *0.5g*, **CARBOHYDRATE** *7g*, **TOTAL SUGARS** *7g*, **SALT** *0.1g*

I love the taste and texture of sautéed padrón peppers from Galicia in Spain. There is a rumour that one in ten are very hot, almost like chilli peppers, but I have been cooking them for ten years now and have never had a hot one.

I like to eat sautéed padrón peppers on their own as a snack, or I serve them to accompany grilled meat or fish. Adding a little garlic and spinach works perfectly; a little spice is also good.

1 tablespoon olive oil

500g fresh whole padrón peppers, with stalks on

2 garlic cloves, crushed

50g baby spinach leaves

freshly ground black pepper

SERVES 4 / **PREP TIME** *5 minutes* / **COOKING TIME** *15 minutes*

1. Heat the olive oil in a large frying pan or wok until hot. Add the peppers and cook, without stirring, over a medium heat until blistered on one side, then turn them over and cook until blistered on the other side. Don't rush this process; it will take about 10–12 minutes in total.

2. Once blistered, add the garlic and sauté with the peppers for a minute or so, then season with black pepper. Stir in the spinach leaves and cook briefly for 20–30 seconds until wilted. Serve straight away.

COOK'S TIP

These sautéed peppers are also delicious served chilled and eaten as a side salad. Once cooked, simply leave them to cool, then chill well before serving.

Exotic fruit salsa

ENERGY *49kcals*, **PROTEIN** *1g*, **FAT** *0.3g*, **SATURATED FAT** *0g*, **CARBOHYDRATE** *11g*, **TOTAL SUGARS** *11g*, **SALT** *0g*

This fruity salsa is great to serve with the Soft Chinese Five-spice Meringues (see page 159) or with lightly grilled meat or fish. A little will go a long way, so use it sparingly.

1 pomegranate

2 kiwi fruit, peeled and finely chopped

seeds and juice from 2 passion fruit

1 small ripe banana, peeled and finely chopped

juice of 1 small lime

4 tablespoons chopped fresh mint

very small pinch of dried chilli flakes

½ teaspoon sweetener (optional)

SERVES 4 / **PREP TIME** *20 minutes, plus 15 minutes chilling* / **COOKING TIME** *none*

1. Roll the pomegranate on a chopping board so you can hear and feel the seeds breaking away on the inside. Cut it in half horizontally and then using a fork, carefully remove the seeds, ensuring that you don't get any of the bitter white pith. It's a bit laborious, but it doesn't take that long.

2. Put the pomegranate seeds in a bowl, then add the kiwi, passion fruit seeds and juice and banana and mix well. Squeeze over the lime juice, then add the mint, chilli flakes and sweetener and mix together really well.

3. Cover and chill for 15 minutes, then stir again and serve.

Spring greens with onions

MED fat 4.4g per 100g LOW sat fat 0.6g per 100g LOW sugars 2.9g per 100g LOW salt 0.1g per 100g

ENERGY *68kcals*, **PROTEIN** *2.8g*, **FAT** *4.7g*, **SATURATED FAT** *0.6g*, **CARBOHYDRATE** *3.9g*, **TOTAL SUGARS** *3.2g*, **SALT** *0.1g*

This recipe sounds very simple and essentially it is, but like all simple dishes the few ingredients used really need to work together well, plus you have to cook it correctly and quickly. The secret is to cook off all the water, leaving perfectly cooked spring greens. I sometimes just eat this on its own, but it's also good served with a roast dinner or with grilled lamb or pork chops.

1 tablespoon olive oil

2 small onions, very thinly sliced

1 tablespoon roughly chopped fresh rosemary leaves

350g spring greens, very finely shredded

pinch of crumbled reduced salt vegetable stock cube

freshly ground black pepper

SERVES 4 / PREP TIME *10 minutes* / **COOKING TIME** *10–15 minutes*

1. Heat the olive oil in a medium, heavy-based saucepan. Add the onions and rosemary and stir over a medium heat for about 5 minutes to soften.

2. Add the spring greens, along with 100ml of water, then sprinkle over the crumbled stock cube. Bring to the boil and stir well, then cover with a tight-fitting lid. Cook over a high heat for 3–4 minutes, stirring occasionally.

3. Once the greens are soft, remove the lid and cook off any excess water.

4. Tip the cooked spring greens into a serving bowl and check the seasoning, adding some black pepper to taste. Serve straight away.

NUTRITION TIP

To reduce the salt content, you can omit the stock cube

Roasted vegetables

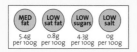

ENERGY *104kcals*, **PROTEIN** *1.8g*, **FAT** *7.8g*, **SATURATED FAT** *1.1g*, **CARBOHYDRATE** *7g*, **TOTAL SUGARS** *6g*, **SALT** *0g*

One of the things I love about roasted vegetables is that you can simply change the mix according to what is in season at the time. Feel free to change this recipe to include carrots, beetroot and fennel; broccoli and cauliflower work well, too, simply adjust the cooking time accordingly.

Mix these roasted veg into a tomato sauce for stirring through hot pasta or topping a pizza, or add them to cooked bulgar wheat or couscous and enjoy with a nice, juicy mushroom steak. This is definitely an ideal recipe to keep in the freezer, so make plenty and freeze in portions.

600g (total prepared weight) mixed vegetables, for example:
  100g red onions
  350g deseeded yellow, red and orange peppers
  100g courgettes
  1 small carrot, peeled
2 garlic cloves, left whole and unpeeled
1 tablespoon olive oil
a handful of fresh basil leaves, shredded
freshly ground black pepper

SERVES 4 / PREP TIME *15 minutes* **/ COOKING TIME** *40–50 minutes*

1. Preheat the oven to 220°C/gas mark 7.

2. Cut the prepared vegetables into chunks of a similar size so that they cook evenly. Spread all the vegetables out in a large roasting dish, then add the garlic cloves. Drizzle over the olive oil and turn the vegetables to coat all over.

3. Roast for about 40–50 minutes until the veg are tender (but not too soft) and beginning to colour at the edges. Turn the vegetables over halfway through the cooking time and let the steam out of the oven.

4. Remove the dish from the oven and season with black pepper. Carefully (as it will be hot) squeeze the roasted garlic from its skin and mix the pulp into the roasted vegetables. Stir in the basil and serve.

Braised baby onions in balsamic

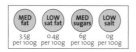

ENERGY *76kcals*, **PROTEIN** *1.2g*, **FAT** *3.9g*, **SATURATED FAT** *0.4g*, **CARBOHYDRATE** *9g*, **TOTAL SUGARS** *7g*, **SALT** *0g*

Braised baby onions can be a great tapas-style starter or a good accompaniment to tray-roasted chicken or the Barley and Mushroom 'Risotto' on page 88.

1 tablespoon olive oil

2 tablespoons balsamic vinegar, plus 1 teaspoon to serve

400g baby (pickling) onions, peeled, roots left on (some halved, if they're difficult to peel)

small bunch of fresh tarragon, snipped

freshly ground black pepper

SERVES 4 / **PREP TIME** *15 minutes* / **COOKING TIME** *30–40 minutes*

1. Preheat the oven to 200°C/gas mark 6.

2. Put the olive oil and 2 tablespoons of the balsamic vinegar into a deep baking dish and stir to mix. Tumble the onions into the oil mixture and toss to coat. Bake, uncovered, for 30–40 minutes until soft, turning once or twice during cooking.

3. Remove from the oven and whilst still hot, drizzle the remaining teaspoon of balsamic vinegar over and season with black pepper. Add the tarragon and mix through lightly.

4. Serve the braised onions with some baby spinach leaves, simply dressed with lemon juice and freshly ground black pepper.

Tomato ketchup

ENERGY *40kcals*, **PROTEIN** *1.5g*, **FAT** *0.2g*, **SATURATED FAT** *0.05g*, **CARBOHYDRATE** *9g*, **TOTAL SUGARS** *8.5g*, **SALT** *0.05g*

This is a nice easy recipe that will give you a ketchup kick. You can use all tomato purée, omitting the can of tomatoes if you prefer, but the colour and taste will be more concentrated. I have not added any extra sweetener as I don't think it's needed, but a little xylitol or Splenda (or similar) can be added, if you prefer a sweeter sauce.

½ small onion, very finely chopped

4 garlic cloves, very finely chopped

400g can chopped tomatoes

100g tomato purée

100ml cider vinegar

1 reduced salt vegetable stock cube (10g)

2 heaped tablespoons Date Paste (see Tip)

½ teaspoon freshly ground black pepper

SERVES 8/MAKES 500ML / **PREP TIME** *10 minutes, plus cooling and chilling* / **COOKING TIME** *15–20 minutes*

1. Put the onion, garlic, tomatoes, tomato purée, cider vinegar and 200ml of water in a stainless steel saucepan. Whisk together well, then bring to a simmer and cook for a minute or two.

2. Stir in the crumbled stock cube, the date paste and black pepper, then simmer, uncovered, over a low heat for 15– 20 minutes until nice and thick, stirring occasionally.

3. Remove from the heat, liquidise and then leave to cool. Check the seasoning, adding a little pepper if needed. Pour the ketchup into a clean sterilised jar, cover and store in the fridge for up to a week.

4. Serve the ketchup straight from the fridge.

COOK'S TIP
To make date paste, place 150g soft dates, pitted and finely chopped, in a small glass bowl. Cover with approximately 150ml boiling filtered water, then heat in the microwave for 1 minute. Leave to cool for at least 30 minutes, then blend the dates together with the soaking water to make a soft paste. Keep the mixture chilled in the fridge before using.

Vegetable gravy base

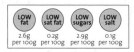

LOW fat	LOW sat fat	LOW sugars	LOW salt
2.6g per 100g	0.2g per 100g	2.9g per 100g	0.1g per 100g

ENERGY *174kcals*, **PROTEIN** *7.3g*, **FAT** *4.3g*, **SATURATED FAT** *1.1g*, **CARBOHYDRATE** *27.2g*, **TOTAL SUGARS** *14.2g*, **SALT** *0.3g*

I have taken the Indian idea of having a few base sauces to add various bits and pieces to. This gravy, as I call it, is packed full of vegetables, flavour, vitamins and minerals, and the recipe here is for adding pretty much anything you like to. For example, a little leftover roasted meat or fresh fish can be simmered in this gravy base. Or, for a curry base, you could add some spices and fresh chilli.

You can make a large batch and freeze it in smaller batches for convenience. To reduce the salt content, omit the stock cube

2 tablespoons oil
6 large onions, finely chopped
6 garlic cloves, roughly chopped
2 tablespoons peeled and finely chopped fresh ginger
400g can chopped tomatoes
2 tablespoons tomato purée
1 reduced salt vegetable stock cube (10g)
400g can haricot or cannellini beans, rinsed and drained
200g firm white cabbage, finely sliced
freshly ground black pepper

SERVES 6 / MAKES ABOUT 1 LITRE / PREP TIME *15 minutes, plus cooling /* **COOKING TIME** *25–30 minutes*

1. Heat the oil in a large saucepan until hot, then add the onions and cook over a high heat to get some colour, about 5 minutes, stirring regularly.

2. Stir in the garlic and ginger, mixing well, then add the tomatoes, tomato purée, crumbled stock cubes, beans and cabbage. Season with the salt and black pepper, then cover with about 700ml water.

3. Bring to the boil, then reduce the heat and simmer uncovered for 10–15 minutes, or until all the veg are cooked and soft, stirring occasionally. You should now have a nice thick vegetable gravy.

4. Remove the pan from the heat, cool slightly, then using a handheld stick blender, purée the mixture to make a smooth gravy base. Check and adjust the seasoning, if necessary.

5. Use as required, or leave to cool, then pour into an airtight container (or divide between freezer bags and seal) and store in the fridge for up to a week (or freeze for up to three months; defrost before use).

Bean & barley gravy base

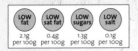

ENERGY *265kcals*, **PROTEIN** *10.7g*, **FAT** *8.5g*, **SATURATED FAT** *1.7g*, **CARBOHYDRATE** *38g*, **TOTAL SUGARS** *5g*, **SALT** *0.5g*

This recipe uses protein-packed beans and barley for a more robust gravy or base. I include mushrooms as they add a lovely 'meaty' flavour and help to bring out the flavours of the other ingredients. I use this base for my Barley and Mushroom 'Risotto' (see page 88). It can also be used as the base of a chicken, turkey or pork sauté or braise, and it's also nice as a soup or broth base. To reduce the salt content, you can omit the stock cube.

2 tablespoons olive oil
3 large onions, thinly sliced
4 garlic cloves, chopped
400g can haricot or cannellini beans, rinsed and drained
400g can chickpeas, rinsed and drained
100g pearl barley
200g button mushrooms, sliced
1 reduced salt vegetable stock cube (10g), crumbled
freshly ground black pepper

SERVES 6 / **PREP TIME** *15 minutes* / **COOKING TIME** *1 hour*

1. Heat the olive oil in a saucepan, then add the onions and cook over a fairly high heat for about 15 minutes to get some colour. The better the colour here, the deeper the end flavour.

2. Add all the remaining ingredients and 1 litre of cold water, covering the ingredients by 3–4cm of water. Bring to the boil, then reduce the heat and simmer uncovered for 35–40 minutes until the barley is cooked through, stirring occasionally. The liquid should now be just below the top of the vegetables – this will ensure you have a nice thick gravy.

3. Remove from the heat and cool briefly, then using a handheld stick blender, carefully blitz the mixture until you have a smooth gravy. Adjust the seasoning to taste, then use as required or cool completely and store in the fridge. It will keep in the fridge for up to 5 days, or freeze for 3 months.

Index

Acknowledgements

A serious book like this doesn't just happen and there are a lot of
people to thank for all the hard work that has gone into checking,
and re-checking the content and nutritional analysis . In particular, I
would like to thank:

Luigi Bonomi and John Rush, my agents and dear friends.

Kyle Cathie and Judith Hannam for keeping the faith, nice lunches,
never hassling me and being straight to the point. Only one slight
problem here, Judith and John Rush are both Arsenal supporters...oh
well, you can't have it all.

Bea for being Bea; her knowledge and expertise are second to
none. Plus she has a dogged determination not only to check but also
to challenge everything.

Hannah Coughlin, Gemma John and Nic Jones from Kyle Books,
great work. Sean Calitz and Annie Rigg, impeccable shots and food
styling. Lou Blair for help with the nutritional analysis.

Pav Kalsi and Shirley Quinn from Diabetes UK for not only
agreeing to check every word, but also to work with us to get
everything spot on. It was very challenging at times but we got there
in the end.

John Packham for responding to my countless emails and helping
me with new ideas/experiments/information with sweeteners, it
was a huge help.

If I've forgotten anyone, I apologise,

Phil